The Hidden Powers of Ritual

The Hidden Powers of Ritual

The Journey of a Lifetime

Bradd Shore

The MIT Press
Cambridge, Massachusetts
London, England

The MIT Press would like to thank the anonymous peer reviewers who provided comments on drafts of this book. The generous work of academic experts is essential for establishing the authority and quality of our publications. We acknowledge with gratitude the contributions of these otherwise uncredited readers.

This book was set in ITC Stone Serif Std and ITC Stone Sans Std by New Best-set Typesetters Ltd. Printed and bound in the United States of America.

Library of Congress Cataloging-in-Publication Data

Names: Shore, Bradd, 1945–, author.
Title: The hidden powers of ritual : the journey of a lifetime / Bradd Shore.
Description: Cambridge, Massachusetts : The MIT Press, 2023. | Includes
    bibliographical references and index.
Identifiers: LCCN 2022052131 (print) | LCCN 2022052132 (ebook) |
    ISBN 9780262546584 (paperback) | ISBN 9780262376556 (epub) |
    ISBN 9780262376549 (pdf)
Subjects: LCSH: Rites and ceremonies. | Ethnopsychology. | Cognition and culture.
Classification: LCC GN473 .S56 2023 (print) | LCC GN473 (ebook) |
    DDC 306.4—dc23/eng/20230105
LC record available at https://lccn.loc.gov/2022052131
LC ebook record available at https://lccn.loc.gov/2022052132

10 9 8 7 6 5 4 3 2 1

Contents

Preface

Welcome to the wonders of ritual and its powers. Some of these powers of ritual are obvious. Others are surprising. Having taught both graduate and undergraduate courses on ritual for many years, I have aimed at a readable but provocative book that, while accessible to those just starting out in ritual studies, would also make a serious contribution to ritual theory. The published literature on ritual is vast and diverse. At the popular end of the publishing spectrum are self-help books on how to benefit from rituals in daily life, whether for personal development, improving family life, or managing workplace relationships. For those wanting a taste of actual rituals, anthropology and religious studies offer a wealth of scholarly studies of religious or civic rituals from around the world. And at the esoteric end of the spectrum, for readers seeking to understand the general dynamics and functions of ritual, there are a fair number of erudite treatises on ritual theory.

In writing *The Hidden Powers of Ritual*, I have tried to straddle all three of these genres by offering a readable and engaging general account of ritual framed as a distinctive kind of human behavior with a fascinating evolutionary history. At the same time, I have organized the book around detailed case studies of rituals I have studied or participated in my lifetime journey through the kingdom of ritual. In this sense, the book is, in part, a personal memoir of a life encompassed by rituals of many kinds. The book's self-help dimension is mostly found in the final chapter called "Harnessing the Power of Ritual." Starting with a ritualized lunch gathering of my friends that has endured for over a quarter century, I offer a set of practical suggestions about how readers might usefully apply some of what they have learned in the book. In this final chapter, I draw on my own life experience as well as things I learned when studying rituals of American family life during the decade I served as director of Emory University's Center for Myth and Ritual in American Life (MARIAL).

The title of the book is borrowed from the name of a course I have been teaching since I retired from Emory in 2020. The online course is sponsored by GEC Academy in Beijing and is mostly for students in China preparing to come to the United States for college. While teaching online, I have been struck by how amazed many of my students have been by my approach to ritual. I offer them a perspective very different from the assumptions they bring with them to the course and a new way to understand human behavior, opening up the concept of ritual in ways they never anticipated.

I suspect this surprise is largely due to the limited range of references of the Chinese word for *ritual*, 仪式 (*yishi*). According to my students, this term generally refers to esoteric, highly stylized performances associated with religion, ancestor commemoration, and, traditionally, the divinity of the emperor. These are the sort of obvious ceremonies I call "big-R-ritual." For example, the ancient Chinese rite known as the Worship of Heavenly Bodies was traditionally both religious and political, focusing on honoring the emperor as the earthly embodiment of the heavenly deities. Closer to home are the annual rites of tomb-sweeping that Chinese clans still practice today during the three-day Qingming Festival honoring clan ancestors. Chinese visit ancestral graves; burn incense; make offerings of food, wine, or tea; and offer ritual paper money. Clan members sweep and weed the ancestors' tombs, adding fresh soil to the graves.

While Chinese people today still practice many traditional rituals at Buddhist temples as well as within the family and clan, these rituals are each named, highly marked by explicit symbolism and formalized practices. Many are related to family rites of passage, ancestor veneration, or the celebration of national identity. Each *yishi* is generally perceived as a ritual rather than as an instance of ritualized behavior. None of these traditional Chinese *yishi* suggests the roots or basic functions of this kind of formalized action.

As in many cultures, the local term for ritual limits its reference to a stock of ready-made, nameable performances. There are rituals in particular but no general phenomenon of ritual. If, as I will be suggesting, ritual develops as a spectrum of formalized behaviors, each culture seems to choose a point on the spectrum where it begins to label a behavior pattern as "a ritual." What is masked by this limitation of reference is the fact that there are many other formalized acts closely related to these so-called rituals but not labeled as rituals. And so the wide range of ritualized action and the general functions of such ritualization become the first of the "hidden" aspects of ritual.

The numerous unrecognized dimensions of ritualized behavior have led me to the title of this book. Our capacity to ritualize behavior is a remarkable part of the human story, a story with many fascinating implications that usually go unnoticed. This is, in part, because the elaborated more obvious rituals often overshadow the humbler ritual moments of life, hiding from us the important work of the junior set of rituals. In this book, I hope to show that the unnoticed rituals, more often studied by sociologists than by specialists in ritual studies, are at least as important as their more recognizable big siblings, the senior set of rituals that usually get all the attention. As we traverse the landscape of ritual, my aim is to offer diverse examples of rituals, major and minor, clarifying their connections by developing a conception of ritual as an evolved form of human behavior of almost unimaginable significance to our species.

1 Discovering the Power of Ritual

Over a long teaching career, I have taught many courses about ritual. Two decades ago, I was eager to find a way to get students not just to understand ritual but also to experience its power. Victor Turner, one of the founding fathers of ritual studies, was said to do this by having his students perform Native American dances all night, as many Native American dancers do. Those students who could muster the stamina to stay with it eventually moved beyond fatigue to an ecstatic state of flow as the rhythmic movements of the dance took over their bodies, liberating their minds from the effort of conscious control. Those students had experienced one of the secret powers of ritual.

Rather than replicating Turner's dance party, I came up with a simpler way for my students to experience the magic of ritual. I was just starting to teach a seminar on ritual with eighteen students. Before the first class, I arranged nineteen seats in a circle. When all the students were seated, I claimed the remaining empty chair. Slowly turning to the student seated to my right, I extended my hand. The student hesitated for a moment but finally shook my hand. I said my name and waited. Looking confused, she said her name in response. I then looked at her and with my eyes directed her attention to the student on her right. She got the message and extended her hand to her neighbor while saying her own name. The guy to her right said his name and, without further prompting, turned to repeat the act with the next student. A new ritual was being born.

The greetings continued around the circle with everyone eventually shaking hands and saying their names. When the last student had said her name, all eyes were on me. I sat silent for a minute. Disarmed by the silence and seeing the teacher sitting still with a bowed head, the students fidgeted uncomfortably, unsure of what to do next. Finally, they got the idea and lowered their heads, joining me in the silence. After a minute of awkward silence, I carried on with my review of the course syllabus, as I always did on the first day of class.

We repeated this greeting ceremony at the start of the second class and every class period after that. By the third class, the students had come to expect it. In no time, it had taken root as the natural way to begin class—at least *this class*. It had moved from being "a ritual" to "our ritual." Then one day, midsemester, preoccupied with a class announcement, I forgot to start class with the greeting circle and went right into announcing a change in a reading assignment. The absence of our greeting ceremony upset many of the students, who quickly reminded me that we had forgotten to begin class with our greeting circle. My little ceremony had a name now and had become essential to the rhythm of this class. The failure to greet each other felt like a disturbing rupture in our class community.

As the semester progressed, I noticed that our greeting had produced some unexpected effects on the students. Students quickly learned everyone's name, and that made it easier for students to talk with each other. Though there was no official rule about where students were to sit, they always took the same seat as they had on the first day of class. Every student had a voice in this course since every class started with each student speaking. I noticed that our class discussions engaged most of the students, which was not always the case with classes.

The simple greeting ritual quickly marked the class as something special for students. And the specialness of our time together was enhanced by our moment of silence, a quiet boundary that set class time apart from outside time. Because it belonged to just this course, our greeting circle gave the students a sense of joint participation in something special. By the third week of class, the class jointly "owned" the ritual. After the semester was over, students would nostalgically recall for me the surprising power of "our ritual."

Once they got used to it, the students were okay with varying the ritual a little. Several times I deliberately changed the greeting. Once I broke off a small piece of chocolate from a large bar and passed the bar along as I announced my name. Without missing a beat, each student broke off a piece of chocolate to eat before passing the chocolate bar on. Students started to bring in other food items to class, which they could pass around during the greeting circle. Another time I altered the ritual by calling out the name of my neighbor whom I was greeting instead of my own name as I shook her hand. The class quickly adapted to the change, each student welcoming their neighbor by name. As long as the ritual retained its basic form, students didn't mind variations. The only change that students resisted was completely omitting the greeting ritual, which made them feel that the class had not really begun.

Ritual is our constant companion, though we do not always know it. Sometimes a ritual is easy to spot. But often we are unaware of its presence. Ritual is sometimes hidden from us in plain sight. At its most exuberant, ritual becomes very showy, demanding our attention. Sacred rites like Catholic masses or Hindu *puja* ceremonies proudly announce their ritual status in the exotic dress of their leaders; their highly formalized and elaborate language, objects, and movements; and the clearly bounded and marked spaces in which the rituals take place. The same is true of elaborate political rites in which a community celebrates its own history and its identity. In the United States, such elaborate national rituals include Thanksgiving, Independence Day (and evening!), and the presidential inauguration. But as we will see, understood as a special kind of behavior, ritual is far more pervasive than these recurring public dramas, penetrating deep into our lives, including our most private moments. A lot of this sort of ritual is more or less unconscious. As the background music of our experiences, our rituals shape the passage of time and punctuate our actions in special ways.

Ritual has always been of special interest to anthropologists. Many of the traditional societies that were the bread and butter of anthropological study have elaborate ritual traditions. In many of these small-scale societies, colorful and elaborate rituals celebrate successful hunting, the coming of age of boys and girls, the installation of chiefs, weddings, funerals, and a host of other important occasions. Studies of Australian aboriginal male initiation rites, Navaho coming-of-age rites for girls, Lunda medicine rites in Africa, Kwakiutl and Haida ritual displays and destruction of wealth, Fijian and Samoan kava ceremonies, Swazi royal installation rituals of kings, Huichol peyote hunts, and the like became standard fare for anthropologists' bookshelves.

When I started graduate school back in the early 1970s, anthropologists often found these rituals to be fascinating objects of study, filled with symbolic objects and acts just begging for interpretation. Rituals seemed to have a special importance in these societies, and exploring their symbols seemed like an exciting entry into an exotic culture. Social scientists like Erving Goffman and Lloyd Warner could apply the same lens to the symbolic life of our own cultures, finding deep shared meanings in small rituals like elevator behavior and more elaborate celebrations like the Catholic Mass, presidential inaugurations, Memorial Day, or Thanksgiving dinner (Goffman 1963a, Warner 1959) .

While a ritual was often an in-your-face kind of thing for anthropologists hunting for something to study, I always sensed that we had never really figured out why ritual is such a special thing for humans. In 2000 I was approached by the Alfred Sloan Foundation and was offered a large grant of research money to set up a major research center at Emory University to study ritual and myth (storytelling) in middle-class American families. Our funders were not expecting to get a general explanation for the pervasiveness of ritual in our lives. The research center was tasked with pursuing a more limited question: "What is the role of ritual and storytelling in the life of southern middle-class families?" And so Emory University's Center on Myth and Ritual in American Life (MARIAL) was born, and over its ten-year existence, several dozen scholars—faculty, graduate students, postdoctoral fellows, and undergraduate fellows—produced dozens of studies focusing on the role of ritual and narrative in creating and nurturing the life of middle-class families.

We learned a lot about the work of rituals in defining and maintaining American families and how the continuity of a family's life and identity rested in great part on its rituals and its family stories. Yet by the time MARIAL had completed its work in 2010, we were still pretty much in the dark about the nature and the power of ritual as a general form of behavior. Having spent a good part of my life interpreting particular rituals in societies around the world (including my own society), I was still not sure why the kind of behavior we call *ritual* mattered so much in human life. Attempting to solve that mystery and uncover the hidden power of ritual, as well as the particular powers of particular rituals, is what has led me, late in my career, to write this book. And it has led me far beyond Southern families and well beyond anthropology.

I hope to figure out that mystery in these pages. But rather than writing another scholarly work aimed only at specialists, I have decided to write this book relatively free of jargon and with a relatively light use of the usual scholarly apparatus. I wanted to write an introduction to ritual studies for a larger and more general audience. Ritual is a fascinating subject and is not just for scholars. It is something all of us can learn to appreciate and use. As we will see in the book's final chapter, the powers of ritual can be harnessed by all of us to help us in our own lives.

The book has benefited from years of reading, researching, and teaching about ritual. That being said, it is intended as a personal account in that its conclusions, while based on a lot of scholarship, are plainly expressed and autobiographically grounded. Take them as academically informed opinions and reflections from a scholar who devoted much of his life to ritual. The examples of ritual discussed in the book constitute a kind of memoir of my personal relationship to rituals I have studied and practiced throughout my life and my career.

The fact that I am writing for a general audience does not mean that I will ignore the many lessons we have learned about ritual from academic research. Our exploration of the hidden powers of ritual will traverse many different fields of knowledge: evolutionary biology, anthropology, sociology, psychology, linguistics, aesthetics, performance theory, and religious studies. While each of these disciplines has managed to shine a light on an important aspect of ritual, I think that no single field has illuminated the big picture. Ritual is more important to us than we might imagine, and I want to illuminate that importance with an especially broad beam of light.

Organization of the Book

Our journey starts in chapter 2 by thinking about ritual as a kind of behavior, specifically as a form of specially constrained behavior. To do this, we need to rethink how we understand behavior. Rather than seeing human behavior as simply an endless stream of actions, it is helpful to think of it as an archaeologist thinks about a research site: as made up of many distinctive layers. Rather than time periods, the layers of behavior represent different degrees of constraint. The outermost layers of behavior might be thought of as relatively free play, behavior that is open to personal choice and easy variation. As we move deeper, our behavior becomes more subject to constraints and control, until finally we arrive at what we call *reflexes*, behavior responses that are more or less automatic and over which we have little control. From this perspective, ritual is viewed in relation to the wide range of ways in which human behavior can vary in terms of a spectrum spanning relative freedom and constraint. While not quite reflex, ritual takes its place on the relatively constrained end of the spectrum.

While many familiar rituals appear as ready-made packages of behavior, it is important to explore ritual as a process, as behavior in formation, recognizing the human capacity to sediment our behaviors into rituals through repetition. This psychological capacity to generate rituals is called "ritualization" and is really more of a cognitive process involving gradual change in brain activity and organization than a static package of actions. Studying the process of ritualization will help us understand where our rituals come from behaviorally. We saw ritualization at work in the gradual transformation of my class greeting circle from what appeared to be a random sequence of actions to a shared ritual framework for starting our class. Understanding the source of our rituals in this way will help us see the important relations between ritual and related forms of constrained behavior like habits and routines. And it will allow us to clarify what we mean by "ritual," a term that is often poorly defined and only vaguely understood.

To provide a break from our more general discussions of ritual, our journey into the world of ritual will take periodic detours into detailed accounts of a variety of rituals that I have both studied and participated in throughout my career. They range from grand public spectacles like the Balinese *ngaben* funeral ceremony to the more homely rituals that shape everyday life. Rather than put all of these examples together in a single section of the book, I have chosen to distribute them throughout the book as a form of ethnographic relief, interlacing our more general and abstract discussions with rich accounts of real rituals. In the spirit of participant observation, that paradoxical methodology shaping anthropological field work, our literary journey through the kingdom of ritual will tack back and forth between discussions of ritual in general and detailed evocations of rituals in particular. This zigzagging alternation between the general and particular is a distinctive aspect of the ethnographic sensibility that anthropologists bring to both their field research and their writing. While the ethnographic chapters will focus on the details of the rituals described, each one will conclude with a commentary in which we mine the ethnographies for general insights that each ritual can provide us about ritual in general.

Chapter 3 is the first of the case studies. It is a personal account of a spectacular mortuary ritual in Bali that I was fortunate enough to witness and photograph in 2008. A former student of mine, whose parents owned a small hotel on the Indonesian island of Bali, had invited me to visit. I was fortunate to arrive just in time to witness a royal cremation ceremony (*ngaben*) in the town of Ubud not far from my hotel. A sister of the former raja (king) of Gianyar Regency had died and was to be cremated along with several hundred other bodies that had been dug up from their graves for the occasion. It was said to be the biggest event of its kind to be mounted on the island in several decades, but even that description did not prepare me for the overwhelming scale and drama of the ritual, which was reported to have attracted a massive crowd of four hundred thousand spectators and participants. The *ngaben* is a splendid example of a classic grand-scale religious ritual, what I call big-R ritual. Coming upon the endless procession of colorfully dressed celebrants, the mesmerizing spiral of gamelan music, the unmistakable sweet scent of clove cigarettes, and the massive, gaudy mortuary structures being carried down the road by thousands of men, no one would have any doubt that we had arrived in the midst of ritual writ large.

Classic studies of animal behavior (e.g., ducks, fish, insects, dogs, and primates) have identified a wide repertory of rituals in nonhuman animals. Some anthropologists have suggested these animal rituals have nothing to do with highly symbolic human ritual and that it is a mistake to call this stereotyped animal behavior *ritual*. While there are clearly some important differences between animal and human rituals, it is worth exploring the possibility that human ritual is an evolutionary elaboration of behaviors found in other animals. So we will take up this question in chapter 4. Here I will describe some of the best-studied ritual behavior in nonhuman animals and compare the biologist's idea of the "ritualization" of animal behavior with the human process of ritualization. Our goal is not to reduce away the important distinctive features of human ritual but to explore the possibility that human rituals, despite their elaboration, have their roots in animal communication. Chapter 4 also considers the important implications for human ritual of the evolution of human language and the dramatic expansion of the human brain, particularly the frontal cortex. In other words, we don't need to reduce away the distinctive qualities of human ritual to appreciate the evolutionary links that human rituals may have with those of other animals.

Chapter 5 deals with gift exchange, a type of ritual that has been very well studied and has been shown to be significant in all human social life. Several case studies are presented describing various forms of ritual exchange. One of the case studies involves a Samoan exchange ritual in which I was involved personally and that turned a friendly exchange of gifts into a kind of ritual warfare. Rather than following the ritual script for exchanging gifts, the circumstances of this ritual in a Samoan village forced me to improvise on an old ritual to create a new and rather dangerous variation.

Chapter 6 discusses ten of the most important specific powers of ritual. Some of these powers are not generally recognized in the literature on ritual. I will discuss each of them in some detail with examples because they make clear why ritual is such an important dimension of human behavior. The longest of the chapters, chapter 6 is the theoretical heart of the book.

Chapters 7 and 8 are two contrasting cases of rituals from the state of Georgia that deal in different ways with how ritual can become enacted social memory. Each chapter focuses on a specific ritual in Georgia that I have studied. Chapter 7 starts by distinguishing between individual memory, as studied by psychologists, and collective or social memory that is shared by a group and becomes part of a group's history. This chapter is based on my five years attending Salem Camp Meeting, a distinctively American Christian religious revival tradition that can be traced back to the founding of the United States in the late eighteenth century. Here we encounter the ritual cultivation of a kind of nostalgic memory for a lost sense of community and family. In dramatic contrast, chapter 8 deals with traumatic memory, an annual ritual reenactment of a lynching of two young black couples in central Georgia back in the 1940s. The Moore's Ford lynching reenactment is ritual remembrance in a minor key, the attempt to keep alive something that many people would rather forget. Both of these Georgia rituals are examined in relation to race relations in their communities and their impact on the individual memories of those involved in the performances.

Chapter 9 deals with the borderland of ritual, when a ritual becomes a game. Focusing on the ritual structure of baseball, the chapter expands its view of ritual to encompass what is called "performance theory," the fascinating relationship between ritual, games, and theater performances. We will confront the problem of distinguishing genres of performance. Ritual, theater, and games have so much in common that it is sometimes hard to tell them apart. Despite their close connections, there are also important differences between the three kinds of performance. The chapter will highlight both the connections and the differences. It's an unusual look at baseball viewed, not as sport but as a distinctively American ritual. By stepping back from the specific events of the game, events that create its excitement for fans, it is possible to see the sport as a ritual performance revealing some important things about American culture. This chapter suggests that organized sports can be understood as both games and rituals, depending on the way they are observed.

Chapter 10 discusses the future of ritual and the impact of modern digital technology on our rituals. The phenomenal growth of the internet starting in the early 1980s has transformed the way the world communicates, and so the digital revolution cannot but have a major impact on how humans do ritual. The chapter will review the development of online rituals, both secular and religious, to see how virtual reality (VR) is transforming our ritual life. The chapter will compare *ritual online*, the use of the internet as a way to broadcast or live-stream traditional rituals, with *online ritual*, more radical implementations of digital simulation to create new kinds of ritual experiences. How cyber rituals cope with the disembodied action and the "displaced" environment of the screen will be a central issue that this chapter will confront.

Chapter 11 takes up the important issue of meaning and asks the fundamental question of whether a ritual necessarily has a meaning. We will consider the objections posed by some scholars that the rituals they studied appeared to be empty actions, whose performers claimed did not have any meaning. Since we have, up until this point, assumed that ritual was meaningful symbolic behavior, this challenge is crucial to our understanding of the work of ritual. If a ritual can be meaningless, why are we claiming it is so important for humans? Obviously, this is a particularly important chapter for this book.

Finally, chapter 12 concludes the book by considering ways in which our newfound understanding of ritual can be used to improve our quality of life. Because the book is intended as a personal memoir of my fifty years engaging with ritual personally and professionally, the chapter begins with the history of a lunch tradition I share with a group of my colleagues, a tradition that evolved over a period of twenty-five years into something much greater than a meal. This lunch ritual will set the stage for a discussion of the role of rituals in shaping our normal daily, weekly, monthly, and yearly cycles and the importance of ritual in giving life its normal rhythms.

These everyday rituals and routines include purely personal rituals that we don't always think of as rituals and we might take for granted. As opposed to the public spectacles linked to religious or civic traditions, everyday rituals come dressed in ordinary garb rather than the formal wear of sacred spectacle. But it is a mistake to assume that everyday social and personal rituals are less important to our lives than their elaborate public counterparts. In some sense these everyday rituals are actually the most important ritual forms, providing us with a taken-for-granted shape to our lives.

This book is titled *The Hidden Powers of Ritual* not because all ritual is necessarily hidden from our view. Much of our ritual life is in plain sight. Our major civic and religious rituals are often matters of intense awareness and attention. Some of our everyday rituals may be understood as hidden in the sense that we take them for granted and don't necessarily think of them as rituals. When I speak of ritual's hidden power, I'm talking about the pervasiveness of ritual in our lives and the surprising implications of ritual that have been touched on in this chapter. In chapter 12, I propose a few important ways in which we can empower ourselves, our communities, and our families by harnessing the hidden power of ritual. So much of our lives is dictated by forces—ecological, economic, political, physiological— over which we have little control. Ritual, on the other hand, gives us all a powerful tool for helping to shape and reshape our lives. This is one of the lessons that I learned during the decade in which I researched American family ritual and spent many hours shadowing families through the ritual cycles of their day, their week, their season, and their year. I came away not only impressed by the resilience of these families but also convinced that their rituals were central ways in which they shaped their family cultures and the culture of their communities. So while the book has taken us into many exotic spaces, I have chosen to end the book by coming home and considering the ways in which we can all harness the hidden powers of ritual to enhance our quality of life and the lives of our families.

2 Rethinking Behavior

Behavioral sciences such as anthropology, psychology, and economics aim to make sense of human behavior. Each field does it in its own way. As an anthropologist, I generally focus on cultural aspects of behavior, local traditions shaping collective behavior that vary from group to group. Psychologists usually study personal and internal motivations that vary among individuals. Economists have traditionally concentrated on exploring the presumed universal rationality of decision-making, studying how people make choices that maximize self-interest and calculate what they call the "marginal utility" of their various options. Despite these differences, all behavioral scientists share the primary goal of accounting for human behavior.

But what counts as "behavior?" Humans are in constant motion, even when asleep. Which of our movements and actions are to be considered our behavior? If I deliberately drop to the ground and roll around, I am clearly behaving (though quite strangely). But am I still "behaving" if I accidentally trip and fall? Are only intentional acts to count as behavior, and is behavior always conscious action? Do we include thinking as behavior, and what about our feelings? Am I behaving when I feel something or only when I express my emotions outwardly to others? What about an involuntary physiological activity like a nervous tic? The closer we look at behavior, the more questions we have, and the definition of behavior becomes more complicated. These questions matter for this book since it treats ritual as a special kind of behavior. To understand ritual, we must begin by rethinking the idea of "behavior."

Even our everyday behavior turns out to be surprisingly complex, a mix of very different kinds of actions. Consider the many types of behavior that

make up the following account of the start of my typical workday during
the years I was teaching at Emory University:

My alarm next to my bed is usually set on school days to wake me at
7:30 a.m. But usually, I get up on my own a few minutes earlier than
that. My "internal clock" heads off the ringing of the alarm. My wife
usually gets up before me, and she is downstairs preparing our morning coffee in the kitchen. Half asleep, I roll out of bed and head for the
bathroom for the usual morning bathroom routine. After my morning
shower, I shave, brush my teeth, take an allergy pill, comb my hair, and
proceed to get dressed in the clothes I had laid out the previous night.

While I usually wear brown slacks, a plain shirt, and, on teaching
days, a tweed sport coat, today I decided to wear one of my colorful
silk aloha shirts. Something different, something cheerful, I think. Once
dressed, I check to see that I have my cell phone with me and look into
my wallet to see how much cash I have on hand for the day. Then I head
downstairs for breakfast.

My coffee waits for me on the kitchen counter, and I put my usual
two slices of rye bread in the toaster. Toast and coffee are my regular
breakfast since I am anxious to get on the road. This morning my wife
suggested adding some vanilla yogurt with a sliced pear she had bought.
After finishing breakfast, I briefly chat with her, discussing her plans for
the day. I kiss her goodbye and head out the back door to the driveway
where my car is parked.

Driving my usual route down several local streets, stopping at two
stop signs and three intersections with traffic lights, I make my way to
the interstate highway that will take me into Atlanta, some forty miles
away. Because the route is so familiar, I do not need the car's GPS, and
the car seems to find its way over the regular route, allowing me to think
about the classes and various meetings I have scheduled for the day.
Noticing that I am low on gas, I exit the highway and turn into a gas
station near the highway entrance to fill up the gas tank.

While I am refueling the car, my cell phone rings. My wife is asking
if I have time to pick up some clothes at a new dry cleaner in Atlanta
that she has recently discovered and is trying out. Checking my watch,
I tell her I'll stop at the cleaners on my way to work. She gives me the
name of the cleaners, and I find their address using my cell phone. I plug

the address into my GPS, which starts broadcasting driving instructions immediately.

Since the diversion to the dry cleaners will take up an extra twenty minutes of my driving time, I find myself driving faster than usual until I notice a police car with a flashing blue light coming up on my left. My heart pounding, I immediately slow down to just below the speed limit and am relieved when the police car passes by me and continues on its way, thankfully ignoring me.

After picking up the laundry, I continue to Emory. Because I arrive later than usual, the parking deck where I always park is full. I circle the deck several times with no luck. So I exit the deck and make my way around the campus, hoping to find another space. Fortunately, I remember that I have an old but still valid, disabled parking tag in the glove compartment from when I had hip surgery several years ago. I finally locate an accessible parking space around the back end of the campus and make my way on foot across the campus.

Arriving at the anthropology building where my office is located, I enter the building. I run into a few of my colleagues, and we briefly chat and exchange small talk. Then I poke my head into the main office and say good morning to the secretaries and the department office manager, who signals me into her office for a chat. Since I am department chair, this is not uncommon. She has some problems scheduling faculty interviews for a job candidate coming next week. We looked over the troublesome interview schedule, and I develop some proposed solutions to her problems. Then I make my way to my office. I have a lot on my plate this morning and did not have time last night to prepare adequately for my upcoming graduate seminar. So instead of leaving my office door open, I close it, alerting casual visitors that I will be busy this morning.

We'll stop here, even though the day was only just beginning. How many behaviors did I perform during the three hours between when I awoke and when I settled into my office? It's hard to say. Human activity does not usually come naturally packaged as countable behaviors despite the attempt of our calendars and to-do lists to make them appear that way. Most of the time, our lives are a continuous flow of actions, interactions, and multitasking, varying in complexity, motivation, consciousness, and tempo.

But when we are asked to recount "what we did," we translate the flow of living into nouns, chunking our motion into activity units and giving them names like "waking up," "having breakfast," "brushing my teeth," "driving to work," and "having a chat." We may conceive of these actions as "behaviors," but none qualify as "raw behaviors." They are abstract concepts created by language, turning the flow of our lives into comprehensible things. Our conviction that our lives are made up of discrete activity chunks is created by the demands of language, forcing us to create behavior boundaries by breaking action into namable clusters.

"Taking my shower" is a complex sequence of acts that allow for many slight variations, such as if and when I reach for the bar of soap or turning down the hot water if the shower is too hot. When exactly does my "taking a shower" begin? When I first think about showering? When I turn on the shower faucet? When I start undressing? In the same way, a detailed description of "driving to work" could break down that cluster into innumerable small actions such as opening the car door, sliding into the seat, putting the key in the starter, adjusting the side mirror, scanning the road, and applying the brakes. And we could even add "breathing" or a beating heart to the mix. This refashioning of action into conceptual chunks is a requirement of storytelling, where, under the rule of language, our actions must be recounted as "one thing after another."

Habits and Routines

My morning was filled with many such action clusters. Some had been repeated so often that I had names for them when asked to describe them. The more minor familiar actions like getting out of bed in a certain way, sleeping on a particular side, twisting open the cap of the toothpaste tube, or putting on socks and shoes are not usually named or even noticed. They are habits, action patterns performed so often that they have become automatic. Habits are the product of the reinforced training of neural networks, brain paths controlling movement, and sequencing. Our habits are not just actions but also brain events. Habituation, the gradual entrainment of a neural network for a small action set, allows us to do things without paying close attention to our actions. Because our brains have been prepared for these habitual acts, habits free up our working memory so we can pay attention to other things.

Habits are behavior modules that can be combined into longer strings of behavior. Psychologists have called these more elaborate strings of repeated behavior *routines*. I described a wake-up routine made up of many habits strung together in a relatively predictable sequence. When we develop specific physical skills through practice, such as learning to play the piano, we characterize the seemingly automatic physical routine as our "muscle memory" at work. Because skilled pianists do not need to focus their attention on the habituated movements of their fingers, hands, and feet, they can focus on higher levels of musical performance like phrasing, intonation, and interpretation. One level of performance has sunk out of awareness so that another can get the attention it needs.

As we saw from my account of my workday morning, much of our everyday behavior is organized into routines. So familiar and automatic are our daily routines that, like our habits, they often elude our awareness. This is why we are often not fully conscious of what we are doing and why we have trouble remembering what we did today when we get home and are asked how our day was. We can usually recall those events that are not routine. Routines generally develop from repeated behavior when a sequence of habitual action is unified into a cluster. Sometimes routines are given a name such as "doing laundry" or "commuting to work." Everyday activity is full of routines ranging from simple routines like preparing a cup of tea in a standard way to more elaborate sequences of behavior such as filling my six medicine trays marked for each day of the week with my pills, which I perform almost automatically every six weeks.

Consider how many behavioral routines you perform on a given day, and you will likely be surprised at just how scripted your behavior is. Routines will vary in terms of how consciously and deliberately they are performed. One of the main functions of routines is to offload behavior from working memory, our immediate awareness of things in which we are currently engaged. We carry out many of our routines almost unconsciously. For example, my wake-up routine had become so familiar that my body unconsciously kept track of the time I needed to get up, making the external guidance of my morning alarm unnecessary.

When we are forced to modify or double-check these routines to make sure they are correctly done, they will move forward from background knowledge into full awareness. Suppose a piano teacher suggests a new way for a pianist to perform a musical passage. In that case, the student no longer relies on the habituated muscle memory of complex strings of notes. Instead, she deliberately refocuses her attention on what her fingers are doing, practicing the new skill until it becomes a habit.

Deliberately bringing a routine to conscious attention is essential as a safety measure in many professions. For example, surgery is often accomplished by teams performing relatively standardized sequences of actions. But the familiar acts are accompanied by a set of verbalized requests and responses among doctors and nurses that serve as a check on commands and create a space for a quick improvisation in case things don't go as planned.

A similar verbal check routine occurs in conversations between pilots and air controllers, where the pilot is required to restate the instructions given by the air controller. This is important not just as a double-check but also because the pilot and controller are often not speaking in their native language, so the repetition routine is a way of making sure the pilot has understood the controller. Airline pilots also perform complex preflight routines checking their controls and settings. Still, they are deliberately given checklists to read and count off aloud to their copilot to double-check that the safety routines are followed. Again, a potentially unconscious action sequence is forced back into a conscious routine to allow the cockpit crew to guard against any performance errors.

In addition to routines, my account includes several actions where I had to be more aware and deliberate about what I was doing. Typically, my route to work was so familiar that I could make the drive without much conscious attention to what I was doing. The route and the driving skills had long ago become matters of habit, allowing me to focus my thoughts on other issues while driving to work. But on this day my attention was shifted back to my driving by the flashing lights of the police car behind me. And when I needed to change my route to make a stop at the new dry cleaner, I could no longer rely on my routine to navigate for me. I now needed to pay attention to my route. Plugging the address into my GPS, I now followed its instructions and relied on its virtual memory. This intrusion of unfamiliar external route instructions (my wife's request plus the GPS directions) made me very aware of where I was and the streets I needed to locate. My actions were no longer automatic and internalized but controlled externally, outwardly constrained. I had to shift from one sort of behavior to another. My familiar routines and the GPS directions are examples of tightly constrained behavior, activities over which I exercise little control.

At the other end of the control spectrum from these fixed action sets are improvised or creative actions over which we exercise a lot of choice and freedom of movement. My decision to wear a brightly colored aloha shirt to work is an example of relatively spontaneous behavior governed by a greater degree of free will. That decision violated my regular dressing routine on workdays. Another example of rather spontaneous behavior was having to come up with a solution to a departmental scheduling problem involving a job candidate. Since this particular situation was far from routine for the department, it involved some conscious strategizing. I turned to creative problem-solving rather than defaulting to a tried-and-true formula. From the perspective of control, we can appreciate the many different kinds of behavior humans are capable of. We can envision a spectrum of behaviors ranging from the relative freedom of spontaneous improvisation to the fixed reflexes over which we have little to no control. It is helpful to think of this spectrum as defining an arc bridging "loose" and "tight" behavior. From this perspective, we can conceive of ritual as a relatively tight sort of behavior.

Kinds of Control of Behavior

We have the least control over our reflexes, such as the startle reflex, or the blinking of the eyes when faced with a threat, or the numerous deep tendon reflexes (like the famous knee-jerk reflex), which are tested by tapping on a tendon and looking for a spontaneous reaction of the adjoining muscle. Reflexes are controlled by a "reflex arc" containing two neurons, a sensory (afferent) neuron and a motor (efferent) neuron. The reflex arc bypasses the brain and eludes conscious control. The synapse linking the two neurons is in the spinal cord rather than in the brain, allowing for quick, automatic responses to threats.

Also relatively self-controlled are the physiological responses like breathing, heart rate, and endocrine secretion under the control of the autonomic nervous system. Unlike reflexes, we can learn to control our breathing, swallowing, and even our heart rhythms through training and concentration. Yogis are famous for using this training to control some autonomic functions. But for most of us, the default control of our autonomic functions is generally left to the autonomic nervous system, which takes over in the absence of conscious control. While these actions may be thought of as our body's behavior, I do not generally think of my reflexes and autonomic functioning as "my behavior." In ordinary usage, considering something as my behavior implies some degree of control and intention on my part.

However, there is a significant intermediate zone where our behavior is under some degree of control and can be considered partly intentional and malleable. Deliberate behavior is subject to a wide variety of different controls. In this zone, we are often held responsible socially and morally for what we do despite some outside control. Here, personal responsibility for one's behavior is often contested and debated. "I was just following orders," or "It's the law!" "She made me do it!" or "Everybody's doing it!" are common ways in which people try to evade responsibility for partly voluntary actions and actions partly under external control.

Sometimes, our behavior's "external" controls come from within our bodies, but the behavior is experienced as coming from beyond the self. Impulsive behavior, habits, or sudden emotional responses like anger are examples of inner causes that may feel external to our conscious selves. Freud called the more impulsive, pleasure-seeking part of the personality the id, or, in German, *das Es* ("the it"), which he opposed to the ego, which he termed *das Ego* ("the self"), suggesting that the id is experienced as impulses alien to the self. But there are also many genuinely external constraints on behavior, such as informal social norms, formal laws, the watching eyes of others, public shaming, imitation of another person's actions, verbal or written instructions, others' responses to our actions, stories that model certain kinds of behavior, or advice from influential people.

Over the course of living, many of these external constraints become internalized, turning behavior regulation into self-control. For instance, well-socialized people do not need to consult the Ten Commandments to know they should honor their parents or refrain from killing or stealing. They do not act out of obedience to the law but out of self-censorship. Much of our learning is the internalization of external constraints on behavior. A skilled musician can memorize a complex musical score, and we say he "knows it by heart." A cook may follow a recipe from a cookbook the first few times she makes a dish. But eventually, she internalizes the instructions and can even improvise on the recipe. The same is true for negative controls that tell us what not to do. What starts as my mother's scolding eventually becomes a remembered inner voice. Controlling emotions like fear, shame, and guilt suggests the power that such internalized controls, born out of genuine or imagined relationships with others, can have over our behavior.

The ability to internalize behavior constraints and invest them with moral authority is a goal of what's called "socialization." In practical activities like getting dressed, this internalization is "learning to do it myself." But in matters of right and wrong behavior, this internalization of behavioral constraints is called "moral development." The Swiss psychologist Jean Piaget studied the gradual emergence of internalized moral rules and described them in his 1932 book *The Moral Development of the Child*. Observing Swiss children playing marbles at different ages, he concluded that children's awareness of rules constraining play develops gradually, unfolding in stages.

At first, children play freely with marbles, with no awareness of rules controlling a game and no sense of social cooperation. This is pure play. By the age of seven, Piaget found that children had begun to cooperate in tournaments, play constrained by social relations. Eventually, children become aware of the rules governing play and start by seeing the rules as absolute and having a kind of immutable external force. Piaget found that children begin to codify the game rules around the age of twelve. Eventually, children recognize that these rules are arbitrary and artificial. Still, they also acknowledge that playing by the rules is necessary for the continuation of the game and the cooperation and coordination of all the players. The freedom of play and the external constraints of games converge.

Interestingly, in this developmental process, Piaget saw the psychic roots of what philosophers have called "the social contract," the human ability to trade the "natural" freedom of action for a degree of social and political control. So-called contract theorists recognized this trade-off as the cornerstone of political and social morality. Piaget saw the most primitive roots of the social cooperation that children achieve in play in the early regularities they developed in their repeated physical movements. Such primitive motor routines allow children their earliest experience of action patterns. Eventually, they learn that these routines can be shared with others and ultimately provide a framework for what psychologists call *intersubjectivity*, socially shared experience. Infants are introduced to these shared routines by the simple interactive routines parents and caregivers develop with the babies, like peek-a-boo games. For Piaget, these routines become the child's first intuition of a shared external compulsion that gradually becomes a sense of law-governed regularity in social play. With the emergence of social games with rules, the idea of "playing by the rules" emerges as the foundation of the very idea of social cooperation. Organized social interaction is born from these simple routines.

Routines fit somewhere in the middle of this behavior spectrum, lying somewhere between fully constrained automatic behaviors like reflexes and spontaneous improvisation. Our daily routines may have been developed by us (with the early help of our parents). Still, once in place, they exercise a degree of compulsion over us and take on the character of quasi-reflexive behavior. Routines are partly responsible for our day going smoothly. Still, they are not reflexes. When necessary, we can permanently alter a routine, skip it entirely, or even replace it with a new routine. This "middle-of-the-road" quality of our habits and routines, sitting midway between tight and loose control, is an integral part of why we have routines in the first place.

Once established through repetition, our routines take a load off of our minds, simplifying the performance of everyday tasks and freeing up cognitive resources for more pressing challenges. But were our practices inflexible and not subject to change and variation, we would always be stuck with doing things the same way. Our lives inevitably change over time, and those changes often require new or modified routines. We need both the stability of routines and the flexibility and creativity they allow in adapting to unique circumstances. Learned routines provide just the right mix of stability and flexibility, giving us a repertory of functional automatic responses but still letting us change the rules of the game when we need to.

Ritual

At last we come to ritual. In exploring routines, we have come very close to ritual. We could almost claim that rituals are just elaborated routines. But that does not quite do justice to ritual. A ritual is a routine but one with a high symbolic load. For the most part, routines simplify and standardize sequences of practical activities like cleaning the house, making scrambled eggs, combing our hair, shopping at the supermarket (where we tend to develop familiar routes through the aisles), and driving a car. Routines have apparent functions, but can we say that they resonate with "meaning?" Usually, our routines get the job done without being especially meaningful.

But under exceptional circumstances, routines can add a significant symbolic load to their practical function. Bathing an infant in a certain way gets the child clean, but it can also become a way of displaying one's competence as a parent or love of a child. It is a routine but has also become a ritual. Barbequing meat on the backyard grill often does more than get the meal made. It can become a way to demonstrate a man's masculine status in the household.

Advertisers know the difference between a ritual and a routine. Ads selling practical items often attempt to add or reinforce a symbolic dimension to our everyday activities, reframing our routines as rituals. Buy this coffee, and you not only have something to drink in the morning, but you will also symbolize your love for your spouse. Once reframed in this way, the advertisements add symbolic value to seemingly practical items. Symbolically loaded, routines become rituals. This way of defining ritual means that there can be no clear distinction between ritual and routine. By definition, every ritual incorporates behavioral routines. Routines become rituals as they gradually develop symbolic significance. Rituals are scripted action sequences that take on repeatable form and symbolic importance over time.

While all rituals are also routines, the opposite is not true. Many of our routines have practical effects but little or no symbolic value for us. For most of us, brushing our teeth every morning might have little "meaning" other than starting the day. When (often aided by advertising) it comes to symbolize our commitment to beauty, social acceptability, or hygiene, however, even brushing teeth can be a ritual. Rituals emerge from routines when they have taken on symbolic importance for those performing or viewing them. This means that, to some extent, the ritual dimension of action lies in the eye of the beholder or the performer. Routine is an easily remembered way of acting. On the other hand, ritual is a special way of experiencing that action. The implication is that the same formalized sequence of activities might be simply a routine to one person but a ritual for another. This is because ritual is part of a more complex spectrum of behavior. Closely related to other behavior genres, a ritual always risks shading off into something else, like a game, a theatrical performance, or a mere routine.

Simple acts are formalized into automatic behaviors through habituation. In the same way, a chain of habits can gradually sediment into stable

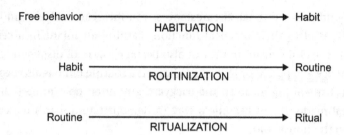

Figure 2.1
Processes of formalization in the emergence of habits, routines, and rituals

routines through a process of routinization. Finally, practical routines may gradually acquire symbolic significance for an individual or a community, a process we call *ritualization*, as a routine takes on meaning beyond its useful function (see figure 2.1 below).

These parallel processes involve the gradual formalization of behavior. In creating routines, this formalization consists of the standardization, stereotyping, and automated sequencing of actions. In addition, ritualization also involves the gradual accretion of symbolic associations. Ritual is experienced as meaningful action, an important aspect of ritual that will be discussed in detail in chapter 11.

Rituals come at many scales and can be personal, social, or sacred. The kind of symbolism of ritual will be different for personal, social, and sacred rituals. To understand these differences, we turn to the matter of ritual scale.

Personal Rituals

Consider the simple act of having a morning cup of coffee, something many of us do. If at breakfast I say, "I'm having a cup of coffee," then drinking it is just a part of breakfast. It might even be part of a morning breakfast routine if I drink coffee regularly. But consider the shift in tone if I say, "I'm having *my* cup of coffee." The use of the personal pronoun suggests that this cup of coffee has taken on special importance for me. In addition to its practical function, this cup of coffee has acquired a "symbolic load." My coffee routine has become a personal ritual, part of how I experience the continuity of my identity. Though no English grammar textbook will use this term, we might call this "my" the *ritual possessive*.

But if coffee drinking has acquired a symbolic load, what might the coffee symbolize? Often this kind of personal symbolism is diffuse rather than specific. I may not be able to say just what the morning coffee represents, only that I feel that my morning coffee matters in making my life meaningful. I'm just not me without my coffee; this day is not a normal day. Because coffee and tea drinking are especially subject to ritualization, terrorists have sometimes targeted coffee shops. By violently disrupting the site of an essential personal ritual, the taken-for-granted fabric of everyday life and the behavioral foundation of one's ordinary identity are shredded. By attacking "my coffee," the familiar horizon I have come to expect for my everyday life is broken. Now too scared to go back to my café, I, along with many others, am the victim of an assault on my taken-for-granted reality.

Personal rituals are the unglamorous hidden rituals that tie together the fabric of everyday life. My personal rituals are unlikely to be recognized as rituals either by me or others. They are usually not named ("my coffee ritual" is more likely to be found in a sociology textbook than in my everyday speech). Their symbolism is not overt or elaborated in the way it is in significant public rituals. We are used to associating the term "ritual" with highly elaborate public celebrations. But more private personal ritual is no less critical. A typical day is filled with small routines that have symbolic significance for people of which they are frequently not fully conscious.

Grooming rituals like "taking my shower" or "applying my makeup" come to have importance both for their practical benefits and as demonstrations of cleanliness, or beauty, or even providing a reassuring activity that marks a particular time of day. Eating is particularly subject to ritualization. Many people ritualize their meal routines: what they eat, when, where, and how. For instance, some people will eat around a plate of food, finishing one food item at a time. Others may mix their dishes with a fork or spoon. If you watch a group of people eat, you will be struck by the degree to which people have ritualized their eating styles. It often turns out that these ritualized eating styles are not random but are instead linked symbolically to other aspects of a person's character or that the eater is unconsciously imitating a parent.

In recent decades, the ritualization of eating has expanded from a personal choice into a conscious social identity. Vegans, vegetarians, those who keep kosher, Muslims who only eat halal meat, pescatarians, devotees of the slow-food movement, fans of the South Beach Diet, and other foodie traditions have become significant identity labels, often with moral or religious overtones. Having acquired a considerable symbolic load, food identities proclaim a ritual status in addition to a practical eating choice. The same goes for fitness routines like jogging, biking, or working out in a gym, which become important rituals displaying to self and others that one is a certain kind of person—a person who takes good care of one's body.

The symbolic nature of the performance is often marked by specially designed clothing or other appurtenances that set apart the wearer as an athlete. Clothing is often a critical symbolic element of personal rituals. Little wonder that companies have marketed their clothing lines so that their prominently displayed name or logos (think Nike or Gucci) serve as ritual symbols for rites of self-definition and can serve as status markers independent of the clothing itself.

Significant transitions are often ritualized. So it is not surprising that we commonly create personal bedtime rituals. A bedtime ritual is famously associated with young children for whom the coming of night and sleep produce potential separation anxiety. Parents learn to ritualize the bedtime routine involving not just the practical routines of changing clothes, bathing, and brushing teeth but also surplus symbolic elements like bedtime stories, cuddling with parents, prayers, special music, special blankets, or stuffed animals or dolls. These ritual add-ons become part of comforting bedtime rituals that encourage a smooth transition from the waking world to the world of sleep. Adults also have their bedtime rituals involving bedtime hygiene and ritualized ways of arranging the bed or watching familiar TV shows or other forms of ritually marked bedtime.

While many personal rituals are performed in public spaces, others are done alone. Our personal rituals do not always need an audience other than ourselves. Personal rituals remind us of who we are, providing the comfort of experiencing a well-worn performance of our identity. Serving as our unique signature inscribed in our actions, our personal rituals are conversations with ourselves about who we are and who we wish to be.

Social Rituals

While my personal rituals belong to me alone, social rituals are interpersonal and are shared by groups or entire communities. Our social lives are like a dance made up of mutually adjusted norm-governed behavior.

Sometimes these interactions are spontaneous, but more often than we realize, they comprise stereotyped and formalized interaction sequences. These ritual frames that shape our interactions with others are what sociologist Erving Goffman made famous in the 1960s and 70s in a series of classic books dealing with "interaction ritual."[1]

Working from philosopher George Herbert Mead's notion of "the social self," Goffman saw the self not as the private possession of an individual but as an ongoing social project, developed in and through ritual interactions with others. One presents "a face" to others whose ritual responses reaffirm or contest the proposed identity. In this influential view of self-creation, the "self" unfolds gradually over time as a ritual coproduction between self and audience. Some of these social rituals are negotiated on the spot, as someone proposes what Goffman calls "a line"—a sense of how they should be viewed and treated by others. This line is either accepted by others or challenged. In this way, the self is revealed, not as a steady identity safely hidden from the effects of social interaction but as a work in progress, utterly dependent on how others respond to our claims to a particular identity. While a relatively stable sense of self can emerge when I get consistent support from others for my sense of who I am, my sense of self can also be put in question by ritual challenges or inconsistent interactions. In this way, the self turns out to be more social than personal.

The ritualization of our interactions is especially obvious in the way we greet or depart from others when we automatically default to familiar ritual forms. Our competence in using our culture's ritual forms is developed over a long period as we grow up. Ritual is a kind of gestural language by which we express the quality of our relationships with others. When we encounter others, we have to choose from various rituals of greeting and departing, relating to our age, gender, social class, and relative social status as well as the history of our relationship. Our options reflect our understanding of our relationship with the person we greet or depart from. In greeting someone, do I shake hands, nod, hug, bow, or squeeze their hands? If I hug, how tightly should I squeeze? How long should the hug last? A brief, restrained hug with stiff arms and minimal body contact is a ritual gesture very different from a long tight, squeezing embrace. Different relationships and different kinds of relationship suggest very different ritual gestures.

While greetings worldwide share some standard features, our culture strongly influences our greeting rituals. In France, they would include the option of a double kiss on both cheeks. For traditional Maoris of New Zealand, greetings might consist of a *hongi*, a rubbing of noses. In Samoa, when passing an acquaintance on the road, you can greet the other by saying goodbye (*tofa*) if you intend to pass them and keep walking or saying hello (*talofa*) if you want to stop for a chat. The most informal Samoan greeting while passing is a mutual raising of the eyebrows. One never passes another on the road without some ritual acknowledgment. If you pass close to someone of higher rank in a small space, you show respect to that person by stooping down and saying *tulou* (excuse me) as you pass.

Throughout Asia, greeting rituals use many forms of bowing, some with hands at one's side, in other places with palms together. The Chinese developed bending into an extreme ritual of submission of inferiors to superiors called kowtow that can still be found in modern China. In kowtow, subservience and respect are shown by kneeling in front of a superior and placing one's forehead on the ground. These rituals of greeting and respect are rarely taught explicitly, but learned by observation and imitation. Royal greetings are an exception. British subjects meeting the Queen or Vatican visitors preparing to meet the Pope must be instructed in the proper ritual forms of greeting and farewell they will have to use. Rather than simple gestures, ritual greetings are always fluid and dynamic indices of the state of relationships. The angle of bowing, the length of hugging, and the degree of stooping are all adjusted to the precise degree of intimacy or distance we want to communicate.

Conversations are also ritualized. More than we realize, we often converse in verbal formulas, beginning and ending our chats with highly predictable exchanges. This is especially true when we do not have a specific conversational agenda with someone we have perhaps met by chance. Unprepared and lacking a preplanned topic for conversation, we default to "empty" ritualized language as a way to provide a shared framework for our interaction. Standard ritual openings like "How are you doing?" or "How's the family?" or "Nice weather we're having?," and, for men, "Did you see the game last night?" act as placeholders for more substantive conversation topics.

Suppose the conversation continues beyond the ritual formalities. In that case, one of the parties will introduce some new information, and the conversation can move beyond the ritual exchange to a more improvised substantive exchange. If not, then the same kind of stereotyped language can end the encounter so that the entire conversation ends up as a series of clichés. In this case, the meaning of such a predictable exchange is simply "I acknowledge your presence." Even the more improvisational parts of the conversation are ritually structured by implicit rules governing turn taking, interruption, topic control, and speech styles. Through conversation ritual, the relative status and intimacy between the participants are negotiated.

Contemplating this sort of empty ritual tends to embarrass Americans. We like to think of ourselves as acting spontaneously and with personal sincerity. The very idea of "ritual conversation" suggests a kind of artificiality and lack of authenticity in our relationships. But that does not prevent our conversations from employing ritual forms. In many cultures, the formality and predictability of conversational ritual are explicit virtues, marking a speaker as cultured and well mannered. This is especially true in societies characterized by social hierarchy, such as traditional Japan or England. For example, in Samoan society, where I lived for five years, status and rank differences between families are tied to their family pedigrees and the importance of the titles held by their *matai* (chiefs). Here, skill in carrying out conversational rituals of greeting and farewell is highly valued. What may come across to Americans as everyday clichés is a highly valued sign of social skill and good breeding to Samoans. Samoans are perfectly aware that they are performing, and they admire it.

When I first arrived in Samoa in 1968, following twelve weeks of Peace Corps training in the Samoan language, I was immediately struck by how much Samoans loved the art of verbal ceremony. When I commented on this to my host family, they expressed surprise that conversations could be made in any other way. In Peace Corps training, we memorized set speeches to exchange with villagers when we walked through a village. We learned to greet people in their houses from the road. If they asked where we were going, even if we carried a towel and soap and were heading to the bathing pool, we learned to reply that we were going to bathe. "Go then," they were supposed to respond. "Have a good bath." To my surprise, Samoans in my village appeared to have memorized the same speeches, often word for word.

Samoans were ritual virtuosos. Every formal Samoan social encounter begins and ends with a conversational ritual in which the dignity of the person and the family being addressed are honored using elevated forms of address. In the most formal ritual settings, special orator chiefs called *tulafale* deliver the speeches. Samoans are well prepared for these encounters, and they occur even in more casual settings, when there is little or no explicit business to conduct. After an exchange of formal greetings, sometimes quite elaborate, the conversation will switch in both content and tone to a more freeform improvisational style in which news is exchanged, requests are made, or other business is conducted. When the conversation is about to end, Samoans will smoothly switch gears again and finish the encounter with appropriate ritual language for a farewell. If there is no news to convey, the formalities will carry the day. There is never a lack of something polite to say.

In any social gathering, from informal chats to the elaborate kava ceremonies, funerals, chiefly installation ceremonies, chiefs' council meetings, and even school staff meetings, I came to expect and eventually to appreciate the elegant verbal embroidery of the speeches that opened and closed the proceedings. When my Samoan had improved enough to allow me to try my hand at translating some of these speeches for non-Samoan visitors, it always amazed me that a five-minute welcome, acknowledging the dignity and honor of the visitors, could only be translated as something like "We welcome the honorable [name] to our village." The other four minutes of speech were largely untranslatable honorific phrases, not content. Form, it turns out, was the point.

We usually call these polite social rituals "etiquette" or "good manners." Our interpersonal encounters cover many different situations, and verbal and gestural formulas cover most of them. Managing social life requires skills both in correctly reading the signs of others and in appropriately responding to them. When I arrived in Samoa, I learned an entirely new set of interpersonal rituals that would eventually propel me smoothly through an ordinary day. After making some embarrassing faux pas, I figured out the difference between a purely polite invitation to dinner that I was supposed to turn down when nothing had been prepared ("Won't you come in and eat?") and a genuine request ("Will you come in and eat?"), which I was free to accept. I learned to remove my shoes and sit immediately when entering a Samoan *fale* (house). In traditional thatched-roof huts in rural villages, I noticed that no one stood up to greet me as they would back home. But in the more European-style houses in town, etiquette had become more European. Social ritual is always sensitive to social context. I eventually got used to sitting for long periods with my legs folded in front of me (slowly growing numb!) since stretching out one's legs in someone else's house without them inviting you to do it was bad manners. I eventually mastered the essential formal verbal exchanges for entering and leaving and the rules for proper turn taking in my conversations.

I eventually figured out how to play humorously with Samoan ritual forms, and Samoans usually loved my joking. My clowning served to shatter the stiff formality that visiting guests—especially foreigners—produced, and both my hosts and I seemed relieved to laugh together. Once you know the rules of good etiquette, you can figure out how to bend them. Skilled ritual interactions usually allowed for a degree of free play once you knew them well enough. My education included many embarrassing mistakes and a lot of careful observation. But eventually, the Samoan ritual code governing social encounters became second nature for me, and island life became much easier and more fun.

Table Manners

Another area of social life that is often ritualized is eating. In English, we talk of good table manners, and etiquette books lay out many of the rules governing social eating. Most Americans will recall being told to keep their elbows off the table, not to slurp their soup, and what to avoid speaking about at the dinner table. High-end restaurants often choreograph food and wine service so that it appears to be a dance performance. Waiters in formal dress move in stylized ways and address diners in a highly deferential and formalized restaurant language ("Would you care to peruse the dessert menu, Madam?"). The opening of a wine bottle and the pouring of the wine are carried out with exaggerated flourishes. In such "high-class" settings, serving and eating are strictly governed by an elaborate ritual code.

The ritualization of eating is closely keyed to social status. The very words for eating are often marked for status. In English, ordinary folks "eat," while those of high status "dine." Similarly, in Samoan, the common term for eating is *'ai*, but chiefs will be said to *taumafa* or *tausami*. The ritualization of eating is dramatically elaborated in the case of politically charged meals such as state dinners in the White House or Buckingham Palace, where places at the tables are set with up to seven or eight glasses for different wines and different courses as well as numerous forks and spoons of various shapes and sizes to accommodate the many courses of the meal.

The ritual elaboration of the meal becomes almost a self-parody. In such settings, guests are presented with a challenge in seeking a smooth path through the meal. The effect is intended to overwhelm the guests with the elegance and the complexity of the meal and the status of the host and those seated at the table. If the dinner at Buckingham Palace is orchestrated like a symphony, the Queen was always the unchallenged conductor, and all guests were warned ahead of time to attend to her subtle signals as to when the meal starts and ends and how long to converse with her.

Formal Samoan meals are also ritually regulated, but the rules are quite different. Guests are seated cross-legged on mats on the floor. One's seating position is determined by the title one holds. Food is served on woven food mats, and one eats in order of social status. The meal begins with a prayer by the host and a speech of welcome. Young untitled men serve the food. A child will be seated in front of each diner, charged with fanning the food to keep flies away (don't ever try to offer the child some of your food). Diners will be given a sizable pile of food, usually more than they can eat. If someone looks like they will finish their food, more will be brought before the mat is empty. No one has to ask for seconds, and guests are not asked if they want more food. There is generally little conversation during the meal.

When someone is done, they call out *Ia, 'ua 'ou ma'ona* ("I'm full"), followed by a speech thanking the family for the abundant food and their gracious hospitality. I memorized one of these thank-you speeches that used poetic metaphor to compare the hosts' generosity to the flow of the sea tide and the rushing water of a river. The hosts were always delighted to hear a foreigner express ritual thanks in this elaborate way. After the speech, and without waiting for others to finish, diners excuse themselves and leave the eating circle. When all the highest status eaters have vacated their places, others of lower status will take their places for their meals. The children, who fan away the flies, will eat last at the back of the house, just before the flies have their fill. On formal occasions in Samoa, eating is a hierarchical, top-down affair.

All social gatherings require a behavioral framework to regulate and coordinate social interactions. So when people gather together, there is always some ritualization of their behavior. The higher the social status of the event, the more pronounced the ritualization. This is why we can easily recognize the state dinner as a ritual but are less likely to notice the ritual regulation of an ordinary family meal or a lunch date at a restaurant with friends. The ritualization of our meals becomes more apparent on special feast days like Thanksgiving or Passover, where everything from the foods served to prayers offered to the seating arrangement around the table is symbolically marked.

Everyday ritual tends to be hidden from view, and we imagine ourselves as more spontaneous than we are. In a society that idealizes individualism and personal freedom, we prefer to think of ourselves as free agents. Nonetheless, the very possibility of social life rests on the shared ritual forms that allow us to interact with one another in a relatively predictable and meaningful way.

Two Kinds of Time

Before there were clocks and calendars, rituals were the heartbeat of a community. Social rituals are the way communities have always kept time, establishing cyclical rhythms for the day, the month, the season, and the year. Whatever the scale of the community, a group of friends, a family, a tribe, a town, or a nation, its experience of continuity has rested on its ritual cycles. Ritual cycles have the power to fold the linear flow of time back on itself, transforming the getting older of things into repeatable rounds, replacing time's corrosive power with a sense of predictable recovery.

My research on family rituals revealed that two very different clocks shape a family's sense of the passage of time (see figure 2.2 below). Our linear sense of family time acknowledges the way family members age chronologically. Yesterday's babies are today's children and tomorrow's teenagers. Eventually, the children become adults and usually establish their own families. The cycle may start again, but now the generations have shifted forward. For their part, parents of children become parents of young adults and eventually enter the

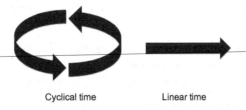

Cyclical time   Linear time

Figure 2.2
Two kinds of time

grandparent generation. We look in the mirror and suddenly see our parents or grandparents staring back at us, and we acknowledge that generational change is a one-way road. This is *chronological time*.

But from another perspective, family time is also experienced as repetitive cycles based on the repeating rhythm of the seasons. From this perspective, the passage of time is shaped by predictable cycles of holidays, birthdays, religious devotion, vacations, weekdays, and weekends. When we think back on our family time, we may alternate between using the long-range lens of generational change (as when we viewed pictures of ourselves when we were children), or we can choose to focus on our time together through the close-up lens of ritual time when family life becomes an unending cycle of Christmases, Thanksgivings, Fourth of July celebrations, summer vacations, and birthday parties. This is ritual time. When we choose to remember our families using ritual time, we often speak in the ritual past tense, recounting what "we used to do" or what "we always did." In this way, the family's ritual life mutes the perception of aging, providing a comforting (if illusory sense) that our ritual cycle can hold back the effects of time.

Sacred Ritual

Ritual studies focuses on studying particular rituals that are presented to us as ready-made institutions. I have introduced ritual by taking a developmental perspective and viewing it as a special kind of behavior that develops out of habits and routines. Viewing ritual as a kind of behavior allows us to clarify the cognitive and social processes—habituation, routinization, ritualization—that produce complex rituals out of simple action patterns. We also can see how rituals will vary in scale and complexity. While it is common to think of ritual as something done by a group, the simplest rituals are personal. Their simplicity often masks their importance in our lives. We are often unaware of these quiet, private performances that are taken-for-granted routines.

Rituals tend to increase in scale and complexity when they belong to communities rather than to individuals. These social rituals are ubiquitous in our interactions with others. They vary in scale, ranging from unnamed stylized interactions framing all social encounters to small group rituals (think "lunch on Tuesdays") that couples or friends may invent, to more conventional rituals shared by larger communities such as families, schools, tribes, or even nations. These social rituals are more likely to be recognized as such, especially those given a special name like Thanksgiving dinner or Passover seder that use prominent symbolic objects, like a birthday cake and candles, a Christmas tree, or the doll at a Mexican girl's quinceañera.

At the far end of the scale are sacred rituals often tied to religious traditions. Sacred rituals are a way that the faithful celebrate and experience their contact with a transcendent power like gods, ancestors, or a spiritual realm. Their symbolic dimension is commonly marked by unique clothing, particular forms of language, music, dissociated mental states, stereotyped movements, and all kinds of holy objects and acts. The result is that the symbolic load of sacred rituals is weighty and obvious for both performers and observers.

While sacred rituals are commonly associated with religious experience, the same ritual scale and intensity also characterizes large-scale civic celebrations of political entities like states, towns, or tribes. Venerated leaders, historical figures, or even flags representing the community's unity serve the same role as the deities of religious rituals. Political leaders have always realized that their power rested on quasi-religious feelings, and political rituals are often indistinguishable in their fervor and unifying power from religious celebrations (Kertzer 1989).

Sacred rituals such as prayer and meditation may be small and understated, but an extraordinary intensity still marks them. In the case of organized religions or cults, sacred rituals are commonly large-scale events that can attract thousands of participants, taking on the form of what we call public spectacle (MacAloon 1984). In the presence of such a spectacle, no one can doubt that they are witnessing a ritual. Many sacred rituals consist of extensive sequences of more minor rituals, which anthropologists usually call "rites." Rituals expand in scale because these more minor rites serve as modules combined with other rites, giving rituals an almost unlimited capacity for expansion and elaboration. Consider the structure of the relatively elaborate Catholic Mass, which comprises four main sections, each containing several specific rites:

1. The introductory rites

   A. Procession of the altar boys, lectors, communion ministers, and the priest

   B. Gathering song

    C. Greeting to the assembly

    D. Penitential rite (reflection on one's sins and a prayer for God's mercy)

    E. Opening prayer

2. The liturgy of the word (the reading of Scripture)

    A. Old Testament reading

    B. Responsorial psalm from the Book of Psalms with a response from the congregation, often sung

    C. Second New Testament reading

    D. Gospel acclamation

    E. Gospel reading from one of the four Gospels

    F. Homily by the priest or deacon based on the scriptural reading

    G. Prayer of the Faithful, to which the congregation responds with "Lord, hear our prayer"

3. The Liturgy of the Eucharist: the sacrament of the Catholic Church's sacrament to increase the sanctifying grace of the devotee's soul. The worshipper consumes the sacred wine and wafer, which, in a moment of transubstantiation, is believed to be converted into the blood and the body of Christ. Before receiving the sacrament, worshippers must confess their sins to a priest and promise not to offend God in the future. The Liturgy of the Eucharist comprises the following rites:

    A. Presentation of the gifts and preparation of the gifts; bread and wine brought to the altar along with monetary offerings for the poor from the congregation

    B. Priest's prayer over the gifts

    C. Eucharistic prayer by a kneeling congregation

    D. Eucharistic acclamations: the Holy, Holy, Holy; the Memorial Acclamation; and the Great Amen sung by the priest and the congregation

    E. The Lord's Prayer

    F. The sign of peace offered by congregants to each other through handshaking and often accompanied by the words "Peace be with you"

    G. Breaking of the bread/lamb of God

    H. Distribution of Communion to congregants wishing to receive communion

    I. Worshippers sitting down or kneel in silent prayer

4. The concluding rites

   A. Solemn blessing by the priest to the entire congregation

   B. Dismissal by the presider, usually by saying, "The mass has ended. You may now go in peace"

   C. A final hymn

   D. Recessional out of the cathedral by the priest

The Catholic Church is noted for its elaboration of sacred rituals. The mass described above is also known as Low Mass and is subject to further elaboration on special occasions. The most elaborated version of the mass is known as *missa solemnis* or solemn mass. Based on the Tridentine Mass (the Traditional Latin Mass), the solemn mass includes a priest, a deacon, and a subdeacon; employs incense; and requires most parts of the mass to be chanted rather than spoken. In the United States, this elaborated mass goes under the name of High Mass.

Even though sacred ritual is experienced as fixed and unchangeable, the modular structure of the ritual allows for its expansion and contraction by the addition and subtraction of rites and holy elements. Some elements (such as the Eucharist) are always considered essential to any mass, while others (like singing or incense) are more optional or reserved for special occasions. Ritual can be thought of as a language that allows for more concise or loquacious communication. Still, any variation of a ritual tends to require of worshippers a rigid and detailed specification of actions. This high degree of formalization of behavior guarantees that participants will experience the ritual as "marked behavior," behavior set apart from ordinary life. Experiencing the ritual with other congregants creates a powerful sense of solidarity and a distance from those who do not share the ritual.

The following chapter will offer an account of a more exotic sacred ritual on the island of Bali during my visit there in 2008. It matches the Catholic Mass in its complexity and exceeds its scale. The Balinese royal cremation ceremony is both a ritual and a spectacle to be enacted as well as viewed. No one watching it can have any doubt that they are in the presence of ritual. In its complexity, this royal ritual is intended to contrast with the simplicity of my classroom greeting ritual described in chapter 1. Rituals can differ dramatically in scale and elaboration, and these differences matter. But they are nonetheless all rituals. We are not yet ready to address why religious experience is so closely associated with ritual. That remains one of the mysteries of ritual, which we will take up in chapter 6.

3 The Balinese *Pelebon*: The Ritual Dissolution of a Body

Chapter 1 described an invented classroom ritual developed in one of my courses. At first, students did not recognize that offering their handshakes and their names were elements of a new ritual. They seemed to be novel (and initially awkward) events. By the third meeting of the class, these events had begun to settle into an expected pattern, a kind of "scripted" behavior that turned the class into a circle of "insiders." We were now class-mates who formally acknowledged each other's presence. A ritual emerged from these repeated actions at the start of class. Since some of our greeting elements were borrowed from everyday greetings, students quickly figured out this was a greeting ceremony. Had I chosen unfamiliar actions for the ritual, the process of ritualization would have taken longer to sink in.

This invented greeting ceremony is an unconventional way to start a class session in American classrooms. It is a deliberate invention of a new ritual, so we see actions in the process of ritualization. This ritual in the making does not fit the standard picture most people have of ritual. Not only was it unexpected, but it was also relatively unadorned. We usually assume that a ritual should be bold and elaborate, featuring distinctive clothing and even special music, highly stylized movements, and speech. In introducing ritual, I have talked about drinking morning coffee, driving to work, brushing teeth, and now an invented class greeting ceremony. But where is the more obvious kind of elaborated sacred ritual we all recognize?

In this chapter, we travel to the Indonesian island of Bali to attend a spectacular funeral ceremony, a performance that leaves us in no doubt of its ritual status. The Balinese *pelebon*, a royal cremation ceremony, is a model of sacred ritual on a grand scale.[1] Here on the beautiful island of Bali, we come face-to-face with an especially showy tradition decked out in

Balinese Hindu splendor. The accompanying photos I took of the event in 2008 leave no doubt that we are in the presence of grand ritual, big-R ritual.

Though the populations of the other islands in the Indonesian archipelago are devout Muslims, almost 90 percent of the 4.3 million Balinese are Hindu. Bali Hindu is a distinctive form of Hinduism that combines Indian religious traditions with beliefs and practices from an older Austronesian spiritual tradition that predates the beginning of Hindu influence around the first century. Traders introduced Indian culture to Bali from the subcontinent, and a Balinese colony was then founded by the Hindu Majapahit empire from East Java. This powerful dynasty flourished between the thirteenth and sixteenth centuries. These Hindu influences in Bali gradually blended with the language and cultural traditions of an Austronesian population, a culture with historical connections to the Philippines and the cultures of Polynesia. The result is a distinctive Balinese culture played out on an island of legendary beauty. So colorful and striking are Balinese traditions that Bali has long been a privileged site for anthropological research and, since the 1980s, a rapidly expanding tourist mecca for visitors seeking a taste of exotic Asia.

The ancient Austronesian traditions and the more recent Indian influences share an emphasis on hierarchy. Like India, Bali is a deeply stratified society, emphasizing inherent caste differences that divide the population into ranked strata. Balinese families belong to one of four castes, derived from the four *varnas* of the Indian caste system. Caste membership is believed to be an inborn trait based on the relative purity of one's blood. As in India, caste also specifies the family's social function. *Sudras* (peasants) are the lowest caste, comprising over 90 percent of Bali's population. *Wesias*, the merchant caste, often includes administrative officials. *Satrias* are the warriors and include most of the ruling nobility and many traditional rajas, Bali's warrior kings. At the apex of the hierarchy are the *Brahmanas*, members of the priestly caste who are in charge of spiritual matters. The dominance of the priestly caste over the warrior kings suggests the characteristic Hindu privileging of the spiritual over earthly affairs.

Having lived and done research among Polynesians, I had always been intrigued by their distant cousins in Bali, and I have been fortunate to have visited the island on three occasions. My first visit was on my honeymoon. Early in 1978, Linda and I, newly married, decided to fly across the world for a Balinese honeymoon. I had learned about Bali from the ethnographic

Figure 3.1
Balinese rice field

writings of Margaret Mead, Gregory Bateson, James Boon, Clifford Geertz, and others, whose accounts of Balinese culture had become standard reading for anthropologists. Bali had assumed the status of a privileged cultural "other" for anthropology, a place where the strong contrast with the West tested the diverse possibilities of human nature.

Bali was a favored site for art, music, and ritual research. In planning for the honeymoon, I contacted Hildred Geertz, a professor at Princeton University's Department of Anthropology. Geertz had done notable fieldwork in Bali with her (then) husband, Clifford. She generously arranged for us to stay in the inland village of Ubud, at the Puri Ubud, the royal palace of the regency (political district) of Gianyar, as guests of the last official Balinese raja who ruled over the regency. The village was surrounded by rice paddies, fed by an intricate irrigation system (figure 3.1).

Our host was Ida Anuk Agung Gde Agung (1921–1999), who was something of a local celebrity. Western educated, with a degree in law and a doctorate in history from the Netherlands, Agung spoke excellent English, having served as Indonesian foreign minister, ambassador to several countries, and president of the East Indonesian government based in Sulawesi. A prominent Indonesian politician, Agung would be declared a national hero of the Republic of Indonesia in 2007, having played a central role in negotiating the country's independence from the Netherlands. A strong supporter of Indonesia's ties to the West, Agung had once been jailed by Indonesian President Sukarno from 1962 to 1966 for his opposition to Sukarno's leftist sympathies and advocacy of a strong central government rather than the loose federation favored by Agung. It was also rumored that Sukarno had felt snubbed by Agung, who had failed to invite him to his father's royal cremation ceremony. Not surprisingly, Agung was a fascinating host.

In 1978, Ubud was a small village despite being home to the raja's family and a center of Balinese arts. At this time, there were no hotels in Ubud, so the royal palace compound was thought to be the best place for a honeymooning foreign couple. Though the administrative center for Gianyar Regency is the town of Gianyar, Ubud had long been a famous cultural and artistic center. Anthropologists Margaret Mead and Gregory Bateson had stayed there during their Balinese fieldwork in the 1930s. In 1978 the village was ringed with extensive art galleries featuring fabulous wooden carvings, intricate traditional pen-and-ink drawings of mythic Hindu themes, and colorful "young people's paintings" of everyday village landscapes. We were given our own guest cottage, which we entered through an intricately carved wooden door, and were assigned a servant to prepare our meals and fetch water for us.

Ubud was an enchanting, almost unreal place full of temples and family compounds filled with statues, shrines, and carved doors (figure 3.2). To outsiders, it had the feeling of an exotic stage set. To the Balinese, it was home. Ubud had neither running water nor electricity at that time, so our honeymoon suite was outfitted with rather basic conveniences that only added to the exotic feel of the place. After a few days, we met the former raja himself, who treated us to an evening of gamelan music from a local gong orchestra and a performance of Balinese dancing as shown in figures 3.3 and 3.4.

Our stay in Bali lasted ten days. We attended many ritual dances, theatrical dramas, and shadow puppet shows (*wayang*), enacting famous scenes from the classic Hindu *Ramayana* and *Mahabharata* epics. Everywhere we went, we encountered Balinese people carrying offerings to religious shrines that were part of every household compound and stopping to offer a prayer as they left off the food offerings. A large part of their day was spent in

Figure 3.2
Ubud in 1978

Figure 3.3
Balinese dance

Figure 3.4
Balinese gamelan orchestra

religious devotion. If ever there was a showcase for a life shaped by ritual, it was Bali. The gorgeous landscape, with its lush vegetation and flowers combined with the vivid colors of the batik cloth from which Balinese clothes were made, the haunting sounds of the gamelan gongs, the intoxicating smell of the clove cigarettes beloved of Indonesians, and the incandescent smiles of our Balinese hosts presented a sensory feast that left Bali lingering in memory long after we returned home.

One would never have guessed that thirteen years earlier, some eighty thousand Balinese, roughly 5 percent of the population, had been massacred by soldiers in what came to be known as the Indonesian genocide that targeted suspected members and sympathizers of the Indonesian Communist Party (Partai Komunis Indonesia). The mass killings claimed the lives of around a million Indonesians with leftist sympathies. Tacitly supported by the United States and other Western nations, the genocide effectively destroyed the power of the Indonesian Communist Party and led to the downfall of Indonesia's left-leaning President Sukarno, allowing General Suharto to assume the role of president. Suharto would rule Indonesia with an iron fist for the next three decades, including the period of our Balinese honeymoon. He oversaw the nation's rapid industrialization and economic expansion, so his government had broad support within Indonesia in the 1970s and 80s. This history means that terror had overtaken Bali a decade before we set foot on the island. It was hard to imagine the losses that many Balinese families had suffered and the horrific wound that lay beneath their bright smiles. One could only wonder at the Balinese ability to keep up their graceful performance of everyday life.

Twelve years later, I returned to Bali to board a cruise ship to act as the port lecturer on a cruise bound for Honolulu. This time I was accompanied by my friend and colleague Frank Manley, a professor of English with whom I regularly cotaught a class on the significance of ritual in plays of Shakespeare. Frank was anxious to see Bali since he had written a short story influenced by Clifford Geertz's famous essay about Balinese cockfighting titled "Deep Play: Notes on the Balinese Cockfight." Flying into Bali's capital city of Denpasar, Frank and I made our way to Ubud, which I was keen to show him. Over the last dozen years, Ubud had been utterly transformed by the dramatic growth of tourism in the 1980s. I was not alone in my fascination with the place. Bali had been discovered.

Hotels had sprung up everywhere, including some five-star resorts catering to well-heeled tourists. Every street now featured cafes, art galleries, and tourist shops filled with T-shirts, mass-produced wooden masks, and cheap souvenirs. English had become the language of commerce and tourism. Young children would come up to us using their few words of English to beg for coins or to sell us souvenirs. Still, Balinese culture still showed through all the glitz produced by tourism. Only now, many of the traditional ritual performances were being performed as tourist spectacles.

Beyond Ubud and the equally crowded resort towns of Sanur and Kuta Beach, I was relieved to see that Bali had not changed dramatically outside the tourist zone. The beautiful town of Semarapura, the administrative center of Klungkung Regency, was famous for the magnificently painted Puri Klungkung (Klungkung Palace) whose walls were filled with grotesque painted images from Hindu epics, most memorably images depicting the horrible tortures awaiting evil-doers after death. I was glad to see that

Klungkung Regency looked much as it had twelve years earlier. But it was also clear that if Klungkung embodied Bali's past, Gianyar and especially Ubud were likely its future.

A Royal Cremation Ritual

My third trip to Bali was in 2008. One of my students, Aaron Collett, a New Zealander whose parents had both moved to Bali as teachers when their sons were young children, invited me to visit the Alam Sari Resort, the eco-friendly hotel his parents had developed in a small village in the cool green hills just north of Ubud. It was an offer too good to pass up.

Once again, Ubud was unrecognizable. It had metamorphosed into a slick international watering hole for fashionable tourists as well as a center of traditional Balinese art. On its way to becoming a small city, Ubud bore no resemblance to the backwater village my wife and I had visited three decades earlier. One was as likely to see Australian, American, or European tourists cruising the crowded sidewalks as locals. Most of the shops advertised their wares in English. Economic prosperity and globalization had produced what seemed to be endless shopping streets stretching as far as the eye could see. The Alam Sari Resort provided a welcome retreat from Ubud's frenzy. It was a serene, low-key place. The village of Keliki where the hotel was located was a rural haven, only twenty minutes but seemingly light-years away from the bustle of Ubud.

To make this third Balinese journey even more tempting, I learned that a significant Hindu ritual had been scheduled in Ubud for the day I arrived. A royal cremation ceremony called pelebon was to take place. Three members of Ubud's royal family were cremated along with the bodies of sixty-eight commoners, which had been disinterred for the collective cremation. I was assured that this cremation promised to be the most elaborate and spectacular pelebon Bali had seen in decades. Determined to get as many pictures of the ritual as I could, I stepped off the plane in Denpasar with a heavy camera bag slung over my shoulder.

Since the 1980s and the start of the tourist boom, cremation rituals had become major tourist attractions. Part solemn ritual, part theatrical spectacle, royal cremations were among Bali's most prominent attractions. Hotels sponsored guided tours to the parade. For their part, the Balinese not only welcomed the tourists but also saw their presence as a sign of respect for

Figure 3.5
Procession through Ubud before cremation

Balinese culture, confirming the high status of the royal family sponsoring the event. Balinese cremation ceremonies, called *ngaben* for commoners and pelebon for royals, are among the most sacred of Balinese rituals. But that doesn't imply that they are stodgy affairs. Royal cremations are impressive theatrical performances, gaudy spectacles intended to attract a vast audience in addition to the tens of thousands of participants who parade through the town to the cremation ground a kilometer away. The gaudiness is a crucial feature of the ritual.

This cremation is said to have attracted several hundred thousand people, though it was impossible to count. What I witnessed in downtown Ubud was a sea of excited Balinese mourners that flooded the town's main streets as far as the eye could see (figure 3.5). Many participants sported brilliantly colored outfits. The female participants were brightly dressed and beautifully coiffed, often wearing plumeria flowers behind their ears. The tens of thousands of participants in the cremation procession were joined by hundreds of tourists hoping to experience Balinese ritual at its grandest.

The *ngaben* is a Balinese adaptation of the four-thousand-year-old Hindu *Agni Sanskar* cremation ritual. This particular royal cremation was being mounted in honor of the late head of Ubud's royal family, Tjokorda Gde Agung Suyasa, his nephew Tjokorda Raka, his aunt Desak Raka, along with the remains of sixty-eight commoner villagers. Heading up the procession were lines of about three hundred women and children from different villages carrying offerings. Each village contingent was distinguished by the color of their sarongs, creating a brilliant undulating rainbow effect on the streets. The offerings were followed by the large and elaborately decorated paper-mâché bull (*lembu*) that served as the *patulangan* (cremation coffin) for the body of Tjokorda Raka, followed by an even larger bull with gold decorations in which the mummified body of Tjokorda Gde Agung Suyasa would be burned (figure 3.6).

Black bulls are usually made for high-caste cremations, while deceased priests are cremated in white bull effigies. Depending on the family's status, other animal effigies might also be used for sarcophagi. But today, it was all bulls. Then came the cremation tower (*bade*) holding the body of Tjokorda Raka (figure 3.7). This bade was followed by the flamboyantly painted undulating *Naga Banda*, the magical dragon symbolizing the human attachment to earthly things. *Naga Banda*'s tail is wrapped around the base of the next bade, the enormous central tower holding the remains of Tjokorda Gde Agung Suyasa, suggesting the deceased's attachments to this world. But when the procession reached the crossroad in front of the palace, the officiating high priest (*padanda*) shot the dragon effigy with an arrow, symbolically killing the dragon and severing the attachment of the deceased's soul to all earthly interests, including acts committed by the deceased in his lifetime. Early that morning, the cremation structures and decorations were ritually purified with water and blessed by prayers by the priest before leaving the family compound.

The procession included a large gamelan percussion orchestra made up of drums and gongs playing the popular *baleganjur* style. Musicians playing different instruments were interspersed throughout the parade so that music was ever-present. The bade is designed to represent the world with its various levels. The spectacular Balinese eagle, the golden-winged Garuda, sits atop the structure (figure 3.8).

The number of levels a bade has signifies the deceased's caste and status. The tallest tower containing the body of Tjokorda Gde Agung Suyasa was around forty feet high and consisted of nine levels. The highest possible bade, with eleven stages, is reserved for the king of Klungkung. These

Figure 3.6
Lembu sarcophagus being carried to cremation ground

Figure 3.7
Massive bade tower holding the body of Tjokorda Gde Agung Suyasa

Figure 3.8
The sacred Garuda eagle

massive towers were carried in one-hundred-yard shifts by teams of two hundred men at a time who shouldered the massive structure along the kilometer-long route from the palace to the *setra* (cremation ground). This tower was said to weigh eleven tons, hence the vast number of carriers. Shouldering the huge bade to the cremation ground ultimately required the coordination of six thousand able-bodied men. So tall was the structure that power lines had to be taken down to pass through the streets of Ubud.

A Boisterous Parade

While we might expect a funeral procession to move in a slow and stately fashion, the Balinese cremation procession was boisterous, even chaotic at times. When the bade came to a significant crossroad, the carriers would maneuver the massive structure in circles. This was done to confuse the witches and other malign forces in the nether world believed to threaten the deceased at crossroads and prevent their souls from leaving the body. The purpose of the cremation ritual was to confuse the evil spirits and discourage them from having their way with the deceased so that the deceased's soul might be released from its mortal remains and begin its journey to eventual deification as an ancestor. The cremation parade and burning took about seven hours. The procession began around noon when the sun had reached its zenith and was moving toward the western horizon. The cremation was scheduled so that the actual immolation of the bodies takes place as the sun goes down, assuring a dramatic fiery shower of sparks ascending to heaven. At the cremation grounds, a tall structure with a long slide had been constructed so that the bodies might be removed from the bade towers and placed in coffins inserted into the hollow bull effigies that would be burned along with the bodies. Gently, the body was removed from the tower and slowly nudged down the slide some forty feet to the ground.

The elaborate cremation structures, including the bulls holding the remains of the deceased, were set afire with blowtorches. Attendants made sure the fire spread quickly. Before long, the structures were consumed by fierce flames, shooting sparks heavenward that the Balinese understand as the newly liberated soul ascending to heaven. I positioned myself close to the structures to get some close-up photos but quickly fell back, fearing that the burning structures were on the verge of collapsing. It was an incredible spectacle but also terrifying. The sight of all the gorgeous decorations and effigies that had been lovingly constructed over several weeks being consumed by fire in a matter of minutes left a strong impression of the ultimate fragility and impermanence of earthly things (figure 3.9).

Balinese royal funerals are not a single ritual. The public cremation ceremony is only one act in an extended funeral drama that plays itself out in several locales over weeks or even months. The cremation ritual presented here is preceded by rites that prepare the body for its cremation. Performing the funeral rites is the responsibility of the son of the deceased or another close male relative. Women are responsible for preparing elaborate decorations and food offerings for the mortuary rituals.

When an individual dies, the family must perform several rites separating itself from the deceased. The deceased's eyelids are closed to make it appear that the body is asleep since a corpse with open eyes is considered frightening. The body is placed on a mat or a bed at the inner entrance of the house with the feet facing south in the direction of Yama, the god of death. To protect the family from ritual impurity, a lamp (*arti*) is placed near the body's head and is kept burning with incense to purify the space

Figure 3.9
Cremation fire consuming the *lemba* and the bodies within it

around the body. This fire rite is derived from the ancient *homa* or *havan* votive fire ritual of the Indian Vedic tradition, also common in Buddhism and Jainism. Sandalwood or ash is placed on the body's forehead to mark it as holy and to distinguish the dead from the living. The deceased's soul is "fed" with drops of holy water or milk, though the body, destined for the flames, no longer needs any nourishment.

We have noted previously that these mortuary rituals were also performed for many deceased commoners from the more than sixty villages in the regency's four residential neighborhoods (*banjar*) who had died over the previous several years (figure 3.10). High-caste families never bury their dead for fear of pollution from the body's contact with the earth. Instead, they embalm the bodies and ritually feed and care for them in their houses during the preparations for the cremation. When the mummified body is ready for cremation, the family washes and dresses it in Balinese attire. It is then sent off with prayers to be carried in procession to the cremation ground, accompanied by gamelan music and singing. Lower-caste Balinese are usually buried in local cemeteries in anticipation of their eventual disinterment and, in this case, their public cremation along with the royals.

Figure 3.10
Commoners carrying the body of their disinterred relatives to be cremated with the royals

The body is viewed as a mortal vessel for an individual's soul, so Balinese show no revulsion at handling an embalmed body or washing the disinterred bones of a deceased loved one. In this, the Balinese view of death and dead bodies contrasts dramatically with our own.

Private Grief and Public Joy

The death of a loved one is experienced as a heartbreaking personal loss everywhere. But Balinese funerals are always a mix of private grief and public joy. The joyful and boisterous mood of the ritual is partly due to the Balinese understanding of death as the beginning of another journey of reincarnation rather than the end of life. The raucous mood created by the music, the dancers, and the crowds in the streets is also a feature of the Balinese worldview. Their conviction that a boisterous ritual produces a spirit of *rame*, a sensory fullness believed to drive away evil spirits. Contrary to our assumption that a funeral ritual must be a sober affair, the Balinese believe that a noisy ritual marked by overwhelming the senses is a way of guaranteeing its sanctity by scaring away hostile forces of destruction.

Cremations are also a joyful celebration because the deceased's soul is liberated from the body to continue its journey in another cycle of reincarnation. In Balinese Hinduism, the body is considered a temporary vessel for the soul, a vessel vulnerable to pollution and attack from witches (*leyak*) and other demonic forces from beyond this world. At death, the soul is thought to hover close to the body, reflecting its attachment to earthly things. This attachment of the soul to its earthly vessel places the soul in danger of being taken over by malign forces from the nether world. The purpose of Balinese funerals is to ritually release the soul from its mortal container and to purify it so that it can eventually return in a reincarnated form. Without the cremation rites, the deceased is in danger of becoming a ghost caught in limbo between this life and the next, a chaotic state that Hindus call *preta*. In such a state, the uncremated body threatens itself and the living. Only by passing through the series of death rituals called *anyesti* can a deceased person move on in the reincarnation cycle and become a deified ancestor.

Reincarnation is part of the cycle of birth, death, and rebirth known in Buddhism as samsara. For high-caste people, the Balinese call it *punarbhawa*. Unlike Indian Hindus, some Balinese believe in a four-generation regenerative cycle. Once freed from its body, the soul of a deceased individual can return after three generations as the deceased's great grandson or granddaughter, transforming the family's loss into a ritually induced cycle of regeneration. But first, the souls of the dead must be freed from the dangers of their mortal bodies.

We can understand the joy and excitement accompanying the rituals surrounding the body's cremation in this context. Cremation is a controlled stepwise dissolution of the body to its base elements and its final scattering at sea. Through the cremation rites, the body is reduced to its five constituent elements: earth (*pertiwi*), water (*apah*), fire (*teja*), air (*bayu*), and ether (*akasa*). Once the body is reduced to its primal elements and returned to the sea, the soul is ritually purified and liberated from the body to begin a new cycle of reincarnation.

Cremations are costly and socially complex productions requiring both money and the coordinated efforts of a large group of people. In the case of royal cremations, the resources necessary are massive. An ordinary commoner cremation can cost anywhere from $1,000 to $20,000 or more, while a royal cremation like I witnessed can cost the family $250,000. While the main expenses are borne by the family, these cremations require the cooperation of thousands of people from many villages in the surrounding area. These contributions include helping to construct the immense cremation structures that are carried through the streets, contributing to the vast stock of food, making decorations and flower offerings required for the cremation, and helping to carry the enormous cremation structures and the offerings to the cremation ground.

Because high-caste Balinese do not bury their dead before cremation, they must raise the financial resources to mount a cremation relatively soon after the death of a family member. Commoners, often lacking financial resources, may have to wait several years to raise the necessary funds. The exact timing of the cremation is usually determined by the priest, who looks for an auspicious date. Families seeking to keep the cremation costs down can wait for a joint cremation ceremony in their neighborhood and pool the costs with their neighbors. Another cost-saving option is for commoners from villages in the regency to wait for a royal cremation to dig up the remains of deceased family members who have been buried over the past few years. As in this pelebon, they cremate the remains of their relatives along with the corpses of the deceased royals, saving a lot of money and basking in the status that comes with having their relatives cremated in royal style. As previously mentioned, in this cremation the disinterred remains of sixty-eight commoners accompanied the royals in their cremation. Many graves throughout the regency were dug up for the occasion.

The cremation fire does not mark the end of Balinese funeral rites. When the flames have died down and the lemba has been consumed by fire, the family (with the priest's help) removes the remains of the incinerated bones from the ashes, arranging them on a white cloth in the form of a human figure. The padanda will then take those parts representing vital organs and grind them up, placing the pulverized remains in an elaborately decorated coconut. This coconut and remains arranged on the white cloth are often transported to Matahari Terbit Beach in the village of Sanur. The mourners board a boat to dispose of the ashes at sea. Because Sanur faces south, it is closely associated with death and is thus considered an ideal place for the final disposal of the remains.

Upon returning from Sanur, the deceased's family performs a ceremony called *mepegat*, which ritually performs the final separation of the deceased's soul (*pitara*) from its body and assures its detachment from all earthly concerns and emotions. The ceremony takes three days, during which the soul is purified so that the deceased can become *dewa pitara*, a divinity. The deceased has now been ritually liberated from all earthly matter and human feeling. Through the work of ritual, a relative becomes an ancestor, and a mortal human becomes a god.

Discussion

It is helpful to remember that social scientists and other outside observers share many assumptions about a ritual that may not be shared with those who practice it. One common assumption of academics is that rituals exercise their primary effects psychologically, affecting people's experience of life, or sociologically, coordinating group action or solidarity. For most social scientists, ritual is assumed to be a human creation with sociological or psychological effects rather than an objective reality that directly works in and on the world. It is humbling to remember that religious traditions often have their own "theories" about how ritual works, convictions that are quite different from our academic accounts. Part of the job of an anthropologist is to interview people to get their understanding of the ritual.

Balinese Hinduism proposes that the world is governed by immutable laws (*santanja dharma*), reflected in the universe's rhythms and cycles. Human rituals are assumed to reflect and perpetuate these eternal cycles, upon which the continuity of life depends. So rituals are not seen as human creations but rather as manifestations of the laws governing the universe. Humans carry out their ritual duties to maintain harmony with the world's fundamental rhythms. The vedas specify many categories of rituals that humans are obliged to perform, and cremation is one of the essential life-cycle rituals (saṃskāra) that humans are obliged to follow. It is impossible to know the degree to which everyone participating in the pelebon holds this view of what they are doing. Still, it is important to remember that an outsider's accounts of a ritual, such as the one offered in these pages, inevitably differ from insiders' experiences, for whom these practices and beliefs may represent taken-for-granted truths rather than comparative data. For anthropologists, it is important to acknowledge and include these insider accounts.

The understanding we have of a ritual will always depend on our relationship to it. As an outsider observing the pelebon for the first time, my ritual experience will be inevitably different from the experience of participating ritualists. For the pelebon described in this chapter, we can distinguish several distinct perspectives from which cremation was experienced, perspectives at different degrees of removal from the ritual action.

At the center of the pelebon are the souls of the deceased, whose interest in the ritual (if we take the Balinese perspective) is to be released from their bodies and all earthly attachments to become deified ancestors. They are at ground zero of the ritual. Then there is the *ratu penanda*, the high priest. He directs the event and is charged with sanctifying and purifying all the essential elements of the ritual to guarantee its effectiveness. A step removed from the priest's engagement are the deceased's close relatives. They have mounted the ritual to carry out their obligations to their relatives to make possible their journey to their next reincarnation. In making possible the cremation, the family members also protect themselves from harm by evil spirits that an uncremated body can produce. In addition to their spiritual engagement, they had to raise sufficient funds and support to mount the ritual. Once the cremation was planned, the deceased's close kin had to protect the status and reputation of their family by putting on an impressive and memorable show.

Beyond the central family members were the families of the commoners who were cremated with the royals and who were carrying out their ritual obligations as well as looking to the pelebon as a way to enhance their own status. The next level of engagement included the thousands of Balinese from neighboring *banjars* who supported the raja's family with their labor and presence. Then there are Balinese from other regencies who came to observe the cremation. These participants are "cultural insiders" to the cremation, sharing a set of understandings about the ritual's purpose and symbolic implications. They can be said to experience the ritual from the "inside."

The remaining participants were all outsiders, watching the ritual either because they were scholars studying Balinese religion, journalists reporting on the event, or tourists, most of whom understood little of what they were seeing but were fascinated by the sheer spectacle of the pelebon. There was wide variation in understanding the rites and in feeling empathy for the deceased among the outsiders. In terms of what was experienced, we might say that there were many pelebons occurring that day in Ubud, distinguished by the level of engagement and understanding of what was taking place.

Do we consider the pelebon I witnessed as a single coherent ritual or an elaborate sequence of different rituals? Should we consider the procession and the cremation as one phase of a more extensive ritual occurring over several weeks? How do we draw the boundaries for "the ritual" we observe? This problem of demarcating the boundary of ritual performance is common to all significant rituals. While the Balinese cremation ceremony is often referred to as a complete, coherent mortuary ritual, it is also clear that the pelebon is actually a complex aggregate of many smaller "rites" that fall into various genres such as purification rites, rites of separation, life-cycle ceremonies, and fire rites. Moreover, the pelebon also plays its part as one extended rite embedded within an even more extensive ritual process, an encompassing ritual that begins with the initial burial of commoners and the mummification and ritual care of the deceased noblemen before the cremation rites, and ends with gathering the remains after the cremation for ritual decomposition and disposal at sea.

This ambiguity is an inherent feature of ritual, reflecting its modular nature. Significant rituals grow in scale and complexity by being combined as links in a chain of other rituals. We often use the term "rite" to specify a subsidiary ritual that is part of a larger and more complex ritual sequence. Though we tend to classify rituals according to their primary function (as in the case of a funeral or wedding ritual), complex rituals usually comprise many different rites, each playing a part in the more significant ceremony. This modular character of rites means that rituals can be expanded or contracted in scale by adding and subtracting component rites.

Despite the common impression that rituals are characterized by their persistence and predictability, this modularity lends to ritual a flexibility that can lead to variations in ritual practice, promoting institutional schism. For example, when Henry VIII broke away from the Roman Church in 1534, establishing the Church of England, a series of controversies ensued over how much of the ritualism of the Roman Catholic Church the new church should follow, arguments that reemerged in the mid and late nineteenth century with the Oxford Movement. These debates involved

the Anglican Church's desire to distinguish itself both from the more ritu-
alistic Catholic Church and the radically simplified rituals of the Protestant
churches. How much could the mass be abridged and remain essentially
the same ritual? Which rites were to be considered optional and which
were deemed essential? Regarding Hindu cremation practices, this inherent
flexibility has made it possible for "traditional" Hindu cremation rites to be
adapted to the hyperritualized Balinese context, while the "same" cremation ceremony could be simplified in the context of the Hindu diaspora in
the United States.

The pelebon is also flexible in another sense. While rituals are often
characterized as rigid, all rituals afford opportunities for improvisation and
free play. While royal cremations can be shown to share a general and predictable format, each mounting of a pelebon is also a unique event. The
scale and length of the ritual are not precisely fixed. Different performances
of the pelebon produce considerable gossip over who showed up for the
ritual, who didn't come, and the different contributions of families and
banjars to the cremation. The actual procession of the pelebon is enacted
boisterously as if it were a spontaneous event. Though the general form of
the cremation procession follows a predictable script, the event's mood is
one of spontaneous energy. Every ritual allows for improvisation, though
the range of variation allowed can vary considerably depending on the
sacredness of the rites and the precise nature of the ritual.

Consider the typical American wedding rite, which combines a relatively
stable core of orthodox elements such as the bride's entry with her father or
a male surrogate, her walk down the aisle, often to a classic wedding march,
the guests standing during her entrance, the positioning of the couple in
front of the officiant, the relatively predictable roles of the best man and
the maid of honor, the symbolism of the wedding cake, and so on. In Jewish weddings, the best-known predictable elements include the wearing of
the yarmulke skullcap by males, the use of the wedding huppah, a portable
canopy under which the bride and groom stand during the ceremony, and
the groom's (or sometimes the bride and groom together) stepping on a
glass placed under a cloth or in a cloth bag to break it. There are several
different interpretations of this act, but its performance always signals the
conclusion of the public ritual, whatever its symbolism. And yet, while
sticking to the scripts, couples strive to personalize their wedding ceremonies so that they are experienced as unique events as well as formulaic rites.

Social changes also underwrite new variations in the script, such as secular weddings, interfaith weddings, or gay weddings. Personal vows often replace scripted traditional marriage vows. Each variation takes pains to invoke familiar forms of the rite while modifying some of the elements to adapt them to personal whim or changing circumstances. It is not a matter of choosing between pure tradition and pure improvisation; the goal is to find an acceptable balance. The interaction of the traditional and the ritual's novel elements always makes for a memorable wedding.

The same is true of the American presidential inauguration, which always includes a familiar seating arrangement for notables, the presence of the chief justice of the Supreme Court, a military band, a swearing in of the new president using a Bible, and a speech by the incoming president. Nonetheless, the event has room for unique variations that historicize the event as a particular inauguration. The choice of the singer of the national anthem or the recitation of an inspirational poem, and even the location of the event, are all subject to modification. In 2021 the presidential inauguration was marked by the absence of the outgoing president, Donald Trump, whose failure to attend was intended as a strong political message about his view of the legitimacy of his successor.

The variability of ritual performances can also reflect essential differences in the social status of the central participants. In the Balinese context, the Hindu cremation rites were gradually integrated into a society that already emphasized social hierarchy. So it is not surprising that the Balinese pelebon functions as a vivid display of social status. Almost every aspect of the ritual reflects the caste status of the primary actors. The very designation of the cremation as a pelebon rather than a *ngaben* marks it as an elite ritual. Commoners are generally buried, sometimes for years, before they are cremated, while high-caste Balinese are mummified and prepared for quick cremation. The scale of the cremation is considered a direct reflection of the deceased's social status and wealth, including the height of the burial tower, the number of levels in the tower, the quantity of food prepared for celebrants, and the color and kind of animal effigy in which the deceased is cremated. Hindu high priests preside over high-status cremations, attracting far more participants and viewers than low-status ceremonies.

How the pelebon mirrors social status is an excellent example of how rituals reflect social differences or mirror changes in a group over time. The role of ritual scale and elaboration in modeling social status is an almost universal characteristic of ritual. But ritual events can also effectively model social change. For example, in the United States, the size, location, and composition of the Thanksgiving dinner can be used to assess the current status and solidarity of American families. The same issues are at play in American wedding celebrations, where who gets invited to the wedding and who gets left off the list can be read as a powerful sign of the current state of relationships.

While outsiders observing the cremation might consider it merely a spectacular show, rituals are always doing some work for those closest to the action. The pelebon is performed as an agent of transformation, gradually reducing a dead body to its elementary components and then dissolving them back into the sea, allowing the soul inhabiting that body to be released. The various subsidiary rites performed before, during, and following the cremation are all effecting some kind of transformation: purification, sanctification, decomposition, separation, and reincorporation.

Rituals are commonly done to perform some kind of transformation. The famous French sociologist Arnold van Gennep highlighted this transformation function of ritual in his book *Rites of Passage*, originally published in 1909. The work focuses on the universal use of rituals to mark changes in status, such as weddings, birthdays, funerals, greetings, and farewells. But there are two distinct ways in which rituals can be understood as agents of transformation: "the symbolic" and "the literal."

One of the distinctive characteristics of ritual is that it is symbolically loaded. Ritual actions are not simply practical techniques as in ordinary routines. In addition to their pragmatic functions, ritual actions stand for other things such as collective sentiments, ideals, unseen spiritual forces, historical events and people, and aspects of identity. Rituals are made up of symbolic actions. When we emphasize the symbolic nature of ritual transformation, it is important to remember that we refer to the change of the ritualists' mindset. This kind of transformation is psychological and social. It works to reframe beliefs, attitudes, feelings, and knowledge of both individuals and communities.

But rituals are also mounted to change the world. We have noted how, for those closest to the pelebon ritual, the ritual actions are not only transforming their understanding of the world but are also understood as acting directly on the world to transform some elements of reality in desired ways. It is not just the idea of the deceased that pelebon transforms from a living relative to a deified ancestor. A body is physically reduced to its primal elements, dissolved into the sea. For the central ritualists, the forces at play in the ritual—gods, humans, witches, holy water, and the like—are all real and directly involved in the transformation.

In other words, while the ritual acts may be symbols, they are rarely considered just symbols. Even modern rites like weddings reflect the dual work of ritual in reframing our understanding of a relationship and transforming the couple's relationship to the world. Couples are not merely symbolically different before and after the wedding rites. They have a new legal status and have assumed financial responsibility for each other. The rites also create a new level of "legitimacy" for their offspring that has consequences for inheritance. Couples who go through a marriage rite are treated differently from those who just live together. Newlyweds who had lived together before their wedding are often surprised by how much their day-to-day life changes once they have gone through the marriage ceremony.

Rituals will always have both symbolic and literal efficacy. But there are essential differences in the relative emphasis on figurative or literal transformation. As an academic observer of the pelebon, I was naturally drawn to explore the complex symbolic changes the ritual makes possible. In other words, I was focused on the work the ritual performed on the minds of the ritualists. The high priest, on the other hand, while having a profound understanding of the ritual's symbolic dimension, was focused on making sure the literal transformations of the deceased's body and the soul were successfully carried out. In one case, an experience was reframed; in the other, the world was transformed.

This shift in emphasis between the symbolic and the literal dimensions of ritual was a central feature of the Protestant Reformation. The ritual centerpiece of the Catholic Mass was the sacrament of Holy Communion known as the Eucharist, which is a ritual reenactment of the last supper Christ had with his disciples. In Catholic practice, the priest's blessing of the communion wafer (the host) and the communion wine were understood to transform them into the actual body and blood of Christ, a literal transformation known as transubstantiation.

One of the critical changes in Protestant practice was to reframe the interpretation of communion as a symbolic act, a "commemoration" of the Last Supper, denying that those taking communion were consuming Christ's body and blood. In this sense, the reformation can be understood as effecting a shift in emphasis from literalist ritual acting directly on the world to symbolic ritual, transforming the minds and hearts of the faithful. This shift is consistent with the Protestant stress on congregants' understanding of the Bible and their inner experience of God, compared with the Catholic emphasis on the performance of sacraments by priests (originally in Latin), with less concern for the worshipper's ability to understand the mass. Catholic rituals are held to work directly on the world, while Protestant rites are held to work on the minds of the worshippers.

In contrast to these debates about the efficacy of Christian rites, the transformations effected by the Balinese pelebon ritual represent an almost perfect balance of symbolic and literal effects. While outsiders might be exclusively engrossed by the symbolic experiential power of the rituals, those close to the center of the ritual clearly understand their ritual actions as transforming both their experience of the world and the world itself. For these insiders, there is no choice to be made.

4 Do Nonhuman Animals Have Rituals?

Discussing animal rituals begins with a question: do only humans have rituals? The question has provoked considerable scholarly debate. Some anthropologists have claimed that ritual requires culture and symbolic thought, exclusively human capacities. From this point of view, culture, a community's invented traditions, tools, and symbols, is essential for ritual. The argument insists that hardwired responses control most of the behavior of the rest of the animal kingdom, so other animals cannot be said to have rituals.

This "only-humans" view of ritual was asserted over fifty years ago in a paper by the distinguished Cambridge anthropologist Sir Edmund Leach. His 1966 essay, "Ritualization in Man in Relation to Conceptual and Social Development," was based on a talk he gave at a Royal Society conference on ritual, organized by biologist Julian Huxley. This gathering brought together the most respected animal behavior scientists of that era along with a handful of eminent cultural anthropologists and psychologists. The scientists debated the meaning and role of ritual in nonhuman animals and humans. Leach opened his remarks by noting that ethologists, those studying behavior from a biological and evolutionary perspective, define "ritual" differently from cultural anthropologists. Ethologists, Leach reminded us, use the term "ritualization" to refer to the evolutionary transformation of behaviors that initially had a practical function into "signals" with a communication function.

Because ritualized behaviors in animals are mostly biologically fixed responses, Leach proposed that the so-called animal rituals were unrelated to those studied by cultural anthropologists and students of religion. "For the ethologist," Leach said, "ritual is adaptive repetitive behaviour which is characteristic of a whole species; for the anthropologist, ritual is occasional behaviour by particular members of a single culture. This contrast is very radical" (Leach 1966, p. 403). While culturally shaped behavior is invented and learned by individuals in a community, Leach argued that species-specific behavior is hardwired and genetically transmitted to a whole species. Therefore, he claimed, animal ritual can have no connection with human ritual, and using the same word for both is misleading. "It cannot be too strongly emphasized," he said, "that ritual, in the anthropologist's sense, is in no way whatsoever a genetic endowment of the species" (Leach 1966, p. 403).

As a student of human culture, Leach emphasized the boundary separating humans from other animals (culture) rather than the evolutionary links connecting them. Humans, the argument goes, are unique in their use of culture. By contrast, animal behavior belongs to "nature," and their behavior is largely under the control of biology. In this view, animal behavior is assumed to be mostly genetically controlled, while human behavior is shaped by learning, invention, and community tradition.

It is a matter of emphasis. Cultural anthropologists tend to focus on differences (both between humans and nonhumans and also between cultures). Ethologists, on the other hand, look for connections linking species and groups. While ethologists also study species differences in behavior, they usually understand those differences in evolutionary terms, gradual divergences due to genetic mutations shaped by natural selection. There are also human ethologists, scientists who specialize in the evolution of human behavior, focusing on innate behaviors common to all humans, both traits found only in Homo sapiens as well as features humans share with closely related species. Ethologists study "the human animal," while cultural anthropologists are interested in "the human non-animal." Ethologists and cultural anthropologists represent two radically different approaches to the study of "human nature."

Leach was right to conclude that ritualization in animals is not the same as human ritual. But in his enthusiasm for human uniqueness, I think Leach drew too rigid a boundary between animal and human rituals. Discovering meaningful connections between animal and human rituals does not imply they are identical. On the contrary, comparing animal and human rituals can reveal for humans the evolutionary foundation for rituals in general while still acknowledging the cultural uniqueness of particular rituals and the distinctive character of human ritual in general. The evolution of the human brain and that capacity for cultural adaptations have massively affected human rituals.

While human rituals cannot be fully explained by instincts, that does not imply that they are purely cultural institutions with no biological basis. Consider human language. Our language capacity is a universal trait of Homo sapiens, grounded in the evolution of speech organs and the human brain. But the historical development of particular languages and their acquisition by members of speech communities is a matter of cultural learning. In this sense, it is no different from ritual. Reducing ritual to just its cultural elaborations ignores neurological processes like habituation and routinization that make ritualized behavior possible. It also overlooks the repertory of innate gestures and emotion expressions that play essential roles in many human rituals and figure as the elementary units of our social interaction rituals. Even the culturally transmitted elements of human rituals rest on a biological foundation. There is a lot to learn in recognizing the fascinating connections between ritualization in human life and that of other animals.

Rigid distinctions between rituals in humans and other animals have also led us to underestimate the role of learning and imitation in animal rituals. Just as humans are part of the natural world, other animals may exhibit the ability to learn, invent, and imitate traits that we associate with human culture. It is true that learned traits in animals are far more limited than in humans. Humans are masters of improvisation. But research on animal behavior has revealed that many animal rituals involve a combination of inherited, learned, and improvised behavior, blurring the old boundary between the presumed biologically programmed animal and the culturally motivated human.

For example, studies of birdsong have revealed that individual birds produce variations on species-based songs. The same mix of genetic, learned. and improvised components has been shown for humpback whale songs. The variations appear rapid and continuous, suggesting they are not hardwired. They also are not seasonal since the songs vary over long periods not linked to seasons. Furthermore, some of these variations in whale songs were picked up by other members of the groups and became integrated into synchronous singing rituals. Whales are not only inventing individual song patterns but also transmitting those variations to other whales. It sounds a lot like cultural learning.

Rituals, whether in humans or other animals, cannot be reduced to an action pattern with a single cause. Ritual is complex behavior shaped by diverse genetic, cultural, and individual influences. While culturally invented and transmitted components are essential to human rituals, so are the biologically transmitted capacities for habituation, routinization, and ritualization. Taking an evolutionary perspective on human ritual does not mean reducing ritual to animal ritualization. Evolution produces both similarities between a species and its ancestors and also changes in the descendants.

Making sense of the similarities between related species presents problems for the ethologist. Similarities between human and animal ritual behavior might be due simply to *convergent evolution*, independent adaptations by species that look similar but have no common genetic origin. Rather than shared genes, these similar traits might come from shared functions, parallel evolutionary solutions to similar problems. Convergent evolution produces *analogies* between traits, organs, or behaviors in two species with similar functions or structures (like the wings of butterflies and birds) that are not genetically linked. Such connections are not simply coincidental and result from shared selection pressures: parallel solutions to parallel challenges. Contrasting with these evolutionary analogies are *homologies*, similarities between species with a more direct biological origin. Homologous traits are the result of the species' shared genetic inheritance. For example, the similarly structured forelimbs of bats, mice, and humans are no coincidence. They are genetically related *homologs* due to common (but distant) ancestry.

So if there are similarities between human and animal rituals, it is not always easy to tell whether the similarities are homologies due to direct evolution or analogies, apparent similarities due to convergent evolution. This uncertainty is a problem that DNA analysis can eventually resolve. Nonetheless, whether the similarities between animal and human rituals turn out to be analogies or homologies, we can still learn a lot from acknowledging the similarities. Furthermore, comparisons of human and animal rituals also reveal important differences, revealing emergent properties in human evolution. Novel human adaptations are just as important as those shared with other species.

In studying human rituals, cultural anthropologists generally focus on these emergent characteristics of human behavior (cultural symbols) and then further limit their focus to culturally specific institutions in specific places. For the student studying cultures, it is all about difference. This stress is reasonable if you are studying culture. For their part, ethologists are often more interested in what is shared or at least analogous between related species. That is also as it should be if you are interested in uncovering evolutionary links. These scientists are simply asking different questions. Connections and differences both matter, and we can learn from both camps. In looking at the relations between animal and human ritual, it makes sense to acknowledge the importance of both cultural and ethological factors. This interest in both similarities and differences between animal and human rituals is the approach we will take in the rest of the chapter.

Communicating with and without Language

No one is sure exactly when early humans acquired the ability to speak. Our ancestral species Homo erectus, which had spread from Africa to the Middle East, Europe, and Asia, a species that had learned how to control fire, coordinate collective hunting, and construct simple huts between a million and four hundred thousand years ago, did not have anything approaching modern speech. The evolution of language—we might call it the *revolution of language*—was a complex process that took a long time and many anatomical and neurological changes. Producing and understanding speech called for a brain able to harness various sound combinations for communication. It needed an oral cavity to make those sounds and a brain/ ear collaboration to distinguish them.

A human language requires a sizable stock of meaningful sounds (what linguists call phonemes) and sound patterns selected from the vast range of sounds the human vocal apparatus can produce. It also involves the evolution of the speech apparatus—the vocal tract, remaking organs originally evolved for breathing and eating into organs equipped for manipulating sound. So, in addition to specialized brain centers controlling the production, combination, and decoding of those sounds, human speech required a long and flexible voice box (larynx), a sturdy set of vocal cords, and a highly flexible tongue to shape sounds rapidly. Human speech was a needy newcomer in human evolution. It colonized a whole array of body parts for its own purposes—teeth, the soft palate, the lips, the throat muscles, the nasal passage, piggybacking on the oral cavity and transforming it from a breathing and eating device into a multitasking speech engine. What developed was the vocal tract, the body's concert hall housing a virtual orchestra of speech organs modified to produce and manipulate sounds.

But sounds were just the start. Those sounds needed to be combined in particular ways into words. Only certain combinations would do for each language. Moreover, those words could themselves be combined into complex sequences by something we call *syntax*. Syntax, a subject taught in "grammar school" that has terrorized generations of students, is a scheme for organizing and manipulating word patterns specific to a language. The syntactic patterns allow clusters of words to cohabit in various ways and effectively paint "pictures" in sound.

With syntax, language could represent all sorts of things that single words could not. For instance, it could distinguish things from actions; specify number (pluralization), temporal, and dynamic relations (verb tense and mode); and indicate subtle variations in how one thing is related to another (prepositions). The particular choice of words, a speech style, could even indicate the relative social status of the speaker and hearer. There were also rules for exchanging speech in conversations. We had to learn what we could say to whom, when we should speak, and when to stay quiet. Language was organized kaleidoscopically in layers, patterns within patterns, from top to bottom. By the time evolution was done with language, most humans could navigate this maze of structures instantly and intuitively. So embedded were our minds in our language that we rarely felt ourselves speaking *in* our language but rather communicating *through* it. Our picture of reality was pretty much oblivious to the speech forms that made it possible.

Moreover, if the patterns were correct and "made sense," those dazzling combinations—basically nothing more than packaged air in motion, could produce "meaning." The meaning of speech was a kind of mental imagery. In most cases, linguistic sense had little inherent connection with the sounds that orchestrated the images. But somehow, the human brain immediately evoked mental pictures of people, actions, relationships, qualities, and ideas from those sounds. Speech communication was a miracle plucked out of thin air for the evolving human species though sometimes (as in onomatopoeia) language forms could be found to be mimicking the things they represented. We are still not sure how humans manage to turn sound into meaning. We cannot even agree on what "meaning" means, but we know when it is missing or impaired.

In producing language, human evolution came up with a miraculous and mysterious way that air could be reshaped to stand for experiences of the world and even picture imaginary things that do not exist. Our everyday reality was grounded in our speech. Because we could create sound shapes for anything our imagination could come up with, language liberated human thought from dependence on what already exists, allowing us to imagine, plan, simulate, and invent things that did not exist. Lest we become too giddy contemplating the godlike powers that language gave us, it is helpful to remember that the potential freedom of thought that language bestowed on our species also meant that humans could lie. Human speech was indeed powerful, but it was also dangerous.

If language is a relatively recent development in human evolution, how did early humans communicate before they could speak? Communication is essential for any social animal, whether or not they can talk. Social animals need to coordinate their behavior and convey important information. Before language was speech, it was gesture. The human body is equipped as a virtuoso communication device. We can use almost any part of our body to communicate with others. While we are not always conscious of how much we depend on gestural communication, we naturally respond to others' body language. A raised eyebrow, a head hung low, a quick shoulder jerk, or a slight frown can speak volumes, letting us know how someone responds to our presence.

Even when we tell white lies to our friends about our feelings, our bodies give us away. Tell someone that you think their ugly shirt is beautiful, and your eyes or your posture will likely contradict your words. We intuitively know this and are constantly watching the body language of others, even as we overlook our own. Gesture is remarkably convincing. When someone's body says something that contradicts their words, we are prone to discard the words and believe the body's message. Still, it is possible to lie with your body. Actors and so-called con artists who have mastered the control of their gestures to entertain or deceive and defraud others can produce fake body language for a living. But it is decidedly harder to lie with gestures than with words. Lying with the body takes practice. Lying with words is a breeze.

Humans never let go of their dependence on their bodies. Despite the evolution of speech, language never completely replaced gestural communication for Homo sapiens (McNeill 1996, 2007; Fast 2014; Kuhnke 2016; Beatty 2004; Reiman 2008). The human body is well equipped for gestural communication. Our hands evolved to allow flexible movement of our fingers and our wrists. While the development of the human hand was propelled by increasing sophistication in toolmaking and tool use, manual dexterity also improved the human ability to communicate with the hands. In both human evolution and ontogenetic development, speech and hand movement are closely linked.

Consider how hand movements always accompany infant babbling and manipulation of sounds. Psychologist Laura Petito and her collaborators studied the hand movements of infants with profoundly deaf parents. They discovered that these infants produced rhythmic hand gestures along with their babbling and that these gestures were different from other uses of their hands. They concluded that "babies are sensitive to rhythmic language patterns and that this sensitivity is key to launching the process of language acquisition" (Petito et al. 2001, p. 35). Hand gestures accompanying speech remain with us throughout life as an important component of human communication. Our facial muscles are also well adapted for gestural as well as speech communication, allowing us to use every part of our head and face, from eyebrows, eyes, and brows to our mouths, for remarkably subtle messaging.

In his book *Origins of the Modern Mind*, Merlin Donald proposed that the evolution of human communication included a prelinguistic phase before humans acquired speech (Donald 1993). He called this phase of evolutionary development "mimetic culture," a period when ancestors to modern humans relied on their formidable gestural skills to communicate. Gestural rituals would have played a key role in coordinating human relationships and transmitting cultural skills and information in such a cultural setting.

In this dependence on gestural communication, early humans were like many other animals. Lacking the capacity for speech, other animals developed communication systems using sound, smell, and body movement to pass messages within their group and to outsiders. Despite their lack of speech-like language, many animal species evolved a repertory of specialized communication aids like the ants' pheromones, chemicals with specific smells that communicate with others and affect behavior in particular ways. The "dances" of honeybees include three types of dance movements (called the "waggle," "the round dance," and "the sickle"). The dance signals to hive mates the location and quality of food sources. This dancing was developed into an analog code for communicating location. The duration of the tail waggle indicates how far away the source is, while the relative liveliness of the dance is proportional to the food's quality. Bees can also transmit vibrational signals from their beating wings by butting the head of a dancing bee to stop the dance because of some perceived danger near that source. Likewise, birdsong is a complex communication system involving both species-specific songs communicating to other species members and individual variations, which allows birds to identify themselves and share their location with mates and offspring.

Ritualization

Nonhuman animals are not endowed with specialized speech organs. Instead, their capacity for communication has expanded by loading specific messages onto behaviors initially dedicated to other, more practical tasks. Just as human breathing and eating organs were borrowed to make speech sounds, these original "functional" movements in animals are repurposed for communication, what ethnologists call "signaling." Ethologists have termed this harnessing of a prior functional movement sequence for communication "ritualization."

Konrad Lorenz, acknowledged as the "father of ethology," noted that ritualization allows for swift and efficient evolution of behavior since it does not require the creation of novel organs or movements (Lorenz 1966a, 1980). Because ritualization "borrows" action patterns that serve functions other than communication, ritualized signals must be distinguished from the original movements to prevent ambiguity or misreading. This clarification of the signal is done by formalization. Through formalization, ordinary movement is exaggerated, intensified, repeated, slowed down, or otherwise marked in a way that sets it apart from the original act. In human performances, this marking of behavior as distinct from "regular" action is called "framing." Framing clearly indicates that "this action is a performance" or "this is 'just pretend' behavior."

In theater, framing uses a stage, a curtain, and the dimming of lights to signal that what the audience is about to witness is a performance. We have all experienced poor acting, which overdoes the formalization of speech and gesture, reminding the audience that they are just playing roles and preventing engagement with their characters. Good actors must master the art of formalizing their gestures and speech just enough to signal "pretend mode" while still allowing the audience to suspend their disbelief and enter into the illusion of real-life action. In his famous paper "A Theory of Play and Fantasy," Gregory Bateson showed how the formalization of behavior that distinguishes the dog's ritual baring of its teeth from an actual bite communicates the paradox common to all play behavior: "This is real/This is not real" (Bateson 1955). While the specific framing techniques differ from species to species, formalizing actions as repeatable communication signals is critical to all ritualized behavior.

Ritualization is commonly found in animal mating behavior. Many courtship ceremonies involve a male offering food to a potential mate, mimicking the feeding behavior of a parent to its offspring. The ritualized offering is usually a token gesture of interest. Since it does not involve enough food to serve as actual feeding, it is not really about the food. Its function has been "displaced" from feeding offspring to wooing a mate. A well-studied example of such redirected food gathering occurs among the great argus pheasant of peninsular Malaysia, where the male pheasant attracts the attention of a potential female mate by pecking the ground in a simulation of food-gathering gestures. The male's pecking alternates with his elaborate fanning displays of ornate tail feathers, underscoring that this is no ordinary food-gathering behavior.

Animal ritual includes displacement gestures, where a potentially destructive or dangerous action is reframed as a relatively harmless display that communicates an uncomfortable or hostile situation. For example, when a dog or wolf bears its teeth to warn a potential enemy to back off, it has formalized the action of biting into a warning signal. Humans also use displacement gestures when they clench their fists (as if to fight), bare their teeth, or "shoot" a glare at someone. Likewise, a father-in-law may greet his daughter's new husband with "a good-natured" slap on the back to welcome him into the family. This "friendly" back slap is loaded with complex messages combining affiliation with displaced hostility, serving both as a welcome and a warning.

In addition to these relatively simple gestures, humans have produced more elaborate displacement activities for aggression like football games, boxing matches, and military war exercises. These displacement rituals all bear a similarity to the displaced acts. But aggression or fear can also be displaced by gestures effectively masking their origin. For example, dogs will yawn or lick their lips when stressed, while humans often yawn, scratch their heads, twirl their hair, or wring their hands. Because we can invent ways to elaborate our body language, humans can also replace such gestures with culturally institutionalized displacements such as worry beads or rosaries.

Displacement gestures in animals sometimes involve an internal conflict between opposing impulses. For example, wild squirrels will show displacement behavior when approached by a human holding out nuts. The squirrel will often freeze, take a few steps toward the nuts, and then scratch itself or display simulated digging behavior in response to the intense approach-avoidance conflict. Consider the ritualized response of many animals to a potential aggressor where conflicting approach/avoidance impulses are fused in an ambivalent signal. In his 1966 Royal Society meeting presentation, Konrad Lorenz described "the triumph ceremony" of the greylag goose (Lorenz 1966b). His detailed account of the ceremony included this kind of ambivalent gesture by the gander, fusing attack and retreat:

> The triumph ceremony of the Greylag Goose serves the double function of holding together a group, in most cases a pair or a family group, and in setting it off, as an independent entity, against other, equivalent groups of conspecifics. The ceremony consists of two subsequent parts, first, the gander's actual or feigned attack on a conspecific, accompanied by a characteristic sound utterance called 'rolling,' and secondly, his return to his mate, during which the rolling subsides and merges into a low-pitched polysyllabic cackling. The attitude of the gander during rolling is that of a display motivated both by aggression and escape drive, the breast is protruded and the neck stretched obliquely upward with the bill opened. (Lorenz 1966b, p. 477)

Here we see an animal ritual with an ambivalent double meaning, similar to the human back slap. Ritualized displacement is commonly a response to approach-avoidance conflict when an animal is threatened and cannot decide whether to attack or retreat. Occasionally, as in the dog's gesture of the bared-teeth growl, we see clearly displayed the fusion of the approach and avoidance impulses in the displacement gesture. However, in other cases, the ambivalence underlying the ritualized act is displaced too far to be evident.

The Structure of Animal Ritual: Displays and Ceremonies

Many animals, ranging from insects, spiders, fish, and birds to mammals, use gestures for communication. Ethologists call these individual ritual gestures *displays*. Animal displays include all sorts of ritualized acts involving various parts of the animal's body. Bright colors, bodily swellings, the fanning of feathers, odorous body chemicals, dance-like movements, gift offerings, distinctive sounds, and facial expressions are all grist for the ritual mill. Specific to a species, ritual displays are mostly hardwired signals rather than learned or imitated. They communicate an animal's intentions and physical or mental states, mainly to members of its own species.

Humans also display some of these hardwired gestures. However, even so-called hardwired gestures are subject to cultural modification by humans. Consider, for example, the smile, a universal human gesture signaling pleasure and affiliation. In the case of humans, the smile is modified and elaborated by cultural display rules so that each culture ends up with its repertory of different smiles. The meaning of a human smile can vary depending on both style and context. Understanding a human smile requires interpretation. The ability to read others' smiles is an aspect of emotional intelligence. Smiles are a universal human gesture, culturally modified, suggesting how the term "universal" can be misleading when applied to human behavior.

Among the best-studied displays in the animal kingdom are the mating rituals used by potential mates to negotiate and synchronize copulation. Among birds, ritualized dances by males are standard courtship displays. The brightly colored and elaborately patterned feathers of male birds are often an essential aspect of the display. The male bird of paradise, whose forty-seven species are found only on remote islands off the coast of Australia and the tropical forests of New Guinea, is well known for its spectacular mating dance. The bird artfully swells and retracts its shiny black feathers, exposing its iridescent blue-green feather "decoration" underneath while gracefully swooping and twirling in its distinctive mating dance. Not surprisingly, the goal of the performance is to attract the attention of a potential mate, a female bird of paradise, who may or may not accept the invitation.

While displays in one sensory mode are common, animal rituals often use multimodal signals to attract mates. For example, I have already noted the use of ritualized feeding display by the male great argus pheasants in conjunction with its elaborate dancing gestures using the sight and sound of its brilliant, fluttering tail feathers as an invitation for copulation. Another example of multimodal displays is the male Anna's Hummingbird, which has two mating displays, a dive display and a stationary shuffle. Both feature a mix of visual and sound stimulation. In the stationary shuffle, the male stations himself directly in front of the female, flares out the colorful patch on his throat, and rocks rhythmically side to side while rotating his tail. In the dive display, the male ascends upward as much as one hundred feet and then abruptly performs a sharp plunge down toward the female, twisting his body and fluttering his tail feathers with a loud buzz as he approaches her. The sheer drama of these displays, with their vivid multi-sensory stimuli, makes them hard for the female to ignore. At the risk of anthropomorphizing bird behavior, it is not hard to see these displays as an eager male hummingbird "showing off" his athletic and artistic prowess in the hopes of winning over a mate.

Butterflies are among the best dancers in the animal kingdom, each species having its distinctive courtship dance. Potential butterfly mates rely on their color patterns to recognize each other. In some butterfly species, the male dances for the female. In others, the male and female dance together in midair, gracefully looping around one another as they synchronize their movements in preparation for mating. Nocturnal moths and butterflies cannot rely on visual displays, so they use distinctive sounds and smells to identify potential mates. Some pheromones emitted by female butterflies can be detected by males miles away. Males seeking mates are initially attracted simply by movement, so they can mistakenly follow other moving insects. But once they get close enough to detect smell and sound, they begin to narrow their search, focusing exclusively on potential mates.

Another well-studied ritual is the agonistic display, often performed at the margins of a group's territory. Agonistic displays are ritual warnings used to ward off a threat to a group or individual. Consider, for example, the dramatic chest-beating display of male mountain gorillas. These gorillas live in close-knit groups led by an older silverback male in the wild. Younger males frequently challenge the silverback's leadership, and the older gorilla's chest-beating response reminds a challenger of the leader's size and strength. The same display can also be directed at a threat to the group from outside. The gorilla's chest-beating display advertises a male's relative size and strength using both sight and sound. Researchers have discovered that the larger the gorilla, the deeper the sound made by chest pounding, allowing gorillas to evaluate differences in the relative size of older and younger gorillas. Thus, not only does a challenger see the silverback's size and strength, but he also hears it.

While many rituals in the animal world are single displays, multiple displays can be sequenced into more complex ritual performances called *ceremonies*. Many species of birds have elaborated courtship ceremonies that make use of multiple displays. One such elaborate courtship ceremony is the property of the remarkable bowerbird. Twenty species of bowerbirds are found in Australia, New Guinea, and the Indonesian territory of West Irian. The male's courtship ceremony starts with an elaborate feat of avian architecture. The bowerbird clears a court area to construct an elaborate "bower"—a cozy enclosure to impress a future mate. Male bowerbirds engage in intense competition for the attention of females, an evolutionary selection process that biologists call *sexual selection*. Females will visit and compare several bowers constructed by potential mates, selecting the most impressive bower builder and the most convincing performer for mating. A single competent male bowerbird may be rewarded by mating with several females. Less successful male bowerbirds are "dumped" by the females and can become full-time bachelors.

Bowers come in two designs. Some species build "maypole bowers," constructed by leaning sticks around a sapling. A roof is added to the bowers of a few species, giving the bowers a hut-like appearance. In others, it is omitted. Other species of bowerbirds build what ornithologists call an "avenue bower" consisting of two parallel walls built from piles of sticks laid on top of each other. Once the basic structures are completed, the bowers are elaborately adorned with colorful objects collected by the birds. Each species has its preferences for decoration. Nuts, berries, shells, stones, flowers, and, in modern times, even bits of broken glass bottles, bullet shells, coins, or colorful pieces of plastic will be repurposed as decorations. Bower birds have even been observed stealing decorations from nearby competitors' bowers.

The finished bowers can be surprisingly large, in some cases up to six feet in length. Males can spend weeks perfecting their constructions. While the basic bower-building strategy is hardwired by species rather than learned, there is some flexibility in how males carry out their construction, reflecting differences in intelligence and aesthetic sense. For example, some bower builders attract females by using an optical illusion, arranging objects in the bower's open court area in a line from smaller to larger things. This design strategy creates an illusion of enhanced scale and distance that seems intended to catch the female's attention.

Once the bower is completed, the bird continues the ceremony with a series of performances for the female. Depending on the species and the individual performer, the displays can include a mesmerizing alternate dilation of the male's right and left pupils, intricate dance movements involving the male's wing rhythmically sweeping in graceful arcs, distinctive clucking sounds, and even imitation of other species' calls. The displays aim to impress the female who looks on with interest. Finally, there are gift displays where the male can offer the female a food gift such as a berry. Unfortunately, a male rival for the female will sometimes barge in on the performance, hoping to interrupt the ceremony and distract the female until she loses interest in the performing bowerbird. The bowerbird courtship ceremony is of particular interest to ethologists. One of the animal kingdom's more complex ceremonies, the bowerbird courting ceremony suggests that calling animal rituals genetically "fixed" may be too simple. Some animals, it appears, can produce "creative" variations of ritual displays within the constraints of the species-specific displays.

Another bird with an elaborate mating ceremony is the blue-footed booby found on the Galapagos Islands. The booby has distinctive bright blue feet, an important part of the mating ritual. Since the blue pigment is difficult for the bird's body to produce, the brightness of the blue color is a reliable sign of the bird's health. Showing them off to a potential mate is a handy way for the female to judge the male's suitability for reproduction. The mating ceremony begins with a male's rhythmic strutting of his blue feet in front of the female. An interested female may mimic his strut. The foot display is followed by a bow of the suitor's head and finally with an elaborate bow with wings extended as if inviting the female to dance. If she finds the male attractive, the female booby begins to mirror the movements of the male until they are stepping and bowing in unison. The male may even offer the female a token food gift to enhance his appeal. Once the pair is synchronized, copulation can begin. Boobies will continue to perform the synchronizing ceremony even after nesting, using their dance as an ongoing bonding ritual.

Comparing the Flexibility of Human and Animal Rituals

There are significant parallels between the organization of human rituals and those of other animals. The three most critical structural parallels between human and animal rituals are (1) modular organization, (2) the increase in the symbolic load of communicative signals, and (3) the process of formalization of an action that frames a performance.

Modular Organization

Individual displays can be combined into more complex sequences in both human and animal rituals. As we saw in the last chapter, significant human rituals like a coronation or a religious mass are elaborated by adding smaller ritual components. These are sometimes called "rites" when they are part of sacred ceremonies. While these ritual components can "harden" over time into inflexible sequences, they always start as modules that can be added or subtracted from the more extensive ritual. For example, the High Mass of the Roman Catholic Church includes rites that are omitted in the ordinary mass. In the same way, a simple English wedding ceremony will resemble the wedding of a future king in its basic form. It will be a recognizable English wedding ritual. However, the royal wedding will always be grander, not just in its opulence but also in its scale—the number and elaboration of its ritual components.

While animal ceremonies can never share the scale or symbolic elaboration of human ritual, they do share its basic modular form. For example, we have seen how displays become ceremonies among certain species of birds by linking various displays together, turning a simple ritual display into a complex ceremony. Significantly, this kind of elaboration is the exception rather than the rule in the animal kingdom. Humans, however, are virtuoso elaborators of rituals. Among humans, simple rituals will often grow in complexity and scale over time as new ritual elements are added. In other cases, rituals can be scaled back as needed by leaving out "optional" features.

Compare the elaboration of the bowerbird's courtship ritual to the modern American wedding. In planning a wedding, the families have to decide on the scale of the event. Scale is often related to the "size" of the wedding—how many people will be invited—which is usually a significant point of contention in wedding planning. The ceremony's scale will also depend on how much money is available to fund the wedding, raising the issue of who will pay. Traditionally, but not always, the bride's family foots the bill. While an elaborate ceremony is theoretically possible with a small number of guests, the scale and size of the wedding are often linked. Bigger weddings will often include more elaborate ceremonies. They will also cost a lot more money. The more guests who attend and the further they have to travel, the more they will expect to see.

The traditional wedding ceremony can include a bride and groom, the father of the bride who escorts the bride down the aisle of the wedding chapel, the groom's best man and the bride's maid of honor, additional bridesmaids and groomsmen, a white wedding dress, a bouquet held by the bride, wedding rings, an officiant who performs the marriage ceremony, and a father figure to "give the bride away." Ultratraditional weddings will also include a set of ritual wedding objects worn by the bride and remembered by the old Victorian English rhyme, "Something old, something new, something borrowed, something blue." Originally, "a sixpence in your shoe" was added to the good luck objects, but it never made it in its translation to the modern American tradition. Today, the cash tends to go to the wedding caterer.

The ceremony starts with the formal entrance and seating of the bride's and groom's close family members. Solemn music usually accompanies the entrance procession. As the bride, escorted by her father or a stand-in, enters the chapel, the officiant asks the audience to stand. The groom turns to face the bride as she walks toward him. Often the music will change to a traditional wedding march, like the wedding march from Felix Mendelssohn's *A Midsummer Night's Dream*. Next, the officiant welcomes the guests to the wedding. If the wedding ceremony follows a religious tradition, the officiant will perform traditional readings and prayers. A secular wedding will feature a short speech of praise, well-wishing, and advice to the bride and groom, followed by readings of poems by the bride and groom to each other.

The bride and groom then exchange their wedding vows, sometimes affirming a traditional set of promises of perpetual fidelity read by the officiant. Alternatively, the bride and groom may read or speak a unique set of wedding vows prepared for the occasion. The wedding rings (often carried by the best man) are handed to the bride and groom, who slip the rings on each other's ring finger. The officiant may ask if anyone in the room can say why this couple should not be legally joined in wedlock. Objections are rare, and the officiant typically proceeds to proclaim the couple "man and wife," informing the groom that he may publicly kiss the bride.

With the official marriage ceremony concluded, the wedding party exits the church in a recessional march, led by the bride and groom arm in arm, followed by the bridesmaids and groomsmen, the grandparents, parents, and siblings of the bride and groom. While the entrance procession was solemn, the recessional appears joyful and spontaneous, suggesting relief that the ceremony has been successfully carried out. Finally, the newlyweds stand outside the chapel, where they are greeted and congratulated by friends and family.

With the marriage ceremony completed, the wedding continues with a series of ritualized postceremony events. The newlyweds are now ritually married, but they are not legally married until they sign a government wedding certificate. So a second "marriage ceremony" occurs backstage with the bride, groom, and a witness signing the documents that marry the couple in the eyes of the law. The legal ceremony, always hidden from public view, can be done before or after the public marriage ceremony. The public ritual continues outside the chapel as the couple prepares for the ritual departure, sometimes an actual departure for a honeymoon trip or, in many cases, a purely ceremonial farewell since the couple reappears at the wedding reception.

In a traditional sendoff, the newlyweds leave the chapel in a waiting car sporting a "just married" banner and dragging a clattering string of tin cans tied to the rear bumper that loudly proclaims the newlyweds' departure to the whole neighborhood. Guests may throw rice at the departing couple, a traditional fertility symbol of a fruitful union. As she departs the chapel, the bride may turn her back to the crowd of well-wishers and throw her bridal bouquet over her shoulder. Sometimes this is done at the reception party. Unmarried girls and women vie to catch the bouquet, a sign that the catcher will soon find a suitable husband (i.e., "a good catch"). In many weddings, the couple and their close family members disappear for an hour or so for the official photo or video shoot of family groupings that will become part of a wedding album.

Wedding receptions are familiar yet optional parts of a wedding. Receptions vary dramatically in scale and cost, and the most elaborate are quasi-theatrical productions produced by a professional wedding planner. Like the marriage ceremony, the wedding reception is a highly ritualized affair with many component rituals. Entering the filled reception hall, the bride and groom are "introduced" to the assembled guests as a "Mr. and Mrs." married couple. A reception can include endless toasts to the couple by the bridesmaid, the best man, close relatives, and friends. Humorous speeches, often "roasting" the bride and groom, are made by the maid of honor, the best man, and sometimes by others. Following an elaborate wedding dinner, a special multitiered wedding cake is dessert. The newlyweds jointly cut the first piece and serve a forkful to each other. Whenever the music begins, there are often special dances featuring the bride and her father, the groom and his mother, and the bride and groom. All of these ritual elements are optional. The larger the scale and the more elaborate the wedding, the more ritual elements are usually included. At Jewish weddings, the bride and groom, each seated in a chair, are often hoisted on the shoulders of celebrants who parade them around the room in a dance of honor.

Because it focuses on the most common wedding formats, my discussion left out many variations in wedding rituals that distinguish one wedding from another. The growth of the wedding industry has expanded the scale of weddings. In recent years, bachelor and bachelorette parties hosted by friends of the groom and bride sometimes precede the wedding ceremony, but they are still parts of the wedding festivities. Moreover, religious affiliation, ethnic elaborations, and military service can add distinctive ritual twists to a wedding ceremony. Since the legalization of gay marriage, there have been modifications to wedding ceremonies to accommodate the union of two women or men.

Ceremonies are also modified to accommodate differences in family circumstances such as deaths or divorces. Many weddings now feature friends as officiants, who may obtain online certification to perform legal weddings. The isolation necessitated by the pandemic has even promoted the invention of online weddings (see chapter 10). However, despite the wide variations in marriage rituals, most American weddings are immediately recognizable as "weddings." Some essential ritual elements are less optional than others. The presence of a couple facing an officiant, the march up the aisle, the exchange of rings and vows, the public proclaiming a couple as married, and the public kiss are all examples of ritual elements likely to be considered essential in the great majority of American wedding ceremonies.

The other wedding elements are optional ritual components that help create a more elaborate ceremony. Conventional optional features include a young boy as a ring bearer, a young girl strewing flower petals on the aisle to prepare the way for the bride's entry, a musical group performing the wedding entrance music, and a rehearsed "surprise" dance performance by the bride and her father. Increasingly, couples come up with new ritual elements to personalize their ceremonies. However, no matter how original a wedding ceremony is, it always includes aspects of traditional rituals. A couple can opt to radically simplify the ceremony by getting married in front of a judge at the local courthouse with a simple legal marriage ceremony and a single witness. No matter how much the wedding is simplified, the primary ritual elements of the marriage ceremony are still evident.

Animal and human ceremonies share a modular structure. They can be elaborated or simplified by adding or eliminating displays. Of course, there is a vast difference between animal and human rituals in the degree of elaboration possible and the resulting scale of the ceremony. Both the bowerbird courting ritual and the American wedding ceremony exhibit this modular format, allowing for some flexibility in the performance scale. However, animal ritual is far more limited than its human counterpart in its elaboration and the range of novel ritual elements that can be used.

Increase in Symbolic Load

Another significant feature common to animal and human rituals is that both develop by adding a symbolic dimension to practical actions. Ethologists long ago recognized that animal displays often "borrowed" everyday practical activities like searching for food, feeding offspring, or building nests and turned them into communicative signs. They called this transformation "the ritualization" of an action. Whether we could consider these signs as symbols would depend on how we understand the term *symbol*. Does the female pheasant interpret the meaning of the male's pecking behavior or his fancy tail display, or do the displays simply trigger a mating response? It is hard to know. In either case, the action can be considered a "communication" whether or not conscious meaning is involved.

The development of human ritual also involves potentially practical actions being repurposed for communication. The behavioral format for ritual is a routine, a sequence of habits for automating practical tasks.

Routines become rituals when the acts take on symbolic significance. This sort of symbolization involves meaning-making through various kinds of associations the actions acquire beyond their practical function. For example, the sequence of security checks the Transportation Security Administration (TSA) carries out at airports has become a familiar routine for air travelers. The TSA might claim that these checks serve the practical purpose of ensuring no passenger carries a dangerous weapon or substance onto a plane. However, for many passengers, the security check has an additional communicative purpose of assuring the public that flying is safe and the government is protecting them. The inspection routine has become a ritual communicating safety and competence for these passengers. So while symbols and signals are not quite the same thing, humans and other animals share the shift from a practical to a communication function.

The Formalization of Ritual Signals

The third similarity between animal and human rituals is the formalizing of communicative actions. In both cases, actions become displays through slight distortions involving framing devices like repetition, exaggeration, slowing down, and other kinds of emphasis that mark the acts as performances. Humans have an extensive repertory of formalizing markers. For example, a ritual drink of wine involves framing gestures like raising the glass or the toastmaster gently tapping on the wineglass with a fork, and special formulaic words, all of which convert a drink into a toast. Likewise, a ritual prayer involves not only special words but also distinctive framing actions like bowing the head, pressing together both hands at the palms, closing the eyes, or chanting intonation. The formalization of gesture in animal rituals is usually less elaborated than in humans, using rhythm, repetition, unique sounds, and exaggeration to formalize ritual behavior. The formalization of action is a defining feature of ritual in both humans and other animals.

The Functions of Animal Ritual

Why do animals perform rituals? There is not a single answer to that question. Ritual is like a behavioral Swiss Army knife for both humans and animals, a single evolutionary capability that does many different things. The major functions of animal rituals are listed and briefly discussed below.

Synchronization and Coordination of Behavior

All social animals face the problem of coordinating their behavior with other group members. Individuals are always capable of some degree of autonomous behavior. The more developed the nervous system, the greater the potential variability in individual behavior. This individual variability is especially pronounced for humans, whose brains have allowed for the elaborate development of personal temperament—what we call "personality"— and a wide range of personal motivations. This variability of response means that coordinated behavior for groups or pairs will always be a problem. Social life always calls for communication that permits coordination and synchronization of individuals to achieve a joint perspective and coordinated activity. This is especially true in mating behavior, where potential mates need to be "on the same page" for intimate reproductive contact. For humans, we call it being "in the mood."

Mating rituals among animals as varied as spiders, butterflies, and salamanders include rhythmic "dances" by which potential mates synchronize their movements in preparing for copulation. For example, synchronized singing is part of the courtship ritual of pacific humpback whales. Variations in the songs of different whales suggest that individual whales invent at least some song elements, and there is also evidence that whales can imitate the songs of others. This variation implies that some animal rituals are not simply hardwired signals but a mix of invented and innate responses.

Imitation is an essential source of coordinated behavior. Birdsong is a well-studied form of animal communication that suggests that songs combine hardwired, imitated, and improvised responses. For example, swamp sparrows can be trained to mimic a range of tempo variations in their song, but those variations can only occur within a specific range of tempos. These limitations appear to be genetically controlled. Young birds early on learn to imitate the song patterns of their fathers. Under experimental conditions, birds retain the ability to mimic introduced song patterns, including recorded songs, and then reproduce them spontaneously.

Years ago, we had a pet cockatiel we named Shadow, a talented student of song. By imitating me, Shadow learned to whistle famous tunes from Mozart, Beethoven, and Schubert. He would often spontaneously break into song, such as the opening section of Mozart's *Eine Kleine Nachtmusik*. These learned tunes became almost as characteristic of its singing as the standard cockatiel whistle. I never tested the limits of his mimicry skills and have wondered what Shadow would have done with hip-hop or twelve-tone music. Different varieties of a bird species appear to be genetically programmed to produce some syllables more readily than others, suggesting interactions between genetic programming and learning.

Migrating flocks of birds and schools of fish show great skill in synchronizing their movements. Watching a school of fish zigzag at high speed through the water in perfect synchrony can put a well-drilled military parade to shame in the speed and accuracy of their coordinated movements. Flamingos are famous for their mating dance, where a large flock of the pink birds will parade in lockstep back and forth for hours while rhythmically turning their heads back and forth. After several weeks of collective dancing, the flamingos pair up for mating. It is unknown how the group marching helps the flamingos find mates, but there seems to be a connection. As among humans, rhythmic movements, often with the aid of colorful swelling of feathers or body parts, are performed among many animals to attract the attention of potential mates. Collective rhythmic movement keeps the animals in synchrony with one another. In addition to facilitating mating, synchrony is essential for maintaining group identity.

Among humans, ritual provides a powerful way for individuals to synchronize social identities and produce fellow-feeling. For example, military training always includes rigidly synchronized behavior such as marching in file. The rhythmic, synchronized movement is an embodied way to experience collective identity. Marching and other drills orient the soldiers to following the commands of a drillmaster (McNeill 1995). Thus synchronized, a collection of individuals becomes a tightly integrated joint unit. Drilling and other collective rituals are used throughout the world to promote unity. For example, sports teams often train using military drill techniques, and many develop distinctive rituals to promote "team spirit." In many schools, classmates will stand and greet the entering teacher in unison. For younger students, lessons often take the form of synchronized chanting of things to be learned, such as times tables. In these schools, uniforms are often worn, supporting the collective identity of schoolmates and loyalty to the institution.

Human mating ritual often involves synchronization through joint rhythmic interactions between potential mates, which we recognize as dancing. Human dancing has evolved into a pleasurable activity and even an art form, attenuating its connections to mating. Human ritual acts are subject to cultural elaborations, often taking them far from their origins. It might be difficult to recognize anything close to a precopulatory synchronization rite in the dance of a prima ballerina. However, many of the most dramatic kinds of formalized dancing like the Argentine tango, the French cancan, the Brazilian samba, the Tahitian *ori*, salsa dancing, and the steamy couple-dancing found in any nightclub retain the erotic movements that link dancing to mating.

In many primates, including humans, synchronization is aided by the presence in the brain of mirror neurons. Mirror neurons fire both when an individual performs an action and when that individual observes someone else performing the same action. The discovery of mirror neurons suggests that primates are cognitively predisposed to imitate observed actions in others. These neurons are thought to be an important factor in promoting empathy and direct imitation (Whitehouse 2022). Traditional Balinese dancing sometimes involves the mirroring of each other's movements by pairs of dancers (figure 4.1), a mimicry skill that reflects the way Balinese

Figure 4.1
Mirroring mimicry in Balinese dance

teach novices to dance by shadowing the movements of experts (Bateson and Mead 1942). Research has demonstrated that the human capacity for imitation is far greater than that of monkeys and apes, allowing for much faster and more complex levels of mimicry. Mimicry was probably central to the transmission of the earliest protohuman toolmaking techniques. Still, as toolmaking became increasingly complex in the course of human evolution, involving increasing levels of hierarchical integration of discrete skills, language was necessary to pass on the toolmaking skills.

Despite the evolution of language, humans still use mimicry in many ways. For example, many duets in human dance exploit the predisposition for mirroring the behavior of others. Also consider the well-known children's game Simon Says that relies on the human penchant for mirroring the observed behavior of others. Simon Says tests the players' ability to resist the natural impulse to mirror behavior whenever the leader fails to say "Simon Says." Mirror neurons are a significant neurological underpinning for synchronous behavior and are likely a factor in the typical transmission of human ritual by observation rather than verbal instruction.

Anxiety Reduction

Repetitive and rhythmic behavior has a calming effect on humans and other animals. This anxiety reduction is evident both for rapidly repeating actions such as tapping one's finger, twirling one's hair, or marching and for regularly repeated complex acts like having a morning cup of coffee or sitting in a familiar easy chair. In the animal world, many mammals such as deer, camels, and rhinos have been observed regularly returning to fixed locations, "home bases," where they prefer to rest for long periods. These homing rituals may become more complex, involving a sequence of acts.

In his 1966 book *On Aggression*, Konrad Lorenz described the ritualized behavior of his pet greylag goose Martina that lived with him in his house, sleeping in an upstairs bedroom. After a day spent outdoors in the yard, it was her habit to enter the dark house and look out of a particular window before heading upstairs. Lorenz recounts an incident when he forgot to let his pet goose Martina in the house at the usual time and only opened the door for her after dusk. The goose, clearly disturbed at the interruption of her usual end-of-day routine, ran frantically into the house and headed straight for the stairs. After she had climbed several stairs, Martina stopped and, stretching her neck in a typical goose display of fear, uttered a cry, turned around and ran down the stairs to her window, and then turned around and gave a display of relief and pleasure as she headed back upstairs for the night. Lorenz saw this amazing scene as an example of how the maintenance of routine behavior is a stress reducer for geese. At the same time, the disruption of the accustomed ritual intensified anxiety.

Caged animals frequently resort to highly formalized repeated movements that appear as responses to the stress of being restrained. For example, farm animals will repeat stationary ritualized actions like nodding, licking, or yawning. In contrast, caged wild animals like bears or lions will resort to ritualized pacing back and forth. Wolves and dogs have a repertory of calming signals and ritual movements in the context of stressful encounters. Like humans, dogs get easily stressed by violence, danger, encounters with strangers, others' anger, and, more generally, anything that produces a loss of control. For example, calming signals can be seen in dogs when they encounter an unfamiliar dog they do not trust or when their human caretakers speak to them harshly.

Calming signals include a wide variety of ritual gestures, including freezing in place, turning the head to the side, or averting the eyes from the source of anxiety, yawning, licking movements, adopting a ritualized invitation to play, or "bowing" to the other dog by stretching forward the front legs. If the threatening dog returns the "let's play" bow, both dogs relax and begin to play with each other. Calming signals like these promote synchronous emotional states between potential antagonists by simultaneously reducing anxiety in both animals. While calming signals in animals have been best studied in dogs, they have also been noted for other mammals like horses and alpacas.

Anthropologists have long noted deep connections between human ritual and anxiety. In the 1920s, based on his research among the Trobriand islanders in the Massim area just off the coast of New Guinea, Bronislaw Malinowski proposed ritual magic as a psychological response to uncertainty and danger. Here is his explanation of the origins of ritual magic used by Trobriand fishermen:

> An interesting and crucial test is provided by fishing in the Trobriand Islands and its magic. While in the villages on the inner Lagoon fishing is done in an easy and absolutely reliable manner by the method of poisoning, yielding abundant results without danger and uncertainty, there are on the shores of the open sea dangerous modes of fishing and also certain types in which the yield varies greatly

according to whether shoals of fish appear beforehand or not. It is most significant that in the Lagoon fishing, where man can rely completely upon his knowledge and skill, magic does not exist, while in the open-sea fishing, full of danger and uncertainty, there is extensive magical ritual. (Homans 1941, p.164–165)

Malinowski explained the use of ritual through psychological principles, focusing on an individual's anxiety (Malinowski 2015). Fellow anthropologist Alfred R. Radcliffe-Brown saw ritual as reflecting a social norm rather than as a product of individual psychology. For him, social ritual expressed collective rather than personal anxiety (Radcliffe-Brown 1922). Despite their differences in emphasis, both anthropologists saw ritual as a response to fear and anxiety, a backdoor means of gaining symbolic control over a stressful situation when ordinary control was not possible.

Among the most common ritual responses to uncertainty are greeting rituals, which are found in many species of mammals. For example, both domesticated and wild dogs display many greeting gestures when encountering others in their pack. Some dogs will run alongside each other or playfully chase one another. Licking is a common form of canid greeting. Greeting rituals often display both fear and friendship, signaling appeasement and reducing anxiety about the possibility of aggression. Here is a description of a greeting ritual found among wild African dogs:

Every dog, regardless of status, displays appeasement signals to any other member of the pack. They crouch low with head and rump, the tail raised stiffly and there is a lot of twittering, whining, squeaking, and locomotory activity in the whole pack. The behaviour is ritualised from infantile food-begging behaviour. Very often, intensive play by some dogs follows the greeting, and this can trigger a mobbing reaction in other pack members, where they "gang up" on one dog, tumble and roll it, but do not actually bite. (Rütten and Fleissner 2004, p. 2)

White-faced capuchin monkeys from Costa Rica have been observed greeting each other by passing sticks back and forth or putting their fingers in each other's noses. Researchers think these greeting rituals are the monkeys' ways of testing friendships and assessing trust (Perry and Smolla 2020). Male Guinea baboons will often mount each other as if they are copulating when greeting each other. Alternately, they may briefly play with each other's penis. These odd greeting rituals are yet another example of how greetings test the trustworthiness of potentially hostile and competitive relationships.

Among humans, greeting someone might not seem a likely candidate for a stressful situation, but think about how you feel when you are about to meet someone. You are likely to experience a bit of low-level anxiety, especially when meeting a stranger or encountering someone you have not seen for a long time. In meeting someone, we face a delicate boundary between our world and someone else's, a boundary that can raise anxious questions. Is this person a friend or a foe? Am I safe? How do I look? What will I say? Will I be understood? Will I commit a faux pas and look silly? Will this person like me or not? The world over, traditional greeting rituals make meeting others more predictable and less stressful.

Ritual greetings are universal but vary widely in form from culture to culture. Most involve mutual ritual gestures such as bowing, bowing the head, raising the eyebrows, shaking hands or elbows, or pressing palms together. Somewhat more intimate greeting signs use various forms of kissing, hugging, or nose rubbing. The common element here is a brief meeting of two bodies, or an inclination of bodies toward each other, movements conveying connection and mutual trust. For example, a mutual bow from the waist, a staple of greetings in Japan, suggests mutual respect. On the other hand, a non-reciprocated one-way bow or curtsy, like the greeting offered to a monarch by a subject, is a gesture of ritual submission, underscoring status distance.

Just as we can easily express subtle differences in our verbal greetings ("I'm *so very* happy to meet you!"), slight variations in our greeting gestures can convey significantly different kinds of relationships. A kiss on the lips is very different from a kiss on the cheek or forehead. Hugs can be stiff and brief or long and tight, conveying very different messages. A handshake can be weak or strong, short or long, one-handed or two-handed, warm or cool. Generally, in the United States, two heterosexual men will hug stiffly, holding back from a complete embrace unless it is between close relatives or very close friends after a long absence.

Ritual Control of Violence

Since ritualization in the animal world involves converting a practical act into a signal, we might not be surprised to learn that one of the functions of animal ritual is replacing direct violence with simulated or threatened violence. Ritual threats are common throughout the animal kingdom. They are used both to ward off potential aggressors and to assert an individual's physical superiority. Actual violence is commonplace in the animal world, ranging from enemy species hunting for food to wolves competing for leadership of a pack to violence between males of a group competing for mates. But violence in the animal world is often measured by estimating the rate of same-species killing, not just attacks.

From that perspective, the most violent mammal in the wild is the meerkat. About 20 percent of all meerkats are killed by members of their own species, many of them as infants. Also at the top of the list of violent mammals are a species of monkey (the blue monkey) and several species of lemurs. Among mammals, primates tend to have the highest rates of same-species violence. There are also surprises. Some of the more violent species, like chinchillas and New Zealand sea lions, are actually more murderous to their own kind than animals most of us think of as violent, like lions and brown bears.

Given the frequency of human-to-human violence reported on the nightly news, we might be surprised to learn that the rate of human homicide is relatively low for modern humans, accounting for around one in every ten thousand deaths. While this rate of intraspecies killing is above the average for mammals, it is still far less than the homicide rates estimated for human populations five hundred to three thousand years ago, which were several hundred times as frequent as modern rates of killing. Thus, while humans are far more violent than the average mammal, our rates of lethal violence are far lower than the average rate for primates. Moreover, these rates have decreased dramatically over historical time. The picture this presents is a bad news, good news portrait. Humans, it seems, are relatively violent mammals but relatively peaceful primates.

Given the increasing toll that violence has exacted on many species in mammalian evolution, it is little wonder that ritual has been harnessed as a way to reduce deadly violence. Appeasement rituals in the animal kingdom involve several strategies. Threat rituals are displays intended to scare off a would-be attacker or competitor. A well-known example is the baring of teeth of wolves and dogs, accompanied by a growl. This display of the canines looks like the animal is about to bite but is intended as a display—a "play" bite but also a warning. Other threat rituals involve making the animal look bigger and thus more threatening. For example, the chest pounding of the silverback male gorilla made famous in the King Kong films conveys a sense of enhanced size and strength produced by the expansion of the chest and the loud thumping.

A common ritual threat strategy is to puff up a part of the body to increase the animal's apparent size. For example, toads can expand their bodies to make themselves look bigger than they are. The numerous puffadder snakes use the same inflation strategy as a threat display. Pufferfish can blow up their elastic stomachs by swallowing water, making them appear too big to be eaten by potential predators. Moreover, this dramatic increase in size also serves as a warning to predators to stay away. For the pufferfish, the warning is no idle threat since it can defend itself with its deadly toxin if a predator does not back off.

Ritualized aggression is the defensive use of fighting gestures as a warning rather than a weapon. For example, spider monkeys will defend their territory from their position high in a tree by dropping branches, urinating, and defecating on potential intruders below. They also use screams or barks to scare away unwanted visitors. Ring-tailed lemurs will ward off intruders with a stink display of noxious fluid they secrete from scent glands on their chests, wrists, or genital area. They rub their long tails over the glands and then wave the smelly tail in the face of an opponent. The smell is not lethal, but it can effectively deter a would-be intruder.

Another kind of ritual that checks violence is appeasement. A potential male rival acknowledges his subordination to an alpha male by lip smacking, grinning, yawning, or averting his gaze. A submissive dog may also cower or lower his body in a kind of appeasement bow. Submissive dogs will also roll over, exposing their bellies, as an appeasement gesture. So, in addition to controlling aggression, ritualized aggression and subordination also serve to sort out leaders from followers for both humans and other animals.

Do Animals Have Rituals?

This book is primarily about human rituals. Nevertheless, this chapter has focused on what ethologists have called "rituals" found among nonhuman animals. We treated ritual in the animal kingdom as a question rather than simply taking for granted that ritual is something animals and humans share because of the contention of some cultural anthropologists that the term "ritual" has been misapplied to the behavior of animals. If ritual turns out to exist only among humans, then studying animal signals can only reveal for the study of ritual what animals other than humans do not have and studies of animal rituals will offer no direct insights into the evolution of human ritual. On the other hand, if there are links between human and animal rituals, we can get some valuable insights from ethologists about the nature and functions of human rituals. So in considering the ritualized signals of animals, each section of this chapter has tried to see if there are relevant parallels for humans without making the mistake of assuming that human and animal rituals are identical.

Clearly, we have shown enough parallels between the structure and function of human and animal rituals to suggest that human ritual is probably homologous to animal ritual and is not just based on misleading analogies. The similarities between human and animal rituals are sufficiently suggestive to justify the term "ritual" for both humans and other creatures, provided that the differences are also acknowledged. Human ritual appears to be linked to the rituals of other mammals as a common evolutionary adaptation. At the same time, our comparisons have also suggested that brain evolution in Homo sapiens and the dramatic expansion of the human capacity for symbolic elaboration have produced significant differences between human and animal rituals.

Recall that the objections to calling animal signals "ritual" stressed the differences between the hardwired signals of animals and the cultural rituals of humans. While it is true that the ritualized signals of animals are more strongly tied to genetic programming than most human rituals, we have also seen that the simple opposition between hardwired animals and cultured humans is also misleading. In chapters 6, we will take a closer look at the many functions of human ritual. Here we will emphasize the distinctive character of rituals for Homo sapiens.

Some elements of animal rituals are clearly learned. For example, individuals improvise some elements of birdsong and bowerbird courting rituals. On the other hand, human rituals are also shaped by genetically controlled capacities for ritualization. Humans possess a repertory of hardwired gestures that communicate information about emotions and relationships. So while the detailed components of any human ritual may be culturally learned and changed, these examples of hardwired elements of human ritual suggest that the "nature-culture" distinction has to be softened. We have seen how genes and learning work together in shaping ritual for both humans and nonhuman creatures. The differences are a matter of the relative influence of biology and learning on animal and human rituals, not a simple dichotomy.

There are basic structural similarities between human and animal rituals. Rituals comprise gestures and (for humans) ritualized language linked into sequences. Moreover, both human and animal rituals are often transformations of practical acts that take on a symbolic significance for humans or a communicative significance for animals. Thus, meaning or at least communication is central to ritual. Finally, both human and animal rituals require the formalization of action, marking it as distinct from ordinary behavior. Formalization helps make ritual action repeatable. The formalization and repeatability of ritual displays for animals are largely genetically controlled. For humans, these aspects of ritualization are a combination of culturally learned responses and innate capabilities of habituation and formalization. In addition to having similar structures, human and animal rituals share many functions. These shared functions constitute the primitive functional substrate of our rituals and reflect the older evolutionary basis of human ritual. However, it is also clear that the functions of human rituals go far beyond animal rituals. Thus, human rituals cannot be entirely understood by finding animal homologs. Reducing human rituals to human versions of animal rituals is as misleading as claiming they have no connection. Many human rituals have no homologous forms in the rest of the animal kingdom.

In conclusion, studying animal rituals has proven helpful in understanding human ritual's evolutionary roots and primitive functions. However, human ethology does not tell the whole story of human ritual, the story of the many remarkable ways people have harnessed the power of ritual in their lives. For that story, we must turn from the animal world back to the cultural worlds of humans to appreciate the extent to which the evolution of culture and the human brain have reshaped our ritual capabilities.

5   Ritual Combat: Gift Exchange as Revenge

> Samoan ceremonial exchange was, and still is, a structure for the transfer of culturally defined wealth, but this "structure" should perhaps be seen as a set of rules to be situationally bent or violated, of possibilities to be manipulated. (Linnekin 1991, p. 3)

We all give and receive gifts. The back-and-forth rhythm of gift exchange sets the tempo of social life, binding us to one another in countless ways. Gifts come in all forms: from birthday presents, dinner invitations, the exchange of polite greetings, cups of sugar borrowed from neighbors, money or cattle exchanged as part of marriage arrangements in Africa, the ceremonial donation of pigs or shell necklaces in parts of New Guinea, thank-you gifts, work done for a friend or family member, to the simple exchange of favors.

In 1925, the French sociologist Marcel Mauss revolutionized the new fields of sociology and anthropology when he published his short book *Essai sur le don*, translated as *The Gift: The Form and Reason for Exchange in Archaic Societies* (Mauss 2002). The book seems to have been directed mainly at economists. Mauss questioned the assumptions of the economics of his day. For example, he asked whether markets and contracts were found only in modern societies. Was it the case that all economic transactions are derived from self-interest? Here is how Mauss put it:

> We shall describe the phenomena of exchange and contract in those societies that are not, as has been claimed, devoid of economic markets—since the market is a human phenomenon that, in our view, is not foreign to any known society—but whose system of exchange is different from ours. In these societies, we shall see the market as it existed before the institution of traders and before their main invention—money proper. We shall see how it functioned both before the

discovery of forms of contract and sale that may be said to be modern (Semitic, Hellenic, Hellenistic, and Roman) and also before money, minted and inscribed. We shall see the morality and the organization that operate in such transactions.

As we shall note that this morality and organization still function in our own societies, in unchanging fashion and, so to speak, hidden, below the surface, and as we believe that in this we have found one of the human foundations on which our societies are built, we shall be able to deduce a few moral conclusions concerning certain problems posed by the crisis in our own law and economic organization. (Mauss 2002, p. 5)

Along with his sociologist uncle, Emile Durkheim, Mauss was convinced that much of the utilitarian school of English sociology and economics had mistakenly assumed that human behavior was guided solely by rational calculation and self-interest. In this view, society was no more than a collection of individuals, and social behavior could be explained by individual acquisitiveness. However, in the exchange rituals of traditional societies, societies that lacked money and physical markets, Mauss saw a way to show that society was based on social rather than individual motives. In other words, Mauss sought to *socialize* social science.

Mauss reviewed the wide range of ritualized gift exchanges found in tribal societies and chiefdoms throughout the South Pacific and among the Native American chiefdoms on the northwest coast of North America. He concluded that hidden in the logic of these ritual exchanges was a rarely acknowledged message: a gift generates an obligation to reciprocate, and reciprocity is the basis of moral society. Every gift was actually two gifts: the original gift and the expected reciprocal return gift. The result of the exchange was the creation or reinforcement of interdependence—a moral relationship of mutual benefit.

Despite the common claim that a gift is freely given ("Oh, it's nothing!"), the giving of a present establishes an implicit obligation on the receiver to give back. Gift exchange tangles the giver and receiver in a series of mutual obligations, obligations that usually propel a relationship forward. When reciprocity fails, the negative aspect of this obligation is shame, guilt, or disrepute. In a successful transaction, the positive side of exchange is pride, a reputation for generosity, honor for oneself and one's group, and the extension of cooperative social relations.

Mauss's insights may seem obvious to social scientists today. His work became the basis of modern exchange theory in anthropology, eventually focusing on marriage exchange as a primary foundation of social order.

Exchange theory inspired a substantial body of work in contemporary social science. However, in Mauss's day, these insights were surprising and profound. Mauss discovered the empirical basis in everyday gift exchange of what political philosophers had called "the social contract."

The social contract was proposed by seventeenth- and eighteenth-century philosophers like Hobbes, Rousseau, Locke, and Kant as the original agreement that had allowed people (originally living in "the state of nature") to voluntarily give up their freedom in exchange for the security and protection of living in a community governed by social obligation. The social contract was the philosophers' attempt to discover the basis of the legitimacy of the modern state in relation to the hypothesized freedom people were believed to have enjoyed in an earlier "state of nature." For anthropologists, this contract went further, accounting for the evolution of social life itself. Gift exchange might prove the key to how individuals are continually being transformed into social beings.

Because the United States had been deliberately created by a group of "founding fathers" gathered at a constitutional convention in Philadelphia, it was easy to imagine the social contract as some document drawn up by a committee and signed by all parties to the agreement. The problem was that this kind of explicit political contract is rare in human history, which is why we display the original copy of the Constitution under glass as a sacred artifact in the National Archives Museum in Washington. If societies were not usually founded by a constitutional convention and a constituting document, was the social contract idea to be dismissed as a philosopher's daydream?

In Mauss's day, people living in tribal societies were thought of as what the Germans called *naturvolk* (nature people) living in "a state of nature," without laws, government, or any common moral code. They were assumed to possess no social contract. What seemed to be the simplest of these societies, bands of hunter-gatherers, were labeled "acephalous societies," headless societies that lacked any government. These mistaken beliefs were one of the pillars on which the nineteenth-century racist theories of cultural evolution were erected. However, if Mauss were correct, no governing body or a legal contract was needed to establish a society. Instead, social morality, the sense of mutual obligation born of gift exchange, provided the necessary mechanism for creating organized social life. Modern states may have legislatures to enact laws, and tribal societies have rituals of gift exchange.

Philosophers, it turned out, were right about the need for a social contract. However, the original social contract turned out to be a ritual process rather than a legal document.

Grand Exchange Rituals

Studying exchange rituals became a mainstay of classic early anthropology. In 1922, three years before Mauss's essay appeared, Bronislaw Malinowski had published his *Argonauts of the Western Pacific*, a detailed account of the *kula* ring, a massive exchange network linking dozens of islands off the southeastern coast of New Guinea (Malinowski 1932). Influential leaders of isolated communities scattered throughout the islands risked their lives to sail on perilous sea voyages to collect valuable shell necklaces (called *soulava*) and shell bracelets (called *mwali*) from traditional trading partners in neighboring islands. While practical trade goods, considered lowly *gimwali*, were quietly exchanged on the sideline, all the emphasis was on the ritual transmission of *vaigu'a*, treasures of great renown, purely ornamental jewelry that had no practical value at all. Malinowski studied the numerous rituals and magical spells that surrounded *kula* exchange. *Soulava* and *mwali* passed around the trade circuit in opposite directions, requiring each participant to have at least two exchange partners on two different islands—one for *soulava* and the other for *mwali*. *Kula* exchanges produced a vast double circuit of exchange where the two kinds of valuables cycled in opposite directions, linking up an extensive network of island societies that were all potential enemies. Malinowski described a detailed example of the social contract at work, a ritual of gift exchange creating a nascent political society out of dozens of isolated communities.

Between 1888 and 1935, the physicist-turned-anthropologist Franz Boas published reports of a different grand exchange system among the Kwakiutl Indians living on and around Vancouver Island off the western coast of Canada.[1] The Kwakiutl are a chiefdom, a ranked society comprising a chiefly class, commoners, and enslaved people acquired in war. The basic kin units called *numayms* are headed by chiefs possessing inherited titles. Chiefs compete fiercely with each other for status and fame.

The Kwakiutl live in villages along the coast. Traditionally, in the summer months, what they call *bakoos* or secular time, they lived in large communal houses often elaborately decorated to give the appearance of animals whose mouth was the house's entrance. They planted huge totem poles outside the houses, featuring elaborately carved and brilliantly painted chains of animals whose forms represented the "crests" or avatars of the ancestral animal spirits associated with the *numaym*.

In the winter months, as the world grew dark, Kwakiutl life moved from a secular condition to a sacred state called *tsetseka*. Now Kwakiutl moved underground to winter lodges, half-buried in the earth. There they confronted the coming winter months by celebrating the taming of the terrifying winter monster, *Baxbakwalanuxsiwae*, "Cannibal-at-the-North-End-of-the-World." They organized a theatrical extravaganza, a winter festival, in which participants from various performing societies danced. As the world grew dark as winter approached, dancers donned masks, assuming the forms of spirit beings. Many of the elaborate dances evoked the imagery of animals eating humans. The most frightening of the dancers was the *hamatsa* dancer, a terrifying cannibal. The *hamatsa* could dance himself into a frenzied trance state, intimidating spectators by threatening to take bites out of the audience. The religious purpose of the winter ceremonial was to "tame" the *hamatsa* and, through him, to tame the destructive forces of the winter season by transforming death into art. The Kwakiutl tamed death by ritualizing it.

The secular summer season also had its rituals. The most important ceremonies were the potlatches, spectacular exchange rituals where important chiefs displayed and enhanced their prestige by ostentatiously giving away vast amounts of wealth to other clans, most often to families related by marriage.[2] Today, potlatch wealth includes piles of woolen blankets, masks, beautifully carved cedar boxes, heraldic copper plaques called *tlakwa*, clothing, preserved food such as dried salmon, and large canoes. Before contact with European trade goods, potlatch wealth included animal skins, furs, and slaves (Codere 1950; Rosman and Rubel 1971; Walens 1982; Goldman 1975; Beck 1993; Drucker and Heizer 1967).

Potlatches were better viewed not as single events but as a chain of reciprocal transactions between *numayms* linked through marriage. A potlatch was a chance for a Kwakiutl chief to display his wealth and his clan's honor as well as a form of reciprocity for previous potlatches in which he had been the recipient. If the families had been linked through marriage, the potlatch might also symbolize a return on earlier marriage payments. As Marcel Mauss had warned us, these lavish gifts were not freely tendered.

In her definitive historical study of the Kwakiutl potlatch, *Fighting with Property*, Helen Codere underscores Mauss's point and goes him one better: "The property received by a man in a potlatch was no free and wanton gift. He was not at liberty to refuse it, even though accepting it obligated him to make a return at another potlatch not only of the original amount but of twice as much, if this return was made, as was usual, in a period of about a year. This gave potlatch-ing its forced loan and investment aspects, since a man was alternately debtor and creditor for amounts that were increasing at a geometrical rate" (Codere 1950, pp. 68–69).

As the potlatch demonstrates, where status, honor, and fame are put to the test, gift exchange can become competitive, a kind of war of contending wealth and generosity. In a consumption-based economy like ours, status competition can emphasize conspicuous consumption as displayed in houses, cars, boats, and yachts. The inherent dynamic is focused on possession, increasing personal wealth. But in many traditional societies, honor and prestige are negotiated not by the possession of property but by its exchange. Prestige requires that we give away our wealth, not hoard it. In these competitive gift exchanges, personal honor and social relations are at stake, much like our own system of exchanging dinner invitations. Fighting with property in this way reveals a tension between self-interest and the more extensive mutual interests of the community. The recipients of the gift are obligated to reciprocate to maintain their honor. In the long run, the competition proposes a win-win battle rather than the enemy's annihilation.

Samoan Gift Exchange

For almost five years, I lived in the island nation of Western Samoa, in the South Pacific, at first as a Peace Corps volunteer in the late 1960s and later as an anthropologist doing research (see figure 5.1). Though Samoa has been transformed by its relations with the West like other Polynesian societies, Western Samoa (now called simply Samoa) has retained many traditional customs and political institutions. Like the Kwakiutl, the Polynesian nation of Samoa is a chiefdom, a stratified society where rank and family honor are matters worth fighting for. When I arrived in the islands, most of the country's quarter-million Samoans lived in villages mostly strung along the coast. Today, many have moved to the country's capital of Apia for work or

Figure 5.1
Author in Samoa 1975

school or overseas to New Zealand, Australia, and the United States as part of the Samoan diaspora.[3]

Samoan families remaining in the islands have come to depend upon regular remittances from their relatives abroad. The political foundation of the society is still the traditional *matai* system of ranked chiefly titles. The governing body of a village is the *fono*, a council of chiefs that meets regularly to enact and enforce village law and to deal with village conflicts and other business of common interest. Figure 5.2 shows a meeting of one village's chiefly *fono*. Samoan families maintain detailed genealogies that trace family connections to their *matai* titles and associated lands. A vacated title is filled by election by the extended family. While both men and women may hold titles, most *matai* are men. The highest titles tend to be inherited by close lineal descendants of previous holders. Significant disputes between contending family branches are either settled by protracted family discussions or by the country's Land and Titles Court.

Samoa was one of the societies Mauss described in his book to illustrate the profound implications of gift giving. Although ritual exchange of valuables, mainly fine mats, accompanied most important occasions like births,

Figure 5.2
Samoan village chiefs' council

funerals, and installation of new chiefs, Mauss focused on the system of gift exchanges during Samoan weddings. In his account, the bride's family traditionally presented "female property," mostly woven mats called *toga*, to the groom's family. The most important mats were the *'ie toga*, "fine mats," finely woven pandanus mats fringed with decorative feathers and valued for their age and the long history of ritual circulation. Important occasions like weddings, funerals, and chiefly entitlement ceremonies always feature elaborate distributions of these mats.

In exchange, the groom's family traditionally presented "male property" such as axes, food, and canoes, classified as *'oloa*. In modern Samoa, the groom's *'oloa* has been translated into gifts of money and Western goods. These traditional wedding exchanges establish a relationship between the bride's and groom's *'aiga* (families). In-laws are called *paolo*, or "shade," suggesting an alliance that can provide a refuge in times of need. Marriages initiate periodic gifts of food and labor between the families, which continue through and beyond the marriage.

Marriage exchange is merely the tip of the iceberg for Samoan exchange ritual. Samoan life is shaped by numerous exchanges, minor and major.

Figure 5.3
An orator (*tulafale*) making a speech on the village central plaza (*malae*)

Samoa has a highly developed tradition of oratory and several levels of speech. Learning Samoan means learning to read situations and responding with appropriate levels of speech. Even casual encounters usually begin with a formal exchange of ritual greetings, where people are addressed with honorific phrases. Important events like births, deaths, marriages, church dedications, greetings, and farewells to guests are all marked by exchanges of food, money, tapa cloth, and mats.

A Funeral of an Important Chief

Funerals of important chiefs can be elaborate and costly affairs lasting several days. During my years in Samoa, I attended several funerals of senior Samoan chiefs. Two of them involved the deaths of men who were surrogate "fathers" to me. Tuato Tualevao Liko was one of the two highest-ranking chiefs in the large village of Sala'ilua (see figure 5.5). I lived with his family back in 1972–1973 when I was studying conflict and social control for my doctoral research. His death was sudden and violent. Tuato, a teacher in the village primary school, was killed by a rifle shot by one

Figure 5.4
Women displaying gifts of fine mats at a funeral

of his colleagues, the son of the other senior village chief, while walking
home from a card game during which Tuato had violently argued with the
younger man. Because Liko's death was a violent murder, the funeral rites
included an *ifoga*, a ritual apology by the family of the murderer to the
family of the victim during which the supplicants kneel outside the house
of the victim, their heads covered with fine mats. The murder triggered a
serious political crisis in the village which necessitated a rare *fono* tauati,
an outdoor assembly of chiefs on the central village green (*malae*) to assess
causes and mete out punishment (figure 5.6). The partly hidden causes of
Tuato's murder and its complex political context were the subjects of my
1982 book *Sala'ilua: A Samoan Mystery*.

Another funeral ceremony of a senior chief was mounted for my
adopted Samoan "father" Memea Papali'i To'afitu Petaia, a high-ranking
and respected chief. I had close association with his large family since first
arriving in Samoa in 1968, and continued to stay with them whenever I

Figure 5.5
Tuato Liko, ranking chief in Sala'ilua Village and head of my family in Sala'ilua, who
was murdered while I was doing research there

Figure 5.6
Rare general outdoor meeting of Sala'ilua families to deal with the murder of their senior chief

returned from the village to town. Memea held two important titles from different villages, one of which tied him closely to the late Samoan head of state, paramount chief Malietoa Tanumafili. The funeral ritual went on for almost a week. It was estimated to have cost my adopted family tens of thousands of dollars, money primarily donated by Memea's eight children and other close kin (including myself). The family hosting the funeral will have to buy vast quantities of food to feed all the visiting guests throughout the funeral.

The Petaia family brought onto the family compound a sizable trailer for safely storing the food provisions, and a small army of young men from the extended family was recruited to help organize the supplies and prepare the food. Hundreds of guests streamed in from all over the islands and overseas, each group bringing fine mats to formally present to the host family in honor of the deceased. These fine mats were ceremonially paraded around the property for all to admire.

Samoan gifts are never given "under the table" but are publicly displayed and acknowledged. Gift transactions are always accompanied by an exchange of speeches from both hosts and guests. Family members are appointed to keep a precise record in a notebook of what each visitor has brought, and each departing guest can expect to receive a return gift of food and money and, in some cases, one or more fine mats. An orator (*tulafale*) representing the host family is responsible for knowing the rank and relation of every visitor to the host family and deciding on an appropriate return gift. Failures of generosity in either direction will be noted. Private grumblings and gossip can follow public politeness in cases where the present or the return gift is deemed inadequate and insulting. The scale of the funeral signals the family's prestige, so every effort is made to mount an impressive event.

Families hosting these rituals will complain that the expenses have bankrupted them. Funerals are just one of the many ritual events families have to sponsor and contribute to, and these events place a significant burden of never-ending financial obligations on families. The more important the family, the greater the burden. No wonder Samoans call such events *fa'alavalave* ("entanglements"), suggesting the ambivalence with which they are viewed. Yet the families almost always find the necessary resources to mount them. When confronted by the need to sponsor a significant ritual, families may have to call upon the generosity of their more distant relatives, in-laws, and political allies.

Thus Samoans spend their lives cultivating their web of relationships so they can call in their debts when the time comes. Though many of these exchanges are said to be zero-sum games in which the wealth coming in matches the money expended on the ritual, there are always suspicions that a family may be profiting from the transactions, keeping more for themselves than they may acknowledge publicly. This is how a ritual can take on the character of a competitive game, as I was to learn in 1976.

Learning to Play the Game

I first arrived in Samoa as a Peace Corps volunteer teacher in 1968. Our group was called Samoa 2 since we were only the second contingent of Peace Corps volunteers to be sent to Samoa. Group 1, agricultural volunteers, had arrived only two months ahead of us, so we had arrived in a country that had virtually no experience with hosting young American volunteers. Even though we had had three months of training in Hawaii, the Peace Corps understood little about Samoa and had struggled to prepare us for life in these beautiful islands. And beautiful they were, just as we had been led to believe by the gorgeous photos in the Peace Corps recruitment brochure that had tempted us to join up. However, looks were not everything. There were also the demands of the culture. We all, Samoans included, would face profound culture shock as we struggled to get used to each other. There was a sizeable gulf between Samoan and American cultures.

Samoans are a handsome, proud, and confident people with consummate social skills. They are also enthusiastic ritualists. Though they were happy to welcome us with their legendary hospitality, many Samoans sensibly insisted that we deal with life there on their terms, not ours. Those terms, which they referred to as the *fa'a Samoa* (the Samoan way), were, in their view, the best of all possible ways to live. The *fa'a Samoa* included a lot of things unfamiliar to young Americans in the 1960s: unquestioning obedience to authority, a passion for fundamentalist Christian belief and practice,[4] a love of ritualized behavior, a puzzling mix of formal etiquette and a tendency to explode into mocking laughter, minute attention to rank and hierarchy, a focus on social relationships rather than self, and a preference for orienting behavior to the shifting demands of social context, at the expense of authenticity and consistency.

At first, I had the impression that Samoans lived life at its surfaces. For an American like myself, accustomed to personal and psychological explanations of behavior, the Samoan inner life was hard to fathom. Always stressing the demands of social etiquette rather than personal feelings, they seemed to live life outside-in. To my American sensibilities, adapting to this cultural overload would prove more challenging than I had anticipated. I was not alone. Forty percent of our group returned home within the first year, unable to adapt to the communal rhythms of Samoan life.

Those of us posted to remote villages were placed with Samoan families, sharing their open *fales*, houses lacking both walls and rooms. The hardest thing to get used to was the thoroughly communal setting and the total lack of privacy. For an introvert like myself, village life in Samoa was like finding myself at a raucous party that never ended. Samoans were cultural extroverts, relentlessly sociable and inescapably charming. We *pisikoa* (Peace Corps Volunteers) had become a source of entertainment for villagers, especially the throngs of kids who followed us everywhere. The bravest of them would run up to us, poking at our skin to see if we were real, screaming out *"Palagi! Palagi!"* ("White person! White person!") and breaking into peals of laughter.

My first months in Samoa were particularly difficult as I struggled to learn the language and adjust to the culture. As I grew more familiar with Samoa, my language skills improved to where I could carry on a conversation with Samoans with reasonable success. Little by little, I came to admire many of the things about Samoa that had initially irritated me. Though still very much an awkward outsider, I was beginning to understand the place from the inside. Rather than parroting the polite phrases we learned from our language manuals, I was becoming familiar enough with the language and culture to play a bit with their customs. Learning to joke in Samoan was a significant relief and seemed to amuse my Samoan family and friends. Humor was a major step forward. I was starting to get a feel for the place.

By 1976, I had spent over four years in Samoa as both a Peace Corps volunteer and a neophyte anthropologist. I had been back in the United States for two years following my dissertation fieldwork and had nearly completed my doctoral dissertation in anthropology at the University of Chicago.[5] I had my first academic job at the Center for South Pacific Studies at the University of California, Santa Cruz, where I taught anthropology courses and worked with Samoan migrant organizations in California.

Along with Margaret Mackenzie, a fellow former graduate student and a medical anthropologist who had done doctoral fieldwork in the Cook Islands, I applied for a summer research grant from the Center for Field Research in Belmont, Massachusetts, to study aging in Samoa, emphasizing the health and social status of the elderly. The Center for Field Research funded short research projects that could use a group of research assistants, who would be given a kind of "field-school" research experience in exchange for helping to fund the project and collecting data as research assistants.

We got the funding, and I assembled a team of four researchers and a travel coordinator. I had arranged for us to stay in the village of Lalomalava on the island of Savai'i as the guests of Tofilau Eti Alesana, an important chief of the village and a distinguished politician who had served as the country's minister of health, minister of finance, and deputy prime minister. Tofilau was later to become Samoa's fifth prime minister. His daughter had been a student of mine at Samoa College during my Peace Corps years, and my status as his daughter's former teacher was useful in my arranging a stay in Tofilau's village.

While the research project required only two months in Samoa, the planning was complex. The Center for Field Work had recruited thirty amateur research assistants to help collect data, whom we divided into two groups, each of which would be with us for a month. We asked each team member to bring some gift items to present at a traditional farewell ceremony at the end of each phase of the project. We also set aside money to distribute to the village as compensation for their participation in the research. Samoan tradition does not encourage direct payments to a village in exchange for hospitality, which is always supposed to appear freely offered. Therefore, compensating the village would have to be in the form of farewell gifts. There would be two gift exchange ceremonies, one for each research group.

We needed to train the thirty assistants in both data collection skills and cross-cultural adjustment. We were all housed in our host's massive *fale tele*, the village's great Samoan meeting house. We slept Samoan style on mats, men on one side of the house and women on the other. A lot of the planning responsibility fell on my shoulders. The village women's committee, which traditionally welcomes important village visitors, was our official host. We also needed to hire translators whose English was good enough to help the researchers do interviews and conduct a village census. The women's committee helped us locate a group of young villagers, students whose English was sufficient for our needs. I was the only member of our team who spoke Samoan.

Despite the complexity of our arrangements, everything went relatively smoothly for the first half of the project. We managed to collect a lot of information on Samoan understandings of aging and the stages of human development and data on the health status and the treatment of the aged. Phase one of the research ended with the planned ritual exchange of gifts. The women's committee presented woven baskets, fans, mats, and jewelry made from seashells and local nuts. I presided over the return presentation of the gifts that the research assistants had brought with them. In addition, we gave the women's committee a sizable amount of money. Cash is always welcome in Samoa as long as it is presented as a gift rather than as payment for hospitality.

Unfortunately, the smooth relations we had developed with the village during phase one would not continue into the project's second phase. Phase two began badly when several newly arrived assistants became ill, probably from drinking the local water unboiled. Fortunately, the illnesses were not serious, and the patients recovered after a few days. However, midway into our research, something more serious happened. One of the translators was caught stealing money from the house we were staying in. We fired the boy discreetly and requested a replacement. What I did not realize at the time was that the lad's aunt was the head of the women's committee, our hosts in the village. While she had surely been dismayed by her nephew's behavior, she was even angrier at us for having fired him and publicly humiliating her family.

Samoans like to say *teu le va*, "look after the relationship." Scrupulously polite and sensitive to matters of honor, they avoid public displays of anger, especially where important visitors are involved. Displeasure is generally expressed indirectly. Unable to read the situation, we remained unaware of the bad feelings the incident had produced. We might well have insisted that we were in the right to have fired the boy, but the village seemed more concerned with its reputation than with the fine points of right and wrong. The village women kept up the appearance of good relations, and until we were preparing to depart the village, we had no idea of the resentment simmering behind the women's smiles.

Two days before our scheduled departure, we were preparing for the ceremonial exchange of gifts at the farewell celebration due to take place the next day. As the only member of our group with any Samoan-speaking skills, I would do my best to serve as the orator for our side. While I was passably competent in conversational Samoan, oratory was something else. Samoans have a highly developed tradition of oratory that uses a lot of arcane, poetic expressions, special "chiefly" forms of Samoan that generally take years for Samoans to perfect.

A great orator was highly valued, and poor oratory signaled a lack of culture and breeding. In addition, every village had a group of orator chiefs who did the public speaking during ceremonies. The *ali'i* (high chiefs) would sit in silence behind an orator who would speak for them. While adult Samoans could usually handle everyday speechmaking, my competence in Samoan was well below what would be expected from any Samoan. I had to count on the villagers' appreciation of my efforts at Samoan speechmaking since hearing a foreigner speak in formal Samoan was a real novelty. At least, I consoled myself, my speech would be entertaining.

As we were preparing ourselves for the farewell, one of my village friends approached me and asked me to follow him. He took me to the women's committee house, where the women had assembled their gifts for us.

"Look," he said, "They're planning to insult you to express their displeasure at your firing the boy. They have almost nothing to give you." He was right. Compared with the impressive pile of handicrafts we had received at the end of phase one, the meager offering prepared by the committee for the following day was laughable. And the joke was to be on us. As my friend explained to me, the women's committee had decided to get their revenge for our firing of the translator by publicly withholding their generosity. Everyone would be smiling, and their speeches would be full of praise, but the paltry gifts would tell the story. Ritual can be a powerful language for expressing discontent. Having insulted them, we were not worthy of their generosity.

As the group's leader, I was faced with a real dilemma. Now that we had been warned of our impending public humiliation, how should we respond? My first impulse was to react as we might in an analogous situation in my own culture: take the high road, accept the gifts with polite thanks, and hope any onlookers would judge for themselves who had acted more honorably. However, this was not the United States. What would be the point of treating the women's committee as if they were Americans? I had done my doctoral research studying how Samoans viewed conflict and conflict resolution rather than understanding conflict from a Western perspective. Now I was being challenged to apply my understanding to a conflict in which I was personally involved.

How, I asked myself, would Samoans deal with this situation? In Samoan terms, my primary job was to protect the honor of my group. We would have to fight back. But we would fight Samoan style, with as much ritual finesse as we could muster. My longtime interest in ritual was about to be put to the test. We could have chosen to fight fire with fire, withholding our generosity and presenting the women's committee with just a few of the many gifts we had prepared. However, that approach did not seem right. That's not, I mused, what Samoans would do. It lacked drama and cultural finesse. And it made us look petty. In addition, it lacked the ambiguity I wanted to display. So instead, we would take the opposite approach and assault the women's committee with excessive generosity. We would "kill" them with our *alofa* (love).

I gathered our group together and explained the situation to them. Not surprisingly, they had not picked up on what was going on. They found it hard to understand what we were about to do. Rather than present our gifts in a single pile of offerings, we would exaggerate our presentation, giving each gift individually, accompanied by a speech. The contrast between their meager gifts and our generous countergifts would be vividly on display. Our final offering would involve a large bolt of beautiful material brought from home by one of our assistants. Her husband sold textiles and had donated about seventy-five yards of elegantly printed cloth that the village women would surely love, probably using it to make a set of new committee uniforms. We spent several hours carefully preparing the cloth for the presentation.

I worked on my speech and practiced it to at least approximate Samoan oratory. I had no hope of pulling off a credible speech, but I hoped the assembled Samoan audience would get the point. My words were edged with irony, carefully tailored to the combative nature of the occasion. Unsure if my manipulation of the exchange ritual would have the desired effect, I would give it my best shot. In Samoan rituals involving hosts and guests, it is important for guests to acknowledge the important families and titles of the host village. The village's history is embedded in a traditional recitation called a *fa'alupega*, a kind of honor roll of village titles and families that visiting orators use to acknowledge and honor their hosts. Fortunately, these greetings had been collected and published in a book that I had brought with me, so I would memorize the local *fa'alupega* and start my speech with the appropriate traditional salute to the chiefs and families of Lalomalava. Hearing a *palagi* visitor recite their traditional greeting would be an unexpected treat for the villagers, but I was also hoping it would alert them to take my speech seriously. They would know that we meant business.

These gift exchange rituals are organized on a gift-counter-gift reciprocal model. The hosts initiate the exchange by formally greeting the visitors, and then the parting gifts from the village are offered. Once the hosts have finished, the ceremony reverses direction (when it involves reciprocal singing, Samoans call this reciprocity "returning the fire"). At this point, the guests offer their formal thanks for the hosts' generosity and then formally present return gifts, which are always treated as freely given rather than expected payments. I was seated on mats just outside the guesthouse where our gifts were stored. Members of our group had lined up inside the house to carry our gifts one by one over to the women's committee, which sat in a group facing us across the lawn. The head of the women's committee made her farewell speech and then presented the meager pile of handicrafts and other gifts they had prepared for us. Following Samoan gift etiquette, I acknowledged each gift brought to us by raising it above my head and thanking the women for their *alofa* (love/generosity).

Then it was our turn. I was nervous since I had never before made this sort of speech in a traditional context and was unsure how it would be received or even whether my Samoan would be understood. Tofilau, the senior chief of the village and our host, sat outside his family's house just across from our guest house. He watched the proceedings with intense interest. Having noticed our elaborate preparations, he suspected that something unusual was about to happen.

I began by acknowledging the village titles and families with the traditional *fa'alupega*. I tried to mimic the orator's stately cadences, though no one would have mistaken my awkward speech for that of a genuine orator. The Samoan audience was taken aback by this recitation, realizing that something unexpected was unfolding. "The river waters are flowing, and the tide is swelling from the generosity of your village," I began, using the poetic idiom of Samoan oratory. "This is the legendary *alofa* that Samoa is so famous for. We humbly acknowledge the love of the women's committee of the village and the care they have given us during our month as their guests. Moreover, we are amazed by the feelings that the women of Lalomalava have expressed to us today by their abundant and beautiful gifts." The sentiments I expressed were appropriate for a farewell speech. However, in the current context, they were bristling with irony.

"There is no way we can match the generosity of the women's committee shown here today. We have no way to equal the bounteous love expressed by these gifts. American love can never be compared with Samoan *alofa*, but we will do our best to make a return on your generosity." By now, it was hard to tell what the women sitting across from us were thinking. Probably they were confused, unsure of what was happening. Had we not understood their implicit insult? They surely realized that something was up, something that no one had expected from a group of foreigners camped in their village.

"Behold American generosity!" I intoned, raising my arm to invite the first offering. Then, one by one, members of our group carried the individual gifts over to the seated women and placed them at their feet. Each gift was announced separately to stretch out the ritual process as long as possible. For half an hour, the gifts kept coming as the mountain of goods rose up in front of the women. We were burying them.

Finally, all other gifts having been delivered, we came to our carefully prepared finale. "In Samoa," I began, "the most important parting gift at a funeral is a special fine mat (cloth) ('ie toga) called 'the cloth of the departing' ('ie o le mavaega). Well, we have prepared a special American 'cloth of the departing' to honor this village for its generosity. Behold the American cloth of the departing." Invoking the "cloth of the departing" in this setting could only be ironic since the 'ie o le mavaega is traditionally used for funerals. My improvisation on Samoan ritual was intended to carry a mixed message that would be hard for villagers to untangle but leave them feeling uncomfortable.

But would they understand my irony? At my signal, our group members filed out of the guest house dramatically carrying the fifty yards of cloth we had prepared. The cloth was carefully paraded in front of the women so that only one side of the material was visible. The bearers circled the seated women, surrounding them with the fabric. The women gaped in amazement at the spectacle we had created, not knowing what to think. It was a familiar ritual form, made strange. Circling the group with the cloth was a carefully orchestrated move since wrapping in cloth is a traditional Polynesian way of making something sacred. But our act was crucially ambiguous since encircling a group is also a way of signaling conquest. Once again, the ambiguity left the audience feeling edgy. They were, it appeared, being both honored and attacked.

With the cloth encircling the women's committee, I concluded my speech with a full dose of irony. "In Samoa, your cloth (mat) is precious on the front side, but you never show what's on the back. Our American cloth, however, is different. We are not afraid to show you the back of our cloth, because the back is even more precious than the front. Behold." In a single dramatic move, the cloth was reversed to show that we had pinned hundreds of dollar bills to the fabric so that it was essentially a fifty-yard train of money. Wide-eyed, the audience gasped as our group began throwing the material in front of the seated women, piling it up until the women were hidden behind the spectacular pile of bill-laden cloth. With that dramatic flourish, our exchange ritual was concluded. The women quickly collected all their gifts and carried them off to the women's committee house on the other side of the village.

Figure 5.7
Lagoon sunset

We were left with some big questions. What did the Samoan onlookers make of our hastily improvised ritual? It was undoubtedly a risky way to handle the situation, one that would be interpreted back home as a rude way to thank your hosts. But this was Samoa, and I am an anthropologist. So I figured, "When in Rome . . ." The question at hand was, Did my response have the effect we intended?

We soon found out. Not long after the exchange had concluded, Tofilau approached me. He was grinning ear to ear. "You just did something amazing!" he said. *"Malo, Peleti* ("Nice going, Bradd"). You beat the Samoans at their own game. Where did you learn to think like a Samoan? It was just the right thing to do in the face of the insult the committee had handed you. I can't believe how you carried your presentation off the way you did. Our village will never forget this day." Tofilau especially liked the way we had pinned our money to the cloth. "I think you've invented a new Samoan tradition," he said. "Maybe next time you visit us, you'll see Lalomalava people pinning money to the back of their fine mats. Whoever thought of doing that?"

We wanted to know whether the women had gotten our message. If we had any doubts, Tofilau put them to rest, saying, "They are so ashamed of what they did. Right now, I suppose they are meeting to find a way to save face. I have a feeling that tomorrow when the bus comes to take you all to the ferry terminal, you may be surprised by what the women will have waiting for you." As promised, the following day, as we boarded the bus to leave the village, we were presented with piles of gifts from the women's committee, all of the gifts that had been withheld at the ceremony the previous day and perhaps more.

Just in time, we left the village with a sense that the mutual harmony that was supposed to emerge from the gift exchange had slipped in at the last possible moment, coaxed into place by our risky deep play with Samoan ritual. Everyone, Samoans and Americans alike, waved goodbye with big smiles on their faces. Just in the nick of time, it seems, our twisted exchange had done the job, setting a troubled world back in order.

6 Ten Powers of Ritual

There are many ways to classify rituals. Rituals have been sorted into such genres as rites of passage, rituals of reaggregation, calendrical rites, and, as described in the previous chapter, rites of exchange. In chapter 4, I took this approach to classification to make sense of animal rituals, specifying numerous genres of animal ritual. Here I will take a different approach in exploring the functions of ritual. Rather than focus on ritual genres, I will discuss ten powers of ritual. Studying ritual's powers rather than its genres has an advantage. Ready-made designations of ritual genres can be helpful, but some rituals will inevitably fit more than one type. In contrast to genres, recognizing a ritual's powers allows clarification of how a single ritual may function in several ways. The ability to specify a ritual's multiple functions underscores the usefulness of ritual.

Chapter 6 examines the following ten powers of ritual:

1. Keeping time
2. Reducing anxiety
3. Coordination
4. Automating action
5. "Taming" violence
6. Creating and maintaining relationships
7. Mediating transitions
8. Commemoration
9. Embodying meaning
10. Reversing agency

1. Keeping Time

Beyond music and poetry, the universe resonates with distinctive rhythms and tempos. No matter at what scale, all matter is defined by its pulse. Even atoms, the traditional basic units of matter, have a rhythm. String theory in physics proposes that atoms are made up of shorter strings, each 10^{-43} cm long, oscillating at 10^{16} Hz. That's a cosmic flutter rate of 10,000,000,000,000,000 cycles per second, a mere 0.000,000,000,000,001 seconds for each cycle. Far grander scales shape our common perceptions of time. Season in our solar system is tied to earth's daily rotation and its annual pilgrimage around the sun. The idea that the universe is ordered assumes that matter and motion are orchestrated to basic beats. The musical metaphor is no accident. Early philosophers like Pythagoras, Plato, and Aristotle believed in a rational cosmology, a universe governed by mathematical proportions. Early cosmologies proposed that heavenly bodies moved according to the same mathematical ratios governing musical intervals, giving off "a music of the heavens." Cosmologists would eventually develop this idea into the notion of "the harmony of the spheres." It is no coincidence that, in addition to his interest in mathematics, Pythagoras was a notable expert on religious rituals.

Biological pulses govern life. Changes in activity levels, age, and health mean that these rhythms will vary over time. For humans, normal respiration ranges between twelve and twenty breaths per minute, about once every six seconds. A healthy heart beats between sixty and one hundred times a minute, typically just out of awareness. For healthy people, the regularity of our "ticker" becomes our most basic assurance that we are alive and well. Predictable and regular rhythms signal wellness, while arrhythmias, skipped beats, and a rapid heart rate (tachycardia) often serve as warnings of mental or physical distress. Though we usually associate our pulse with heart rate, every organ has its beat. Our bodies hum along at the intersection of our many pulses.

For example, our retina's rods and cones resonate to light at the rate of between 10^{14} and 10^{15} HZ. The human brain oscillates at 0.1 seconds, while the healthy heart beats close to once each second, giving us an ever-present biological intuition of the clock's second. While Western medicine focuses on measuring the rhythms of the heart, Chinese and Tibetan doctors take advantage of these various organ pulses in their diagnoses of disorders.

Biologists have documented how the coordination of these biorhythms maintains *homeostasis*, a process of harmonizing these cycles. For humans, maintaining the homeostasis of our many rhythms is critical to the optimal functioning of bodies and minds. Arrhythmia implies disorder.

In recent decades we have witnessed the emergence of *chronobiology*, focusing on the significance of circadian rhythms in all living things (Foster and Kreitzman 2004). Circadian rhythms are the alternating night-day rhythms that govern cycles of sleep and wakefulness that underlie our basic activity schedules. Recent discoveries have shown that the regulation of the basic twenty-four-hour cycle (biologically speaking, just over twenty-four hours) of sleep and wakefulness is built into the mammalian brain. Our circadian clock, the suprachiasmatic nuclei (SCN), is located in a small area of the ventral hypothalamus, on the underside of the brain, just below the thalamus and above the pituitary gland.

While the SCN governs circadian rhythm, the daily sleep-wake cycle is reset every day by the effect of light and darkness perceived by photo-sensitive receptors, our eyes. The SCN sets the daily circadian cycle of 10^5 seconds, producing a monthly lunar cycle that is 10^6 seconds. The interaction of the internal (brain-based) and external (light-based) controls on our activity patterns allows for the resetting of the circadian clock due to changes in season, location, and, in the case of humans, individual sleeping schedules. The internal clock limits the range of variation possible in circadian rhythms so that repeated violations of our biological rhythms (such as dysfunctional work schedules, sleep disorders, or jet lag) can lead to severe physical and mental disorders, including, in the most extreme cases, death.

Temporal pacing also shapes the everyday experience of time and action. The invention of mechanical timekeeping utterly transformed human life. Control of clock time became a powerful source of political control. Long before there were clocks, the experience of time was shaped by patterns of regular activities. Our reliance on the predictable rhythms of our activities is often unconscious, coming into awareness only when the beat is disrupted. The rhythms of life become apparent every time we check our watches to see if we are "on time," check the position of the sun in the sky, consult our calendars to see what is coming up on our schedules, or when we take note of the neighborhood Christmas lights that have started to appear.

All around us are reminders of our dependence on the beats punctuating the flow of time. While many of these rhythms are the product of forces beyond our control, like planetary rhythms, seasonal changes, and biological regulators, humans also have the power to invent and regulate their activity patterns. Because of the complexity and variability of human lives, our biological rhythms cannot provide a sufficient framework for scaffolding our activities. Humans also depend on flexible and programmable activities that mimic natural rhythms. Human evolution supplied a programmable rhythmic brain that made possible activity patterns that felt natural and automatic while remaining open to reprogramming.

Before the mechanization of timekeeping, life was paced by both natural cycles and by ritual time. When we speak of "dinner time," "teatime," "Christmas time," or "bedtime," we are consulting our ritual clock by which we pace the programmable cycles of our lives. The fact that rituals are inherently repeatable makes them excellent timekeepers. Activity patterns create rhythms of living. Our routines and rituals are the pulses built into our daily, weekly, monthly, or yearly activities. However, while our routines and rituals have a certain compulsive quality, they never permanently lock us into that pulse but can be reshaped by social, environmental, historical circumstances, or individual inclination. New routines can be added to our schedules. While there is no intrinsic limit to the frequency of a ritual, rituals repeated too often can become dysfunctional compulsions. In contrast, rituals rarely repeated face extinction, losing their grip on our minds and bodies, and dimming our sense of inevitable recurrence. Eventually, such weakened rituals are experienced as merely unique or occasional events.

Rituals coordinated with clocks and calendars can mark time for us at a wide range of time intervals, effectively marking hours, days, weeks, months, years, and lifetimes. The modular nature of ritual allows single acts to be stretched into larger units, and so rituals and routines operate at widely variable time scales. At the short end of the spectrum are single quick acts like playing with worry beads, a meaningful wink, or a nod of greeting. At the other end of the spectrum are extended rituals drawn out over many years.

Consider the *Sigui* festival practiced by the Dogon people of the West African nation of Mali. The *Sigui* is a male initiation ritual signaling the elders' passing of sacred secrets to the younger generation. Timed by the position of the star Sirius (the brightest star in the night sky), the *Sigui* is mounted approximately every sixty years. It requires initiates to learn a secret language and work together to carve a sizable sacred mask about six feet long, known as *Imina*. The presence of the *Imina* transforms a space into a sacred dance ground, allowing the novices to perform a sacred dance from village to village. The last Sigui began in 1967 and concluded in 1973, and the next one is scheduled to start in 2032.

In the early 2000s, I spent two years studying "family time," the ritual lives of four families in a small town in Georgia. I spent several hours a week talking with each family about the various ritual cycles that engaged them as a family. We started our discussions with the day and then moved on to the week, the month, the season, and the year. For each cycle, the families could relive their family ritual time together in their stories. I also participated in a few of their family celebrations. The families I studied shared American cultural themes—typical holidays, familiar American routines, and shared religious traditions. Each family had developed its own ritual life, a distinctive family culture. Thanksgiving celebrations were all very similar, but there were always distinctive dishes, practices, and family crises that made each family's Thanksgiving its own.

Through their rituals and the stories they produced, families come to own their time together. The stories were structured by phrases that create a sense of "ritual time," phrases that began like "we always" or "we usually" or "when the kids were small, they used to." What is remembered in the stories are the ritual patterns of family time and the exceptions to the patterns when things changed. Together, the patterns and the changes make up a family history (Shore and Kauko 2018). These discussions inevitably produced disagreements about what was and was not typical for the family. The stories of some family members, the better or most dominant storytellers, often became the default family memories. The collective recollection of ritual time is often punctuated by memorable events, such as crises or other unique changes in family life. In one family, a child's death in a car accident provoked a tragic landmark in the family's history. The family would now reference its time by a break, life before and after the tragedy. In addition to losses like deaths and divorces, family histories are often shaped by children leaving home for school or relocating to new houses and neighborhoods.

American middle-class families are often mobile, and relocating to a new house is commonly remembered as a chapter in the family's life story. Families often segment the "chapters" of their family history by the neighborhoods in which they lived. All the homes were full of mementos of past times in the family's life. Family photos and photo books are popular ways of creating a legacy of what people call "family memories." I took a tour of each house, which triggered powerful memories about family time for families.

We all experience our lives in two rather different ways: through linear time and cyclical time. Linear time is time passing and people aging. Cyclical time is things recurring. Ritual is an important way that we transform linear time into cyclical time. Our most intimate experience with cyclical time in nature is the constant change and return of the seasons. Seasonal cycles provide a natural scaffold for our year, ordering time as a set of recurring annual cycles. Human activity schedules like agriculture, school, holidays, and even clothing styles are often keyed to the time of year. Through our rituals, cyclical time runs parallel to linear historical time, which is cumulative, defining centuries, decades, and eras. Ritual is a powerful way that humans can convert time passing to time recovered, muting the disturbing sense of time as getting ever later, running down, or running out. Spring festival rituals welcome the return of spring. Winter festivals like Christmas, Chanukah, or the Kwakiutl Winter Ceremony, performed as the days grow shorter and darkness envelops the world, are a ritual challenge to death and an invitation for spring renewal. In this way, ritual can replace the experience of getting older with the intimation of what the historian of religion Mircea Eliade called a myth of "eternal return" (Eliade 1954). Our birthday keeps cycling back on schedule, every year.

Ritual cycles can involve more than just the rhythms of time. In his brilliant and influential study of ritual pig slaughter by the Maring Tsembaga tribe in Papua New Guinea, *Pigs for the Ancestors: Ritual in the Ecology of a New Guinea People* (Rappaport 1968), anthropologist Roy Rappaport studied the relationship between cycles of warfare, land degradation, pig production, and the ritual slaughter of pigs. He characterized the Tsembaga rituals as a regulatory force through which the Tsembaga people maintained an ecological balance between the carrying capacity of their land (for feeding pigs) and the need for protein in times of warfare. In Rappaport's view, Tsembaga ritual served to control energy exchanges between the people and their environment, while the Tsembaga explained their rituals as a way to discharge their debts to their gods. Rappaport believed that the ecological control involving the ritual was an uncognized function of their ritual, not recognized as such by those performing it. Rappaport proposed that the Tsembaga ritual had evolved in the society to regulate cycles of energy exchange between a people and its natural environment. Here, cyclical time involves the interaction of human and natural cycles of growth, consumption and activity.

In addition to shifting our sense of time from a moving line to a circle, our rituals can produce some complex interactions between linear and cyclical time. They have the power to engage both temporal modes simultaneously. Consider birthday rituals. Annual birthday celebrations mute the linear passage of time by emphasizing the yearly recurrence of the day we were born. At the same time, landmark birthday celebrations such as the Mexican quinceañera for girls when they turn fifteen, American and Canadian sweet-sixteen celebrations, or a hundredth birthday party for a grandparent all combine the recurrent birthday celebration with a linear emphasis on reaching a certain age. Our birthday comes around on schedule every year. But we only turn fifty once. In this way, birthday rituals have the power to blur the passage of time while also marking it.

The same can be said of celebrations of historical events like Guy Fawkes Day (or Bonfire Night) in Great Britain, Cinqo de Mayo in Mexico, or Independence Day in the United States. As historical commemorations these celebrations recall unique foundational events in the history of a nation. But as recurring annual celebrations, these national celebrations are detached from their historical roots and reified into perpetual, recurrent symbols of national identity. They manage to both acknowledge a nation's history and transcend it.

2. Reducing Anxiety

Have you ever found yourself tapping your fingers, twirling your hair, or saying a prayer when you are anxious? Some religions have even come up with prayer beads you can methodically pass through your fingers while you mutter a prayer to calm your nerves. You can, quite literally, count on ritual to calm yourself. It is hardly surprising that the predictability of ritual rhythm is a powerful antidote for anxiety. Those devoted to meditation have always known it, and religious practice implicitly acknowledges it. The underside of ritual comfort is that terrorists, seeking to inject fear into the heart of our everyday life, have learned how to turn our dependence on ritual against us when they attack coffee shops, synagogues, mosques, and other ritual sites, both secular and sacred, sowing seeds of unpredictability and disquiet by disrupting those places where we seek ritual comfort in our lives.

Long ago, anthropologists were struck by how rituals were performed by the people they studied during uncertain and dangerous times and appeared to reduce anxiety. Chapter 4 reviewed a debate about ritual between Bronislaw Malinowski and Arthur Radcliffe-Brown in the first half of the twentieth century. Both anthropologists had noted in their field studies how rituals and ritual magic appeared at times of uncertainty. They agreed that ritual relieved anxiety by providing an assuring sense of control, differing only about whether that relief was psychological or social in nature.

Edward Schieffelin describes how the Kaluli people from the New Guinea highlands use ritual as a response to collective fear and uncertainty:

> [C]eremonies retain a character independent of the events they usually celebrate. Kaluli sometimes perform them in the absence of critical social transactions, in times of fearful portents, such as when the first airplane flew over the plateau or at the approach of epidemic disease. In the latter case, the community may perform sickness-warding magic and invite another community to perform a ceremony that night. If sickness is already in the longhouse and there have been several deaths, magic is dispensed with, and, in a mood of panicky anxiety, people announce their imminent arrival to another community and go there to dance. (Schieffelin 1976, p. 27–28)

Schieffelin's account straddles the line between psychological and social anxiety and does not require the reader to choose between them. The "mood of panicky anxiety" experienced by the Kaluli is an example of *collective anxiety*, psychological anxiety that would likely be experienced individually but is amplified and transformed into a coordinated response.

This observation brings us to an influential theory of ritual that seeks to link all ritualization to stress and anxiety. Pascal Boyer, an anthropologist, and Pierre Liénhard, a psychologist, have proposed that ritualization is an innate human response to danger. They suggest that the dysfunctional compulsive acts of people suffering from obsessive-compulsive disorder (OCD) are an excellent place to start in understanding the root of ritual behavior. People suffering from OCD suffer from recurring intrusive thoughts and respond by compulsive repetition of acts like hand-washing, organizing clothes or other objects, counting (steps or actions), or checking for nonexistent dangers.

The compulsive acts, which are usually unrelated to the person's fears, never really relieve the anxiety that brings them on, leading the sufferer to repeat them. The repeated actions of the OCD sufferer are intensely ritualized. They are rituals run wild. Neurologically, OCD is tied to a neural circuit dysfunction, specifically the cortical-striato-pallidal-thalamic circuit. More specifically, OCD is an anomaly in the brain's basal ganglia.

Boyer and Liénhard make inferences from OCD behavior to explain customary ritual. They propose that the anxiety caused by a perception of danger triggers a "vigilance-precaution system" within the human nervous system (Boyer and Liénard 2006). This system produces a dramatic shift in an individual's attention from the normal "midlevel" activities we usually notice (e.g., "making dinner" or "driving the car") to more specific lower-level gestures ("chopping onions" or "turning the steering wheel"). Noting that people under unusual stress, like pregnant women and new parents, tend to become obsessed with details of the fetus's or infant's behavior, they propose that this downward shift in attention is adaptive for people facing a precarious situation (like new parenting), forcing them to attend to things at a much finer level of focus.

This connection between ritual and anxiety for some rituals is convincing. Experimental research on the relationship between stress and the ritualization of behavior supports the vigilance-precaution hypothesis. One study focused on the effects of religious rituals on stress (Anastasi and Newberg 2008). Thirty students in a Catholic college were divided into two groups. Twelve students recited the rosary, while the remaining eighteen viewed a religiously themed video. Both groups were tested for signs of anxiety before and after the intervention, using a State-Trait Anxiety Inventory. The testing revealed that the students reciting the rosary experienced a significant drop in their anxiety levels, while those watching the film did not.

More recent experimental research on the effects of religious rituals in reducing anxiety was carried out in a Marathi community on the island of Mauritius (Lang, Krátký, and Xygalatas 2020). Marathi Hindu women were divided into a ritual group of thirty-two and a control group of forty-three. Both groups were fitted with monitoring devices measuring both heart rate and variability in heart rate as well as signs of ritualization in body movements. The control group was tested in a rented laboratory space consisting of two rooms with tables and chairs. In contrast, the ritual group met in the prayer room of a Marathi Hindu temple, about the same size as the laboratory space. Both groups were asked to sit quietly for five minutes, after which the women were each presented with the same stressful task. They would be given three minutes to develop a public speech on preparing for natural disasters (common in Mauritius). The speech would be recorded and evaluated by government officials. The task was intended to be inherently stressful.

Participants completed surveys at the beginning and end of the experiment. The first survey was a seven-item generalized anxiety disorder questionnaire that assesses proneness to anxiety. The exit survey asked the women how much stress they were experiencing during and after the experiment. The control group was asked to sit in silence for several minutes and were then informed they would not have to deliver a speech after all. The ritual group was also given three minutes to prepare a speech, at which point they were led to an adjacent prayer room and asked to perform their customary Hindu rituals alone. They had access to all necessary ritual paraphernalia like fruit, flowers, incense sticks, and oil lamps. Participants were instructed to perform the ceremony in their usual way. After completing their ritual, the women returned to the main temple hall, where they were told that they would not have to record their speech. While both groups experienced the same stressor, one group performed religious rituals, while the control group did not. The physiological stress data showed a significant difference in the responses of the two groups to the stress. The control group recorded stress levels twice those of the ritual group. In this experiment, performing religious rituals seemed to have a significant effect on reducing anxiety.

In sum, the hazard-precaution theory does seem to account for the frequently observed links between ritual and anxiety. Nevertheless, it leaves some questions unanswered. For example, what turns the ordinarily functional vigilance-precaution system into a dysfunctional case of OCD? Is OCD to be understood as a dysfunctional form of ordinary ritualization or something else? More important, how do we explain rituals not produced by stressors, like family dinner, tailgating parties, casual small talk, and traditional cheers at a football match?

The vigilance-precaution theory understands ritual as heightening attention by shifting focal awareness downward to small gestures. Here ritual increases self-consciousness. While this explanation makes sense of compulsive rituals aimed at preventing danger, it ignores the many rituals that produce semiautomatic behavior, where we are just going through the motions. Learning a strange ritual will increase cognitive load and may shift attention away from sources of stress. The vigilance-precaution theory sees this redirection of stress as the source of ritual effectiveness. But frequently repeated ritual acts that have become automated seem to have a different effect from a ritual that has just been learned. Rather than producing hyper-vigilance, the ritualization of everyday activities promotes a calming effect by reducing cognitive load. The body feels like it is on autopilot. It seems that Boyer and Liénard offer a compelling theory of obsessive ritual, but not an explanation of ritual in general.

3. Coordination

In his book about the rituals of the Kaluli people in Papua New Guinea, Edward Schieffelin vividly describes a ritual dance/chant called the *ulab* through which Kaluli project a sense of community and solidarity of purpose:

> As people are standing around waiting to do something, a few men, sensing the moment, suddenly jump up, shouting "Bruh! Bruh!" in deep-throated tones and begin stamping and bouncing up and down together in place. Others immediately run to join the circle, everyone bouncing vigorously, waving axes over their heads, twanging their bowstrings. Shouts of "Bruh! Bruh!" give way to a low note, "ccccc" which increases in intensity until the stamping, pressing men in the circle suddenly bring their waving axes and bows down together and end their motion abruptly with a single unified shout: *"UUUU!"* Then all rush off to do what they were about to do. The noise and motion of *ulab* projects an atmosphere of vitality and exuberant spirit. The stamping and shouting not only synchronize their noise and motion but are a real exertion. The men pound the earth dancing themselves into tune with each other, working each other up into a mutually vigorous and wonderful state. *Ulab* is performed to initiate a garden planting or to announce a successful murder of someone in the forest by a raiding party. It announces the approach of visitors in the forest bringing gifts and concludes an arrival display in front of an *aa*. Through *ulab* a group unifies itself, projects its energy, and declares itself as a force to be reckoned with. It is a means by which male energy can be visibly mobilized in cooperative social action. (Schieffelin 1976, p. 134)

Scheiffelin's account powerfully evokes the way that ritual can coordinate focus and action of a group and create a visceral experience of collective identification. We have all experienced ritual cheers or group dancing that do essentially the same thing.

Rituals promoting social coordination are all around us. Simple rituals introduce infants to the world of social relations. Parents will often get to know their infants through interaction rituals like peek-a-boo or shaking a rattle in the space between their eyes and their baby's and then smiling or softly speaking to the child. For parent–infant relations, the rattle provides a mediating object of "joint attention" for the baby and its parents, a stand-in for the more basic direct parent–child connection. Sports teams will often do a collective cheer in a huddle before taking the field, while fans will chant cheers and sing loyalty songs, bonding with both their team and each other. Many elementary schools will start the week with an assembly where everyone stands and sings a patriotic or a school song. When I was a child, we always began our school day with a collective pledge of allegiance to the flag. These activities are examples of how we use rituals to promote social coordination.

Why do we need a ritual to bring people together? Confucius saw the wisdom in performing rituals to foster social harmony as one of the four basic tenets of his philosophy. All social animals live and work in groups and coordinate their activities. Communication systems can be effective means of coordinating action. We have already explored how animals communicate with one another through smells (e.g., ants' pheromones), vocal signals (e.g., bird song), and bodily movements (e.g., honeybee "dances"). Humans are also opportunistic communicators using the full range of communication media: gesture, vocalization, and even smells to coordinate with friends and foes. And, of course, there is also language, a tool that has given humans astonishing powers of communication.

However, the evolution of the human brain and the remarkable communicative skills it bestowed on our species have also created coordination problems for humans. Evolution made possible human social organizations of immense scale, variation, and complexity. To navigate complex social worlds humans required large and complex brains. Anthropologists have suggested that the evolution of the scale and complexity of human societies was a significant factor in the evolution of the human nervous system.

The brain evolution that allowed us to navigate a complex landscape also produced significant cognitive variation in individual responses. Members of groups are also individuals, with minds of their own. For humans, individual temperaments evolved into differences in "personality," further complicating the job of social coordination. Moreover, once we had language, we could never be sure what someone else was thinking and feeling, giving rise to the ever-present possibility of dishonest relationships. Thus, brain evolution endowed humans with a double life—and an inner subjective life that made possible autonomous experience and a social life that made humans interdependent.

This double life implies the difference between *subjectivity*, the private life of personal thoughts and feelings, and what the philosopher Edmund Husserl called *intersubjectivity*, the interchange of conscious and unconscious thoughts and feelings between two or more people. The capacity for intersubjective understanding is commonly called *empathy*. A degree of empathy is considered essential in adapting to a complex social system. To get along with one another, we need to read each other's minds and develop what psychologists call "shared intentionality" (Tomasello 1990, 2009). According to the Swiss psychologist Jean Piaget, subjectivity comes first, and infants enter the world with an egocentric perspective on the world.[1] The development of the child's ability to coordinate its perspective with others and develop a sense of "us" occurs initially through the simple rituals parents develop with their infants. Parents and babies gaze at an everyday object like a rattle that links them. The rattle and the rituals themselves become objects of joint attention. Babies have an innate predisposition to gaze directly into the eyes of their caretakers. This gaze is the basis of what psychologists call "primary intersubjectivity," a mutual gaze, the first "us." When a mother and baby are face-to-face and the mother withdraws her attention from the baby, the baby will retreat into its subjective state and stop engaging with the mother. The link of primary intersubjectivity is broken.

The infant-parent rituals using play objects harness and extend the infant's capacity for empathy by cultivating a "secondary intersubjectivity," a three-way relationship where parent and infant cooperate in jointly gazing at an object (Delafield and Trevarthan 2013). These simple rituals support the ability of the child to take part in acts of joint attention. Through such rituals, infants learn to coordinate their attention with others. The transition from primary to secondary intersubjectivity has been of great interest to developmental psychologists for the last fifty years:

> From the point of view of earlier phenomena of infant social interaction, joint attention is the capstone of a long process that begins as newborn infants interact with adults face to face in "primary intersubjectivity," which ends as they

begin to participate in bouts of "secondary intersubjectivity" with adults. . . . Secondary intersubjectivity, or joint attention, allows infants to incorporate a third element into their dyadic interactions with other persons, thus making possible many kinds of triadic social interactions with people and objects. (Carpenter et al. 1998, p. 2)

The rituals with our caretakers that promote joint attention are our first rituals, introducing us to the universe of social rituals we will participate in for the rest of our lives.

These elementary infantile rites are just the start of our ritual lives. Ritual coordination will require us to participate in increasingly complex kinds of rituals. Consider, for example, the two basic types of ritual coordination. The most basic way ritual works to promote coordination of behavior is through *simple synchronization*, where people all perform the same actions (Whitehouse 2022). This kind of synchronization is evident in military-style drills, marching, and some dance routines, performances that use symmetrical coordination to transform individuals into a collective unit (McNeill 1995). Symmetrical ritual coordination is supported by mirror neurons in our brains that fire both when we perform an action and when we watch someone else perform. The human attraction to mimicry might be called the "Simon Says effect" since it underlies the challenge of that game to resist mirroring the motions of a leader. Rituals promoting simple synchronization such as marching or reciting things in unison are probably the most basic sources of ritual coordination and are often the foundation of rote education.

However, socialization also requires a more complex *asymmetrical coordination* that brings together people not through mirroring each other's actions but through complementary differences in their actions. Whereas symmetrical coordination is based on the idea that "you do this, I do this," asymmetrical rituals are based on "you do this, I do that," a ritualized division of labor. The most basic asymmetrical rituals are about status differences. While greeting rituals between equals generally use mirroring to suggest status equality (shaking hands, hugging, mutual bowing, etc.), greetings between those of different statuses are usually asymmetrical—a subject bows or curtsies to a monarch, who does not return the gesture. In complex social performances, the integration of roles requires considerable practice and the cooperation of all participants, suggesting a different sort of complexity from the symmetrical coordination of marching in step.

Whether a simple cheer by a group of football fans or a complex ritual like a marriage rite, ritual is one of the most important ways humans coordinate their relations.

4. Automating Action

There is a big difference in the effort required to learn a new ritual compared with performing a tried-and-true ritual. Wedding rehearsals can be very stressful because they are rare and symbolically important events. The process of getting used to a new behavior pattern generally results in a significant reduction in both stress and focus.

Consider the "ritual" of commuting to work described in chapter 2. Before GPS, commuting to a new job in an unfamiliar place involved considerable stress. You did not want to be late for work on your first day, so you might have left extra driving time if you got lost. Perhaps you had a set of directions that highlighted landmarks and streets to watch for. Alternatively, you could have used a street map that you needed to consult frequently while driving. The stress you probably would have experienced was tied to what psychologists call the task's "cognitive load." Watching for streets or landmarks or checking the map would have distracted attention from the act of driving. Nothing looked familiar. Since you could not rely on experience, you had to be attentive to everything at once. You probably had to consult the map or the directions every time you commuted for the first week or so.

Eventually, the job of driving to work became a familiar routine. While you had to remain alert for driving hazards or traffic detours, the complex sequences of driving to work had settled into the everyday commuting routine. You even found yourself thinking about other things as you drove, not fully aware of your route or even of your driving. Your routine had receded in your memory. Psychologists would say that your knowledge of the route and driving skills had shifted from your "working memory" to procedural memory, our background memory of "knowing how" to perform familiar tasks. The routinization of the drive had offloaded the cognitive demands of your commute, which now felt more automatic. Not focusing on these tasks meant that your attention could be shifted to other things. One advantage of the reduction of cognitive load is efficiency; an automated action set requires less energy and less conscious attention.

There is a less obvious advantage to reducing cognitive load, enabling hierarchical learning. Many complex skills are learned in stages, where a basic framework is learned first and then is refined by adding new layers of complexity. Separating the learning into "stages" that are each routinized before moving on to the next one has made highly complex skills possible. Consider the acquisition of piano playing. First, there is familiarization with the keys and learning the fundamental interactions between the fingers and the keys. Learning to manipulate the pedals will usually come later and be added to the skill set. Simple exercises can start once the piano student gets used to stretching her fingers across the keys and striking them one finger at a time. The skills learned in this way include sequencing the key strikes, combinations of strikes making chords, and changes in key pressure that produces variations in loudness. Two-hand playing requires separate actions from each hand. At some point, the feet can be added as the students learn to integrate the pedals with the movement of the keys. Each skill level is repeated many times in what is known as piano practice. The goal is the routinization of each kind of movement.

Once the student masters one level of action, it can be combined with new levels, like scales and simple songs. Again, these need to be routinized into automatic patterns. Even experienced professionals will regularly repeat playing scales to ready themselves for a performance. As each level of playing is mastered and automated, it is integrated with the earlier levels. Eventually, the pianist no longer has to focus on the basics of playing. She has developed technique and can play a complex piano composition without noticing her fingers or feet. The practice has also allowed her to "sight read" new pieces with considerable skill because basic playing patterns have been automated. Once the physical skills have been mastered and coordinated, the pianist can focus on subtle aspects of the music—dynamics, tone, and interpretation.

The progress of skill acquisition is made possible by the progressive routinization of more fundamental levels of action, freeing up the musician's focus and shifting attention to higher levels of performance skill. Without the progressive offloading of cognitive resources like attention and memory, we would never be able to refine skilled performances. The high levels of performance of professional musicians, dancers, and athletes are only possible because of this human capacity for shifting cognitive resources through hierarchical routinization.

5. "Taming" Violence

As noted in chapter 5, the Kwakiutl people from Vancouver Island are renowned for their spectacular carved masks, totem poles, and theatrical performances. Their religion promotes cycles of regeneration of animal and human life. Keyed to seasonal changes, the sacred side of Kwakiutl ritual life occurs in the winter months when the days grow short and the world is overcome by darkness and cold. Their rituals of regeneration occur during their annual ceremonial season in the sacred winter period known as *tsetsequa*, which means "secrets." In opposition to the secular summer months, where most productive hunting, fishing, and agricultural work is done, the *tsetsequa* period is devoted to spiritual matters when supernatural forces inhabit the village.

There are also summer rituals that focus on transmitting names and privileges within family groups (*numayms*). The winter months are periods of communication between *numayms* and between humans and supernatural beings. Initiation into secret societies is a central activity of the *tsetsequa* period. Spirit protectors give society members the right to perform specific dances in the theatrical spectacles that highlight the annual Kwakiutl winter ceremonial, the time when dance society members don elaborate costumes and masks to dance out stories featuring the animal and demon spirits that populate their legends.

Most famous among these masked dancers are the *hamatsas*, the most prestigious dance society. We have already encountered these terrifying figures in chapter 5. The *hamatsa* dancer represents the spirit of *Baxbakwalanuxsiwae*, "Cannibal-at-the-North-End-of-the-World," the Kwakiutl embodiment of the violence of hunger and oral destruction. Many of the *hamatsas* appeared in the spectacular masks of the raven, "the crooked beak of heaven," with huge beaks that flap open and close, gestures of consuming violence. The purpose of the ritual dance is to "tame" the dancer and the cannibal spirit it embodies with the dancer.

The ritualization of the cannibal's violence reframes the violence so that the destruction inherent in eating becomes the regeneration of life through feeding. In his 1982 book *Feasting with Cannibals: An Essay on Kwakiutl Cosmology*, Stanley Walens shows how the act of killing is reframed as new life.

> For the Kwakiutl, the animal world, like the human world, is predicated on two opposing principles: the principle of hunger—the need and desire for food, which

drives humans and animals alike to kill—and the principle of sociality, the principle by which humans and animals consciously suppress their hunger for the benefit of their associates. Just as humans share food at feasts, so do the animals share food with their conspecifics: parent birds regurgitate food for their nestlings, gregarious scavengers congregate at a kill site to share a carcass, raccoons kill crayfish for their young, wolves bring food to their dens for those members of the pack who did not hunt that day. (Walens 1982, p. 98)

Kwakiutl ritual turns images of oral destruction (biting, swallowing) back on themselves, transforming swallowing into vomiting, life-taking into life-giving. Some of their cannibal poles depict carvings of animals hanging from the mouths of other animals, a deliberately ambiguous visual pun. Swallowing becomes vomiting, the dominant Kwakwaka'wakw image of birth.

Just as death is metaphorized in oral terms, so is creation visualized as an oral process. The power of life resides not in semen but in vomit; fertilization is believed to occur only if the mother eats certain foods. To bring life to their unborn children, parents must perform rituals that transfer the life-giving power from the tongues of frogs into the mouths of children. Many rituals mimic acts of eating and vomiting and are considered to directly affect the behavior of the child both in the womb and during labor; especially feared is breech birth, which is counteracted by a large number of ritual oral gestures (Walens 1982, p. 15).

The Kwakiutl conception of ritual as a taming of the *hamatsa* is a vivid example of how ritual can control violence. Rather than denying violence, ritual often acknowledges it but reverses or tames violence, suggesting the power of ritual to reframe experience by performing and reversing the meaning of critical symbols. This taming of violence is not unique to the Kwakiutl. The Catholic Eucharist, the consumption of the bread and wine of Christ's "Last Supper," is first converted into an act of oral destruction, the literal consumption of the body and blood of Christ through the "transubstantiation" of food symbols into the real thing. Those symbols of death are then transmuted into tokens of eternal life through the incorporation of Christ into one's own body. Thus, the suffering and death of Christ are ritually reframed as the rebirth of a soul nourished by Christ's body and blood. Violence is acknowledged and then transformed.

Ritualized violence is violence at play. The human capacity for violence is as great as our capacity for generosity and love. Having found no way to eliminate violence, humans have had to settle for taming their violent proclivities by "playing" them into submission. Our ability to transform our actions into "performances" governed by rules or scripts is the key to the ritual taming of violence. Through theater, rituals, and games, we can simulate violence while limiting its destructive power. Boys in our culture engage in a lot of play fighting, involving simulated violence. Because kids are aware that the fighting is "just play," play fighting encourages violence in a tamed form. As children age, simulated fighting takes the form of games and organized sports. Sports can flirt with disaster when play fighting spills over into the real thing, a phenomenon I have called *marginal play*.[2] Outbreaks of real violence are well known in sports like football and hockey. Professional wrestling goes so far as to model this eruption of real fighting in wrestling matches, and fans are often unsure whether the violence in the ring is real or simulated.

A well-known example of marginal play is "soccer hooliganism," where British soccer fans turn the competitive play of their teams into actual violence against opposing teams' fans (Buford 1990; Giulinotti, Bonney, and Hepworth 1994). In the United States, football, boxing, and wrestling come the closest to all-out violence, but even here, the violence is constrained by the rules of the game and by referees. With the advent of computer games, we could simulate violent combat with avatars fighting for us. Even real warfare is regulated by "rules of engagement" like US military Standing Rules of Engagement governing situations when the United States is not legally at war and subject to Wartime Rules of Engagement regulating active warfare. The military also carries out "war games" as practice for actual combat, closely simulating actual fighting conditions.

Games are not rituals, but they are very closely related, and the two are sometimes hard to tell apart (see Chapter 10). Like rituals, games are a form of scripted behavior. However, in games, the relations involved are competitive rather than cooperative. The script (the rules of play) regulates the interactions but not the conclusion, which is left open like an actual event. The rule-governed "violence" of competitive games is elaborated throughout modern societies as competitive business dealings, electoral politics, and legal disputes. The fact that we do not generally refer to these activities as violence attests to the effectiveness of ritualization in simultaneously expressing and suppressing violence.

In a well-known essay, Clifford Geertz analyzes a Balinese cockfight as a game and a ritual. As a game, the fighting cocks draw Balinese men into what Geertz terms "deep play," where they are willing to bet heavily on the outcome of a match, especially when the bet is close to even odds and against someone of similar social status. At stake are status and honor. While killing a neighbor to gain social prestige is discouraged in Bali, the Balinese let their cocks do the fighting, so the battles are "just play."

> As any art form—for that, finally, is what we are dealing with—the cockfight renders ordinary, everyday experience comprehensible by presenting it in terms of acts and objects which have had their practical consequences removed and been reduced (or, if you prefer, raised) to the level of sheer appearances, where their meaning can be more powerfully articulated and more exactly perceived. The cockfight is "really real" only to the cocks—it does not kill anyone, castrate anyone, reduce anyone to animal status, alter the hierarchical relations among people, nor refashion the hierarchy; it does not even redistribute income in any significant way. What it does is what, for other peoples with other temperaments and other conventions, *Lear* and *Crime and Punishment* do; it catches up these themes—death, masculinity, rage, pride, loss, beneficence, chance-and, ordering them into an encompassing structure, presents them in such a way as to throw into relief a particular view of their essential nature. (Geertz 2005, p. 79)

As a ritual, the cockfight expresses powerful and ambivalent themes of status competition and repressed violence, themes simultaneously discouraged in Balinese life and encouraged in Balinese play. When seen as a ritual, the contest has the same meaning whether one wins or loses.

> In the cockfight, man and beast, good and evil, ego and id, the creative power of aroused masculinity and the destructive power of loosened animality fuse in a bloody drama of hatred, cruelty, violence, and death. It is little wonder that when, as is the invariable rule, the owner of the winning cock takes the carcass of the loser—often torn limb from limb by its enraged owner—home to eat, he does so with a mixture of social embarrassment, moral satisfaction, aesthetic disgust, and cannibal joy. Or that a man who has lost an important fight is sometimes driven to wreck his family shrines and curse the gods, an act of metaphysical (and social) suicide. Or that in seeking earthly analogues for heaven and hell the Balinese compare the former to the mood of a man whose cock has just won, the latter to that of a man whose cock has just lost. (Geertz 2005, p. 79)

Different kinds of performances like rituals, games, and theatrical drama take their place on the spectrum of performance genres. As a result, they are not easily categorized. Moreover, a single performance may exemplify more than one kind of performance. For example, the Balinese cockfight and the Kwakiutl winter ceremonial may be viewed as rituals, theater, or games, depending on whether one emphasizes the perspective of the performer, the audience, or the competition. These ambiguities are inherent in human performances and are central to modern performance theory (see chapter 9).[3]

6. Creating and Maintaining Relationships

Samoans have a saying that serves as a kind of Golden Rule. *Teu le va* literally translates to "Take care of the between." "The between" refers to the space between people—what we usually call the relationship. The "taking care" (also implying putting in order) is where ritual comes in, most commonly ritual exchanges. Much of Samoan life is governed by this apparently simple phrase which turns out to be quite complicated . Chapter 5 described several gift-giving rituals, focusing on traditional and nontraditional ritual exchanges in Samoa. Anthropologists have highlighted the large-scale ritual exchanges of goods like woven mats, pigs, jewelry, and food items that make up the exchange ceremonies commonly found in preindustrial societies. We have analyzed marriage arrangements as forms of alliance-creating exchange. However, ritualized exchanges are found in all corners of human life. Every day, we engage in exchanges of many kinds with family, friends, colleagues, and neighbors. Within the web of connections created by these exchanges, small and large, lies the universe of human social relations.

Many of these exchanges are so casual that they are not easily recognized as rituals. They are rituals because they are governed by a general script, a set of implicit rules that we rarely are aware of until someone breaks the rules, and we sense that something has gone wrong. There is much more hidden in our exchanges than we might realize. For example, an odd feature of everyday exchange is that we usually do not openly acknowledge our offerings as "exchanges." Only rarely, as in the Samoan gift exchange described in chapter 5, are gifts exchanged in both directions simultaneously. Instead, most of our exchanges are framed as gifts ("giving")—one-way tokens of favor or love. The reciprocity involved is often delayed, sometimes by months or even years. Commonly, the status of a gift as a return is unacknowledged unless the return gift fails to materialize. Anthropologists call these long cycles of exchange "delayed reciprocity." This delay is a more important aspect of gift exchange than we might realize. Try returning a borrowed egg to a neighbor the same day you got it or offering a return favor at the time it is given. Your offer will risk being taken as an insult.

The most puzzling thing about exchange rituals is that they rarely acknowledge the expectation of exchange. Often, they emphasize the generosity, benevolence, thoughtfulness of the giving, and gratefulness in receiving. The exchange dimension of the transaction is usually masked. This denial of reciprocity explains why everyday gifts and favors do not feel like rituals. This ritual dimension is implicit but hidden. The obligation to pay back transforms any gift from a unique event into an implied future sequence of exchanges. Because reciprocity is not generally acknowledged, the ritual nature of the gift as an exchange is also denied. Exchange ritual usually involves a tacit agreement by both donor and recipient to treat a gift as given freely and without expectation of return. It would be bad form for any recipient of a gift to even hint at the obligation of reciprocity involved in the transaction. That would spoil the sense of goodwill that any gift is intended to promote.

The delay in repayment not only masks the reciprocity it obligates but also represents the trust inherent in a relationship of good faith. Failure to reciprocate amounts to a denial of the relationship. Even banks that make cash loans to individuals often call themselves "trust companies," suggesting the voluntary and friendly nature of the loan rather than its legal character. The power of the gift to create alliances of goodwill seems to require the masking of the obligation that lies behind it: in other words, the masking of its essentially ritual character. An explicit emphasis on reciprocity suggests coercion and self-interest, undercutting the spirit of amity gifts are intended to represent.

While we normally think of gift exchange as the passing of valuable objects between individuals or groups, exchange rituals also involves more abstract aspects of relationships. The rules of exchange apply to such apparently innocuous things as invitations, favors, compliments, turn-taking in conversations, and interest expressed in the lives of others, all of which are governed by expectations of reciprocity. We all live within a vast economy of exchange, the rules of which are rarely made explicit. Yet if you listen carefully to some of the gossip around you, you may find that much of it consists of hurt or angry expressions of resentment at failures of reciprocity in social exchange. As hidden as exchange rituals seem to be in their everyday manifestations, we tend to be hyper-aware of violations in their expected forms. The violations point to our tacit awareness of the expected obligations that are implicit in the moral economy of ritual exchanges.

7. Mediating Transitions

Many years ago, I had the pleasure of visiting Japan at the invitation of the family of one of my students, who lived in a beautiful traditional Japanese house in the port city of Yaizu in Shizuoka Prefecture midway between Tokyo and Kyoto. Neither speaking nor reading Japanese, I was dependent on the excellent translating ability of my student, who accompanied me everywhere during my three-week stay. In addition to being fluent in English, Tomohisa was a keen student of anthropology. He clearly enjoyed helping me understand the intricacies of Japanese family life and social behavior, though I fear that the rigors of nonstop translating and making clear the many rules of Japanese social life had worn him out by the end of my stay.

I was struck by how attentive the Japanese were to different kinds of space. A pure zone could be defiled by the unwelcomed introduction of "dirt" from the outside even if the "dirt" was purely conceptual (Douglas 1966). Central to Shinto religious belief is the Japanese concept of *kegare*, referring to pollution, corruption, or defilement by association with any act or unclean condition such as death, disease, menstrual blood, or rape. To counteract pollution, the Japanese have numerous purification rituals. *Misogi* (ritual bathing) and *hiraegushi* (the waving of a purification wand over a person, object, or place by a Shinto priest) are prominent Shinto rites of purification.

While the most extreme forms of pollution are associated with death and disease, Japanese people are very conscious in their everyday behavior of avoiding polluting important "inside" spaces with the dirt from the "outside." Nowhere is this more evident than in entering a Japanese home. One of the Japanese terms for "family" is *uchi*, which also means "inside." The Japanese take the distinction between inside and outside very seriously regarding domestic space. Movement into a home from the outside is ritually marked by removing one's shoes (being careful not to touch the bottom of the shoes with your hand) and sliding into slippers waiting at the entrance.[4]

The transition zone into a house is the *genkan*, a porch platform separating the outside ground and the house entrance. Since Samoans also remove their footwear before entering a house, I automatically removed my shoes and slipped into the waiting slippers when first entering Tomohisa's house.

Noticing how he bristled as I headed into the house, I asked him what the problem was. He explained that I had left my outdoor shoes carelessly on the *genkan* without aligning them with the toes facing the entrance door. "The *genkan* is the border between two worlds. We pay careful attention to how we move between them," he said, turning the ritual theory I had taught him back on me.

This interest in shoes does not end at the house entrance. Japanese people will often change their shoes as they transition between spaces, even within the house. Once inside, they will usually remove the house slippers when entering a room with *tatami* mats. Western hotels in Japan are distinguished from traditional Japanese inns (*ryokan*). Street shoes are acceptable inside Western-style hotels but are swapped for slippers when entering a *ryokan*. However, when entering a *ryokan* bathroom, an individual will typically exchange the house slippers for special bright yellow bathroom slippers. Ryokan sleeping rooms should never be in contact with footwear used in the toilet area.

I would confront these notions of pollution again when we visited a beautiful Buddhist temple in Kyoto. Like Japanese houses, temples and other historic buildings are treated as sacred inside spaces, and therefore outdoor shoes could not be worn inside. Since people walked from building to building in their stocking feet, the paths between the temples had narrow, slightly raised walkways, allowing visitors to move between buildings without putting on their shoes. As I walked on the walkway, I met another visitor coming in the opposite direction. I briefly stepped down onto the ground to make room for the other person and was taken aback by the looks of shock that greeted the sight of someone touching the dirt with his stocking feet. I felt like I had defiled the entire temple complex.

These Japanese practices highlight the role of ritualizing transitions. As we move through life, we encounter all kinds of transitions, changes in space, social status, age, and relationships. We enter new areas and cross boundaries. We greet strangers and friends as they enter our space and say goodbye as they exit. As we move through the stages of our lives, our identity is repeatedly updated along with our age. We become new selves as we take on new roles. Everything changes; nothing stays still. Transition is the unsteady state of life. Because transitions bring us face-to-face with the unknown and the unpredictable, they are often a source of anxiety. And so transitions beg for ritual.

Rites of transition, like the Japanese changing of shoes at the threshold of the house, provide an oasis of predictability and order as we confront change. Transition rituals punctuate our social relations, both separating and uniting two different dimensions of experience. Think of how you feel when you are introduced to someone new. Depending on the situation, you may or may not look forward to the meeting. Inevitably you will be a bit anxious. "How do I look?" you may ask yourself. "Will they like me? What sort of self am I presenting to these strangers? What impression will I make? What face do I prepare for this encounter?"

Fortunately, culture usually comes to the rescue with default ritual greetings on which we can always rely. We might improvise a memorable greeting if we are confident. But usually, we default to familiar greetings to get us over the hump. The same goes for departures. We all have a handy stock of farewell rituals. The ritual words and gestures we choose to say goodbye both smooth the departure and speak volumes about the nature of the relationship. As competent members of our culture, we learn very early on to ritually say our hellos and goodbyes.

The best-studied transition rites are the rites of passage, marking significant transitions in social identity, ceremonies like birth rites, weddings, baptisms, and funerals. The most famous work on rites of passage is a slim volume published in French in 1909 as *Les Rites de Passage* by the French sociologist Arnold van Gennep and translated into English as *Rites of Passage*. Van Gennep introduced the concept of a rite of passage by noting how the path from one territory or country to another is often marked by elaborate legal and ceremonial protocol. Boundaries, Van Gennep noted, were often considered sacred, and crossing them demanded great attention and care. Van Gennep's chief contribution was recognizing that rites of passage typically have a three-part form. Here is how he put it:

> It will be noted that the rites carried out on the threshold itself are transition rites. "Purifications" (washing, cleansing, etc.) constitute rites of separation from previous surroundings; there follow rites of incorporation (presentation of salt, a shared meal, etc.). The rites of the threshold are therefore not "union" ceremonies, properly speaking, but rites of preparation for union, themselves preceded by rites of preparation for the transitional stage. Consequently, I propose to call the rites of separation from a previous world, preliminal rites, those executed during the transitional stage liminal (or threshold) rites, and the ceremonies of incorporation into the new world postliminal rites. (Van Gennep 1969, p. 20–21)

According to Van Gennep, ritual transitions often included distinct ritual phases of separation, transition, and reincorporation.

While not every rite of passage follows this three-step scheme, Van Gennep's insight makes sense of many transition rites. For example, entry into a Japanese house discussed above begins with moving from the dirt onto the *genkan* and removing one's shoes, a rite of separation. Next, changing from shoes to house slippers at the Japanese *genkan* would mark the "liminal" or transitional phase, while stepping up into the house through the entry door completes the transition, incorporating the individual into the household. The critical space in the ritual is the *genkan*, which is neither outside nor inside. In Van Gennep's formulation, the *genkan* is the liminal zone of transformation that Victor Turner would make famous as the "betwixt-and-between" stage of rites of passage (Turner 1969). Rites of passage turn a sudden change in status, location, and identity into a stepwise process of transformation. Ritualizing transitions allows participants and audiences to sense a structure to change and to adapt to the changes unfolding around them. Turner has a lot to say about this liminal zone. His work features liminal spaces, statuses, and states of being that he views as spaces of possibility and creation. Hanging between one state and another, liminal phenomena not only beg for transition but themselves can embody extraordinary power in human life.

8. Commemoration

Commemorative ritual serves as both a storehouse and a workshop of memory. Whether it is a holiday or a holy day, every commemoration is an act of remembering. In most cases, what is "remembered" has never been directly experienced by the celebrants, so it is not literally remembered. Historical memory is only directly available to those members of the first generation of celebrants present at the commemorated event and for whom it recreates an actual memory. For subsequent generations of participants in commemorative rites, the remembered person or circumstance is not, strictly speaking, a memory. Instead, the ritual creates a simulated memory for these latter-day celebrants, replicating an alleged historical event through ritual. The event is remembered as ritual.

Commemoration means remembering together. Individuals can use rituals for purely personal recollection, such as the Jewish tradition of lighting a *yuhrzeli* candle on the anniversary of a loved one's death. However, commemoration is usually done by a community, whether a family, an ethnic group, a town, or a nation. Commemorative rites are important sources of collective or social memory, as a community gathers to recall historical events or persons essential to its identity. Remembering together produces a special kind of memory.

The remembered event can have actual historical roots, as in the case of the annual American Thanksgiving celebration. But the object of commemoration is often elaborated or even transformed over time. For example, Thanksgiving can be traced to an actual event, a three-day feast organized in November of 1621 by the Pilgrim colony Governor William Bradford to mark the Pilgrims' first corn harvest. The governor invited the colony's Native American allies, including the Wampanoag chief Massasoit to join in the feast. However, by the time George Washington issued the first official Thanksgiving proclamation in 1789, Thanksgiving had become an expression of gratitude for the success of the American war of independence and the ratification of the US Constitution.

In 1827, the journalist Sara Josepha Hale launched a campaign to make Thanksgiving an official national holiday, a campaign which would take thirty-six years to bear fruit. The campaign finally succeeded in 1863, when President Abraham Lincoln proclaimed an official national day of Thanksgiving. The Civil War was at its height, and the expressed purpose of the Thanksgiving celebration was once again updated. According to Lincoln, Thanksgiving was proclaimed to "commend to [God's] tender care all those who have become widows, orphans, mourners or sufferers in the lamentable civil strife" and to "heal the wounds of the nation." Thanksgiving has remained one of the most beloved American holidays. However, what is being remembered will vary significantly over time and between families. The inherent flexibility of the concept of Thanksgiving is key to the continued vitality of the celebration.

"Remembering" is a slippery idea. Commemoration rituals are subject to many kinds of manipulation. They are rarely straightforward reflections of historical events. For example, Eva Batista writes of the use of manipulated history of the Battle of Boyne in Northern Ireland to underwrite the creation of a new commemorative festival called Orangefest, which was intended to celebrate the continuity and legitimacy of Protestant and British rule in Ulster:

The myth of the Battle of Boyne has enabled individuals to create their own tradition, which distinguishes them from others by their heroic past. Societies evolve around mythologies, testifying of their origin and sanctifying their norms. Misreadings of the past can become cherished myths. They become comprehended as a true story, which through re-telling and re-enactment renews the social order and the image of the world. In this sense, the myth creates sacred history and thus validates ideologies, which justify social order and social change.

The Battle of Boyne commemoration has been an active factor in social identification. It celebrates one version of history and uses one method of remembering it, thus excluding Others. . . . War commemoration in Northern Ireland conveys the meaning of sameness and the continuity of the Protestant community. In order to justify and maintain this tradition, war commemoration has been redefined and reshaped on many occasions. (Batista 2009, p. 6)

Commemorative rites are inherently political in their use of historical memory to legitimize certain definitions of community while often marginalizing or "forgetting" others.

It is hardly surprising that commemorative rites often produce controversy as alternative readings of the histories they recall are proposed. A contemporary example of such a controversy is the fate of Columbus Day in the United States. This holiday has traditionally celebrated the "discovery" of the "New World" by Christopher Columbus in 1492. Native Americans and their supporters have two significant objections to honoring Columbus. First, the Americas were initially populated by ancestors of contemporary Native American populations so that America had already been "discovered" long before Columbus arrived. Second, Columbus enslaved and mistreated the Native people he encountered in the Caribbean. On his first day in the New World, Columbus had six members of the island's indigenous population seized as servants. Later on, he had thousands of Taino Indians from the island of Hispaniola sent back to Spain to be sold as slaves, many of whom died before reaching the country. This alternative reading of the historical "facts" of Columbus's discovery of the New World suggests to many dissidents that he should not be held up as a hero of American history.

The contested commemoration of Columbus gradually became a movement to replace Columbus Day with Indigenous Peoples' Day. Shifting the object of commemoration from Columbus to Native populations is significant. What had been remembered would be forgotten, and what had been sidelined by the earlier ritual would now be remembered. A new history would emerge from a change in the commemoration ritual. Indigenous Peoples' Day was first proposed in 1977 by the International Conference on Discrimination against Indigenous Populations in the Americas, sponsored by the United Nations. Around the same time, a group of Native Americans in Boston began to protest the celebration of Thanksgiving as misrepresenting the relationships between the Pilgrim settlers and the Native populations as a collaboration.

In 1990, representatives of indigenous American populations gathered in Quito, Ecuador, at the First Continental Conference on 500 Years of Indian Resistance. They agreed to devote 1992, the five hundredth anniversary of Columbus's first voyage, to advocating continental unity and liberation for indigenous populations. In 1992, the city council of Berkeley, California, voted to replace Columbus Day with Indigenous Peoples' Day to commemorate what they called the death and forced assimilation of generations of Native Americans that followed upon Columbus's "discovery." Several other California cities followed Berkeley's lead.

The rewriting of history occasioned by the Columbus Day controversy appears to be gradually having its intended effect. Today at least a dozen states no longer recognize Columbus Day. State legislatures regularly introduce legislation to replace Columbus Day with Indigenous Peoples' Day, but the proposals always generate considerable controversy over whose history will get acknowledged. Commemorations are always a mix of remembering and forgetting, and whose versions of history become certified through ritualization and whose history is officially forgotten is inevitably a sensitive and divisive political issue.

9. Embodying Meaning

"In the beginning," the New Testament assures us, "was the Word." However, the record of human evolution tells a different story. In the evolution of human communication, ritual preceded language by several million years. In fact, ritual communication is much older than our species and was probably used by our primate ancestors long before the Homo line evolved. But once language did develop in Neanderthals or early Homo sapiens, it produced a revolution in how humans understood and interacted with the world.

The advantages that language afforded our species were extraordinary. So powerful was the effect of language on human life that one might have assumed that the ancient ritual mode of communication would have become extinct. But that never happened. Ritual has remained a significant dimension of communication for humans everywhere. Human nature never transcended its dependence on ritual. But why? To answer that question, we need to consider a characteristic of ritual that distinguishes it from ordinary language: embodiment. Unlike speech, ritual is inherently gestural communication. It speaks by way of the body. This fact gives ritual powers with which language cannot compete.

But isn't language also anchored in the body? Calling language disembodied communication needs some qualification. It is true that speech depends on the body in at least four ways. First, there is the physical articulation of speech sounds. For that, language colonized bodily organs that serve for breathing and eating. Second, language required the evolution of numerous new brain centers. When we talk, it is our brains speaking through our mouths. Damage those brain centers, and language is impaired. The third way language depends on the body is in meaning-making. Bodily experience is essential to semantics—how words make meaning. Metaphor theorists like Mark Johnson and George Lakoff have proposed that bodily metaphors are at the root of linguistic meaning, a view now shared by many linguists (Lakoff and Johnson 1980). The abstract concepts language makes possible are supported by concrete images linked to bodily experience. Mental models, what Johnson calls "image schemas," serve to bridge concepts and physical experience. This conceptual bridging is what the philosopher Mark Johnson has called "the body in the mind." (Johnson 1990). So language digs deep into our bodies as well as our minds. Finally, there is gesturing. We inevitably accompany our speech with physical gestures. Our body insists on having its say. Words are not enough.

Despite these ties between speech and the body, there are several significant ways in which language resists and transcends the body. Without gestures, there is no ritual. But language is different. We can disconnect language from physical speech and store it in writing or electronic code. With the advent of digital coding, language can be converted into many different codes and stored in many media. Although rooted in the body, language directs our minds outward and upward, away from the body and toward abstract "concepts." Language makes possible ideas like freedom, innocence, and intolerance, concepts without an apparent concrete reference. Language also makes it easy to lie. With its freedom to represent anything, real or not, it gave us a powerful way to deceive others. In contrast, our bodies are more closely tied to our thoughts and feelings. While the body can be trained to lie, it is much more difficult to deceive others with our body language than with words. That is why we intuitively watch someone's body language when we want to assess whether they are speaking the truth. It usually takes skilled actors or con artists to lie convincingly with their body language.

The relative freedom of language has many advantages. Consider the power to paraphrase. Language enables us to say the same thing in different ways. With language, we can discard one way of saying something and find another. We can even translate foreign languages into approximations of each other. Language is "discursive," discoursing around things. Language is not a thing in itself. Puffs of air, our words are not things but concepts, or more specifically airy vessel for transmitting concepts. Other than a magician or a god, no one can talk something into existence. We can only talk about something, moving around a subject. However, with ritual, we do not communicate about something; we present something. There are no two ways about a ritual because the performance is the ritual. What ritual says is inseparable from how it says.

Despite these differences between language and ritual, words proved too valuable a tool to be wholly separate from ritual. Language gave humans a new ritual medium. It could be "ritualized," converting speech into rigid, repeatable units. Words could be made into verbalized ritual gestures. The co-opting of language by ritual meant that the freedom and mobility of ordinary language had to be suppressed and transformed. Language had to become embodied, captured by ritual, frozen, and made sacred as ritual language becomes "word magic."

Once ritualized, a world of verbal ritual forms opened up: prayers, speeches, chants, verbal etiquette, curses, and blessings. Ritual speech would become an essential part of our ritual toolkit. Ritualization could magically transform ordinary words, rendering them sacred, enchanted, prophetic, or demonic. Thus, the power of ritual language is not the power of ordinary language. Common words are often transparent and interchangeable, while the evocative power of ritual language lies in the body of the words, the material articulation of the sounds.

The invariance of ritual language, its materiality, has proven challenging to the Catholic Church. Consider the Roman Catholic Vatican II proclamation allowing the Mass to be "translated" into the vernacular language of the people. Not only was the decision greeted with considerable resistance from traditionalists, but the church was forced to suggest that Mass in English was not quite the same Mass as the traditional Latin version. The translation came dangerously close to generating a new ritual. The Catholic Church now distinguished between the traditional Latin Tridentine Mass and its translated "versions."

The 1962 Tridentine Mass is often called the *usus antiquior* (older use) to distinguish it from the vernacular Mass of Pope Paul VI. In 2007, Pope Benedict XVI issued a personal letter authorizing the performance of the 1962 Tridentine Mass by Catholic priests but only in masses celebrated without the common people. These Latin masses, the document read, "may . . . also be attended by faithful who, of their own free will, ask to be admitted." It is tempting to read the statement as an admission that the traditional Tridentine Mass in Latin was the "real Mass," to be practiced by the most devout followers. The issue of multiple masses has proven a delicate one for the church, with inevitable political overtones. Recognizing the danger inherent in acknowledging that the church universal had more than one Mass, Pope Benedict XVI denied that the 1962 Tridentine Mass and the new vernacular masses were separate rites. Instead, he explained that it is simply a matter of "a twofold use" of the same Roman rite. Instead of splitting hairs, Benedict attempted to reunite them.

The power of embodiment appears to override the power of authenticity. Once the English version of the Mass had become standard, congregants began to attach themselves to the English wording of the new Mass with the same intensity with which they had formerly devoted themselves to the older Latin wording. By 2011, the English Mass had begun to evoke in congregants the same sense of ritual sanctity that the Latin Mass had produced half a century earlier. However, in November of 2011, the Catholic Church officially adopted a new translation of the Roman Missal. The translation was said to be more "authentic" in more accurately following the original Latin. The US Conference of Catholic Bishops authorized this new translation for all English-speaking dioceses.

The bishops had hoped to bring the English mass closer to its Latin source. But the small changes in wording outraged many devout Catholics. For them, the sanctity of the Mass had been violated. American church leaders defended the changes, insisting that a new translation did not make it a new Mass. The Most Reverend Joseph P. McFadden, bishop of Harrisburg (Pennsylvania), insisted that the new translation will allow Catholics to "rediscover the mystery of the mass, enter into it more fully and find their identities and destinies."[5] But not everyone was convinced. George Worgul, chairman of the Department of Theology at Duquesne University, countered that changing the translation would disrupt the automatic flow of familiar words that renders the Mass so powerful for parishioners. As a result, rote recitation would be disrupted. "You can do so much more when you aren't struggling for words," he argued. "It doesn't mean you're not involved. You could be more involved. We don't have to think; we can just let God work on us and in us."[6]

What is true for ritual language is even more true for ritual gestures. The resistance to deviations in ritual performance is fierce. Psychologists have conducted elaborate experiments on how individuals react to even minor violations of ritual practice. In one set of experiments, various minor deviations from orthodox ritual practice by group members in religious and civic rituals produced "moral outrage" from in-group members, as measured by punishments meted out to the violators. These experiments focused less on ritual language than on action patterns such as standing for the American Pledge of Allegiance or the ritual performance of the *brit*, the Jewish circumcisions.

Even when changes in ritual practice were acknowledged as beneficial (for health or convenience), changes in ritual gestures, objects, or the order of actions consistently produced strong aversion. The authors concluded that the failure to perform rituals precisely was seen as rejecting the community's moral values. For these researchers, this denial of group values appeared to trigger the outrage.

> Across seven studies, we show that group members who alter group rituals invoke stronger moral outrage and punishment from other group members than those who do not alter the rituals, even when the alterations are minor or beneficial. Furthermore, altering group activities with more (vs. fewer) ritualistic features provokes more moral outrage and punishment. This outrage is amplified among individuals who are most committed to their group and see the ritual as most strongly symbolizing the group's values. (Stein et al. 2021, p. 6)

The conclusion of this study was the importance of the in-group in enforcing its values on group members. In other words, ritual compliance was understood as a form of social control.

While social control of ritual may well be an essential aspect of group psychology, it overlooks the self-enforcing power of ritualized action. In changing the Catholic Mass, the authorities supported and even mandated the changes. Conforming to group values was not at risk in complying with the changes. What dissident worshippers stressed was the effect of these changes on their experience of the ritual. Whatever social factors were involved in their objections to the new Mass, their stated emphasis was on how the changes affected their relationship to their faith. The old ritual forms had become their embodied connection to the Catholic Church. At issue was not the meaning of the words but something more primitive: the loss of connection to the physical articulation of the sounds. Bodily experience had certified the ritual's authenticity.

Describing a ritual experience is like describing dancing, not the audience's view of the dancer but the dancer's experience of her body moving in space. In *The Divine Horsemen: The Living Gods of Haiti*, the legendary filmmaker and author Maya Deren struggles to describe her experience of spirit possession by a Voodoun *loa* (god) while she participated in a ritual dance:

> As sometimes in dreams, so here I can observe myself, can note with pleasure how the full hem of my white skirt plays with the rhythms, can watch, as if in a mirror, how the smile begins with a softening of the lips, spreads imperceptibly into a radiance which, surely, is lovelier than any I have ever seen. It is when I turn, as if to a neighbor, to say, "Look! See how lovely that is!" and see that the others are removed to a distance, withdrawn to a circle which is already watching, that I realize, like a shaft of terror struck through me, that it is no longer myself whom I watch. Yet it *is* myself, for as that terror strikes, we two are made one again, joined by and upon the point of the left leg which is as if rooted to the earth. Now there is only terror. "This is it!" Resting upon that leg I feel a strange numbness enter it from the earth itself and mount, within the very marrow of the bone, as slowly and richly as sap might mount the trunk of a tree. I say numbness, but that is inaccurate. To be precise, I must say what, even to me, is pure recollection, but not otherwise conceivable: I must call it a white darkness, its whiteness a glory and its darkness, terror. It is the, terror which has the greater force, and with a supreme effort I wrench the leg loose—I must keep moving! must keep moving!—and pick up the dancing rhythm of the drums as something to grasp at, something to keep my feet from resting upon the dangerous earth. (Deren 1983, p. 258–259)

Deren is forced to turn to a poetic idiom, a somewhat tortured one, as she tries to convey the effects of the drumming and dancing on her body. It is hard to follow her account as her words struggle to convey an experience she calls "pure recollection, but not otherwise conceivable." In the end, Deren resorts to a metaphorical paradox, describing possession as a "white darkness," an impossible mix of glory and terror. Ritual experience will always elude accurate description.

10. Reversing Agency

When I was growing up, the Shore kids dreaded Passover, the holiday my grandmother called *Pesach*. Every spring, we would roll our eyes as we contemplated the tedious ritual that awaited us, unfolding in a language we did not understand. What seemed like hours of Hebrew chanting by my devout uncle stood between us and a delicious Passover dinner. Once again, we would have to repeat the same meaningless prayers, sing the same songs (which we had learned by heart even though we knew not what we were singing), and, as we got older, take turns reciting the same stories from the Haggadah that guided us through the seder. "It's all empty ritual," we complained. Only years later did we realize that the comfort we felt celebrating the seder with our own children was intimately connected to those early years when we thought we were just "going through the motions" of Passover. Passover had turned on us.

There is nothing uniquely boring about Passover. Any elaborate ritual will elicit the same adverse reaction from many kids and adults alike. The very idea of ritual can inspire the rolling of eyes. How many times have you heard someone complain that a celebration was "an empty ritual?" "Going through the motions" is a common complaint about ritual. However, this picture of ritual is too simple. Even as we acknowledge that ritual often feels empty, we confront a fascinating paradox. Somehow, the same ceremony that produces the sense of pointless repetition can also inspire an intimation of the sacred. Oddly, rituals can produce both boredom and awe, sometimes simultaneously.

The feature of ritual that accounts for this paradox is what I call *agency reversal*. The label "agency reversal" is my own coining since the concept it names is not commonly acknowledged. Although it has gone largely unrecognized, agency reversal is among ritual's most important powers. Agency reversal accompanies all habituated behavior. Once it becomes a habit, behavior becomes increasingly automatic. What is true for habit is also true for ritual. A frequently practiced ritual can turn the tables on us. Instead of our performing the ritual, it seems to be performing us. The sense of who's in control, what social scientists call "agency," is reversed. Agency reversal is the feeling that a pattern of behavior has taken over, controlling our bodies. We are, as we say, "moved" by the experience.[7]

The most extreme forms of agency reversal are trance states induced by rhythmic behavior like dancing. A well-documented example of ritually induced trance is experienced by the so-called whirling dervishes of Turkey and Iran. The dancers (also known as *semazens*), who belong to certain Muslim religious orders originating in Persia, form a circle and spin gracefully and rapidly around the room, allowing their skirts to flare out dramatically as they turn. The whirling is an act of meditation goal aimed at emptying the worshippers' minds as they attempt to achieve a perfect connection with God. Empty experience is the point of the rite, not the problem.

Other examples of trance states aim at "possessing" the celebrant by a deity or other spirit. Haitian Voodoun religious services, discussed above, aim at inducing a *loa* (god) to take over the body of a celebrant, mounting the celebrant's body as a rider mounts a horse. Through intense ritual drumming, dancing, and spinning, the worshipper is temporarily possessed by a god, losing touch with her own soul.

A third well-known example of ritual possession are Bali's *kris* dancers, who are featured in a famous Bali Hindu ritual drama (figure 6.1). The ritual enacts in music and dance the contest between the witch *Calon Arang* or *Rangda* ("widow"), a devouring mother figure and queen of the demon world, and the beneficent lion/dragon *Barong*, the chief protector who seeks to tame her. The drama portrays the eternal struggle between evil and good. The *kris* dancers, named after the razor-sharp daggers that they wield, attempt to kill the witch, but she magically turns their blades back on their own bodies.

What follows is a trance-induced dance in which the dancers threaten to stab themselves, the daggers' tips poised menacingly on the dancers' chests. However, the result is not suicide but a moral standoff. With the forces of good and evil counterposed in perfect balance, the dancers writhe in agony as they struggle to keep from stabbing themselves. The battle between good and evil is embodied in the tension between impulses for self-destruction

Figure 6.1
Balinese *kris* dancers in a trance

and control, resulting in the perfectly poised dagger, as the male dancers are possessed by the spirits of the two mythical figures.

Of course, not all ritual leads to possession, which is the most extreme form of agency reversal. While most rituals do not involve possession, this extreme example of agency reversal points to an essential characteristic of all rituals. Once ritualized, behavior patterns come to be experienced as external to the performer. The more intense the ritual, the greater the sense that it is being performed *on* or *in* the actor by an outside force. A sociologist might say that the behavior pattern becomes experienced as an "institution" rather than an individual action. Human behavior institutions owe their existence to the human capacity for ritualization. Once ritualized, behavior can be conceived of as external to the performer. Once it is detachable, it becomes a potential social institution, a behavior pattern we can name and share with others. Or it can be a divinity or demon that has taken over one's body.

Back in 1968, I was on the Hawaiian island of Molokai for a Peace Corps training program to prepare us for Samoa. Every day of the three-month training period, we would have five hours of language classes in Samoan taught by a group of Samoan college students studying in Hawaii. Our language textbook featured dialogues that we had to memorize: what to say when walking through a village and people greet you from their houses, greeting and farewell scenarios, how to shop at a village shop, what to say when you see someone heading to bathe in the village pool, and so on. When training was done and we flew to Samoa, I was posted to live with a family on an island far away from the capital of Apia. As I walked through the village, I was astonished to discover that villagers had apparently also read our textbook. The speeches I heard were identical—word for word—with our textbook exercises. There seemed to be a set speech, call, and response for every occasion.

My first reaction was dismay. I felt as if I had entered a robot society where automated speech had replaced real conversation. We Americans had our own ritual greetings, but Samoan etiquette struck me as far more constrained and rote. Eventually, I arrived at a more subtle understanding of Samoan verbal ritual. By making their greetings predictable and automatic, Samoans had created a community attuned to the smooth flow of social relations. Not just the particular words but also the back-and-forth rhythm of these rituals was incorporated into Samoan social life and became part of the habitual behavioral repertory of individual Samoans. Much of Samoan social life took place *within* these shared ritual forms.

When I was walking down the village road toward the bathing pool, towel and soap in hand, I was no longer irritated by the endless calls from each house politely inquiring where I was going, as if it were not obvious. I had realized people were simply acknowledging my presence in their village and letting me know that I was now part of their lives. What I had thought of as "formal noise" turned out to be the grease that oiled everyday social relations. I was always free to walk on if there was nothing more to say. But if there was news of any kind, I could stop and chat, turning a purely ritual encounter into a real conversation.

Years later, I rethought these early experiences and realized that the "meaningless" back-and-forth of ritual speeches was a tuning device for the give-and-take of social life. Anonymity and privacy were not virtues in Samoa. You didn't ignore people; you acknowledged them even if the words were purely formal. This rhythm of simple verbal exchange—every ritual phrase had its ritual response—set the tempo of mutuality in more complex social relations. No one dominated a conversation; people rarely lectured you, and there were few extended monologues as is, unfortunately, commonplace in our society. These clichés set the tempo of social life. Thanks to agency reversal, the fundamental rhythm of social exchange would become automatic, like the greetings themselves. The conversation was "out there" on the street before it was in our mouths.

The power of agency reversal resolves one of the biggest riddles about the origins of human social life. Their big brains allowed Homo sapiens to adapt to a wide variety of ecological niches by inventing all kinds of extensions of their bodies. When these inventions took the form of objects, we often call them "tools." But humans also developed more abstract tools, including ideas, stories, recipes, names, and techniques. Among these abstract inventions were chunks of repeatable behavior that could efficiently coordinate human interactions and direct practical activities. The framework for smooth interaction was ready-made, and, in Samoa, we did not have to apologize for inhabiting it.

We possessed a stock of tools for getting things done and a stock of ready-made behaviors that would allow for predictable relationships with one another. Our social rituals would simplify tasks, so we didn't need to improvise new ways of acting every time we faced a challenge. We had greetings and farewells, forms for expressing deference and power, verbal and gestural formulas (small talk) for casual interactions, and a host of other patterned actions—a ritual for every occasion. Like axes and knives, these patterns were tools. They created a set of standard techniques, expectations, and understandings that we recognize as our culture. As shared institutions, these interaction patterns were not just within our minds. They were projected into the world as shared objects shaping our behavior.

But there was one problem. Although communities might invent their interaction patterns, we did not want to feel they were simply our inventions. These behaviors had to be regarded as obligatory by community members. As arbitrary patterns, they would have no moral force. The feeling of arbitrariness might encourage individuals to go their own way, refusing to participate in the community. As we know, this does happen. One solution is to promulgate laws enforcing behavior, and punishments for violating the laws. But while laws could force compliance with accepted behaviors, motivating personal compliance from within was much more effective—members of a community needed to feel a sense of obligation to conform to social institutions.

You could always make laws to force people to act appropriately, and for some extreme behaviors, laws work. But ritualization of action proved to have many advantages over the force of law since it derives its authority from agency reversal. With ritual, our social "institutions" could be naturalized. We would feel a compulsion to conform to social norms as they take hold of us. Our local customs might be relatively arbitrary, but they do not usually feel arbitrary. Ritualized behavior feels natural. For the most part, we perform our social roles as habits. As the French sociologist Pierre Bourdieu puts it, our everyday interactions become our habitus (Bourdieu 1977).

Agency reversal has its dangers, of course, as is clear from watching films of Nazi mass rallies. But for greasing the wheels of everyday social life, ritual agency reversal solved a big problem. If we were to transcend complete genetic control of our social interactions, we faced a paradox. We needed to invent behaviors that were ultimately flexible and negotiable but would still be experienced as obligatory. The "cultural" would have to feel "natural." The answer was ritualized behavior that could "socialize" our most basic interaction patterns. Law could be brought in for the rest.

Agency reversal is also one of the reasons ritual is a common feature of religious experience. Through ritual, the faithful can experience an external agent controlling their behavior. Ritual makes possible the direct experience of transcendent power, and experiencing transcendence is at the heart of religious life.[8] Much of the power of spiritual experience can be attributed to the effects of this ritual reverse of control. Though agency reversal is not often recognized as a power of ritual, it turns out to be one of ritual's most potent legacies—if you will, God's gift to human adaptation.

7 Nostalgic Commemoration: Salem Camp Meeting

Ritual is a kind of remembering. Among ritual's numerous powers is the ability to shape social memory. Social memory is collective remembering by a group or a community, memories evoked by stories, photographs, histories, plays, novels, memorials, or celebrations. While we usually assume remembering is done by individuals, many of our recollections are formed through collective activity and are about things experienced with others. In rare cases, social memory is a recollection of something directly experienced. More commonly, however, it is simulated, a recollection of something that the group has not directly experienced. In most commemorations, what people actually recall are the repeated performances of commemoration rather than the event or person being commemorated. The original experience is an imagined memory.

In this chapter, we will witness some moments in the creation of a collective memory of family by listening to longtime campers who attend an annual camp meeting in central Georgia. Family memory is often inscribed in stories, anecdotes, photographs, or, increasingly, videos (Barclay and Koefoed 2021; Shore and Kauko 2018). Family memories are also evoked by things, whether simple objects or treasured family heirlooms. Another important source of family memory are collective rituals such as the annual camp meetings, religiously inspired revivals that occur throughout the United States every summer.

Commemorations come in various keys, triggering different emotions. Nostalgic recollections unfold in a major key, celebrating treasured memories that are sweetened by regular repetition. Powered by an impulse to idealize, nostalgic memory views history through "rose-colored glasses." Sometimes nostalgia involves recalling actual events, memories positively framed, as when we recount fond memories of childhood or family outings. Nostalgic memories are summoned by photos, treasured objects, or, more diffusely, by smells and tastes that bring to mind earlier times. The current craze for cell phone photography has produced "prospective memories" of family life, family photos and videos taken to provide anticipated future memories of family time.

In addition to nostalgia for our past experiences, there is also an imagined nostalgia for a place or a time that never existed. We have no words to distinguish nostalgia for places, people, and things in our past from the nostalgia we experience for an imagined experience. Imagined nostalgia rests on simulated memories, filling a wished-for place that is absent from our experience. We enter Disneyland's Magic Kingdom by stepping onto Main Street, USA, a nostalgic simulation of an idealized American small town from bygone times. By reducing the scale of the buildings to three-fourths on the first floor, five-eighths on the second floor, and half scale on the third, Disney's "Imagineers" have produced an illusion intended to trigger a sense of control and comfort. The general reduction in scale creates a realistic playscape rather than a real town. The reduction of scale on upper stories makes the buildings appear higher than they are. An exception is the Town Square Exhibition Hall, which is recreated full scale to block the view of the Contemporary Resort. Walt Disney wanted no distractions from the illusion of a return to a simpler times. This is how nostalgia can be architecturally choreographed.

Camp Meetings

For five years, as part of a research project on ritual and family memory in Georgia, I attended a camp meeting gathering held every July at Salem Campground in Newton County, Georgia. Salem Camp Meeting recreates a spiritual revival gathering of mostly white Protestant families in a nostalgic setting that simulates a small rural village. Camp meeting is one of America's oldest religious traditions. Camp meeting revivals sprang up at the end of the 1790s on the heels of American independence along the American frontier, in places like Tennessee and Kentucky.

The tradition spread rapidly between 1795 and 1830, the period known as the Second Great Awakening of American religious fervor. Because settlers were scattered along the frontier, far from neighbors, there were often no established churches with regular services. The settlers depended on roving Methodist and Presbyterian preachers who traveled the frontier on horseback ministering to the population. Early camp meetings, known as "brush arbor meetings," took place in a temporary "brush arbor," a crude open-air shelter constructed in a clearing. The shelter would take several days to erect as it involved clearing land and cutting trees for the roof structure. Local men would cooperate in the construction work (Bruce 1974; Johnson 1985; Weiss 1998; Eslinger 1999).

The first camp meeting was conceived by James McGready, a charismatic Presbyterian minister, who, in the late 1790s, came up with the idea of a traveling church service in the hill country of Kentucky. The camp meeting revival quickly caught on and spread throughout the frontier. So popular were some of these early meetings that several temporary brush arbors had to be constructed to accommodate all the worshippers, who enjoyed the spiritual renewal and the chance to gather with others to exchange news stories and gossip. Camp meeting preachers were often charismatic speakers, and their sermons and the accompanying hymns sometimes produced ecstatic seizures in campers.

The camp meeting tradition is still popular in the United States. Today there are over two thousand campgrounds throughout the country, mostly Methodist and Presbyterian but also camps run by Evangelical churches. While campgrounds are found throughout the country, the epicenter of the camp meeting movement has always been in the American South. The original chain of campgrounds throughout the South and the Ozarks came to define the Bible Belt. The camp meeting tradition has spread beyond the United States to Canada, and there are even several annual camp meetings in England, but camp meeting is largely an American religious tradition.

Salem Camp Meeting

In July of 2005, I was engaged in a research project on ritual and middle-class family culture in Newton County, Georgia, about forty miles east of Atlanta. Sam Ramsey, the mayor of Covington, Newton's county seat, invited me to attend Salem Campground to experience a camp meeting. "If you want to know about ritual and family traditions," he said with a wide grin, "you just gotta come to Salem." This would be the first of my

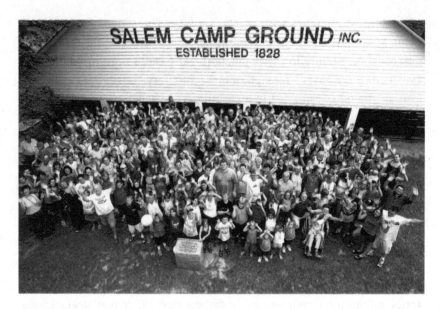

Figure 7.1
Campers gathered in front of the tabernacle at Salem Campground

five years attending Salem Camp Meeting. Families have gathered at Salem Campground every year since the camp meeting was founded in 1828 (see figure 7.1). Families, predominantly white, Protestant, and middle class from Newton and neighboring Rockdale counties, have been attending the camp meeting for generations. For many, attendance at the annual ritual reunion is an essential part of their lives and identity.

Though originally located deep "in the country," miles from any population center, Salem is now surrounded by sprawling suburban subdivisions and strip malls. Salem Road sees a steady stream of cars and trucks that have begun to intrude on the campground's tranquility. Nonetheless, the busy road and everything it represents is still considered by campers to be "out there" beyond the magic circle of the campground (figure 7.2). This magic circle is felt to envelop campers for the week they are there. "Look at that traffic," complained one woman, sitting with her adult daughter on the porch of their tent and pointing to the traffic on Salem Road. "I just don't want to even go out there." Her daughter threw up her hands in agreement. "I'm tired of it," she said, "But I don't know where you go. My son is at school in Atlanta. My husband works in Duluth. I'm in Buckhead, and my

Figure 7.2
Salem Campground

daughter's here in Conyers. That's crazy!" "It really is," her mother replied, "But what can you do?" For these folks, camp meeting is one answer to that question. The campground represents both a sacred space and a kind of time travel, linking them to each other, to an imagined past, and giving the campers a sense of wholeness missing in their everyday lives. As one man put it, "I don't know if you'd call it stepping back in time. But it's real symbolic to me. To come off of that road to here, it's like traveling ten million miles."

While the explicit agenda of the weeklong gathering every July is spiritual revival and fellowship, the annual ritual gathering is also an essential source of extended family renewal. Family members, many now scattered far beyond Georgia, celebrate their family identities by gathering as extended family clans. Most families stay on the campground for the week in their family "tents," which are now small cottages with sitting and dining areas, a kitchen, several bedrooms, each with multiple beds and bunks, and a front porch filled with rocking chairs or other comfortable seating (figure 7.3). Most tents are named after the clan that stays there. The tent's name is often featured on a sign posted outside the house, and a few even

Figure 7.3
Family "tent"

have family banners or flags prominently displayed in front. While the tents are intended as rustic throwbacks to an earlier time, some have televisions providing a diversion from campground socializing. These modern amenities have long been frowned upon at Salem as contrary to the spirit of camp meeting. Most tents still have sawdust floors. The oldest of the tents are more like rustic barns than houses and lack air conditioning (figure 7.4).

The tents surround the huge open-air tabernacle with rows of pews facing a large stage outfitted with a preaching pulpit and two grand pianos (figure 7.5). The center of collective activity, the tabernacle is the latter-day version of the brush arbor meeting house. The tabernacle at Salem Campground is currently listed on the National Register of Historic Places. In contrast to the open tabernacle, the surrounding tents are centers of private family activity. The front porches of the tents serve as a transition between the collective Salem family and the individual families who sleep in the tents. Family members spend much of the day and evening visiting other tents, and everyone is welcome to sit on the porch of any tent and chat.

Figure 7.4
The oldest tent at Salem Campground

Figure 7.5
The Salem tabernacle

Since 1933, Salem has had a hotel on the campground, a sizable wooden structure with twenty-two hotel rooms, a large dining room and kitchen, and surrounded by a wide, inviting porch lined with rocking chairs. Initially built to house visiting preachers, the hotel also houses campers who do not have their own tents and some older campers who prefer the comforts of air-conditioned hotel rooms to the more primitive accommodations of the family tents. The dining room seats about eighty diners. With tasty Southern cooking and attractively low prices, the hotel dining room will host most tenters for a few meals during camp meeting week along with the campers who rent rooms in the hotel. The hotel is also available for family reunions and religious gatherings throughout the year.

The Unchanging Schedule

The daily schedule during Salem Camp Meeting week is simple and fixed. Judging from old camp meeting schedules, campers have followed the same pattern of activities since at least the 1930s. Each year, two visiting preachers are invited by Salem's governing board to spend the week leading the

Figure 7.6
Salem Campground's musicians

daily services. The choice of preachers is considered an essential part of the camp meeting, and the board tries hard to invite preachers who are powerful and effective speakers. Salem Camp Meeting is not a church, tenters will remind you, and there is no regular pastor. Pastors are there at the invitation and the pleasure of the campers.

Preaching at Salem is considered both an honor and a challenge. "Salem is a tough pulpit," Sam Ramsey explained to me. Preachers who cannot meet the high expectations of the campers for the sermons at the camp meeting are rarely invited back. Following a service, campers will often discuss the sermon among themselves, commenting on both the message and the delivery. There are two church services in the tabernacle every day, at 11 a.m. and 7:30 p.m., with the two pastors usually alternating as speakers. A bell just outside the tabernacle is sounded to remind campers to head to the tabernacle. Most services feature a visiting choir from a local church.

For many years, hymns have been accompanied by two talented pianists, identical twin sisters Becky Ramsey (Sam's wife) and Alice Griffin (figure 7.6). In addition to morning and evening services, an early sunrise service called Morning Watch begins at 7:30 a.m. from Monday through

Friday. These early services are well attended despite the early hour. Kids can be seen making their way to Morning Watch in their pajamas, barely awake. On the last night, the campers gather for a communion service and a candlelight parade featuring younger campers. After the prayer service, there are Bible classes for all ages. Every evening, Salem Campground sponsors organized activities for older children and young adults. On Saturday morning, the campground supports a sports program for children called "Wide World of Sports."

When campers are not joining in these camp-wide activities, they are usually back at their tents. Women spend a lot of time in the tent kitchens preparing family meals. Otherwise, families can usually be found sitting on their porches chatting with family members and neighbors. Repeated every year, these activities lend a powerful rhythm to camp meeting as members shuttle back and forth from the relative privacy of family tents to the collective prayer services in the tabernacle and then back again to their tents. This rhythm alternately unites campers into a single Salem family and divides them into their clan families. Camp meeting is a "homecoming" ritual in several senses.

The porches offered our research team easy access to any tent for interviews. We strolled over to a porch and were immediately invited to have a seat. Over the years I spent at Salem Camp Meeting, I spent many pleasant hours chatting with family members on the front porch of almost every tent at the campground. In the process, I gradually found myself engaged in a web of stories about Salem families, memorable events featuring key people present and past, living and dead. For some campers, Salem Camp Meeting was a way of vividly recalling deceased family members. The tents are full of framed photos of deceased family members, who are felt to be with the families during the week. In the words of a young woman, camp meeting is a time "to remind everyone of our faith. They are here. The communion of saints is gathered on the other side. The dead are with us."

I toured many of the tents, accompanied by stories, photographs, and height markers of adult campers from when they were kids (figure 7.7). Families will hold up framed photos of long-deceased relatives against the cheeks of young children and comment on resemblances. "Bless you, mama," said Susan as she placed the photo of her deceased mother on a shelf above the picnic table in her tent's dining area. "I brought her so she

Figure 7.7
Memories on the walls

could look over us." Another woman held up a large photo of her parents and commented, "When I come out to Salem, I feel like our whole family is here. Like my dad, he's still out on the front porch with us." Because the campground and its rhythm of activities do not change perceptibly from year to year, it is easy for campers to sense the presence of dead family members. Time seems to stand still. Campers will stand next to their height markers or handprints from years past to note both growth and continuity. Every object, every photo, and every piece of furniture has a story to tell and a memory to recall.

Eventually, the anecdotes converge as the details came together as a coherent picture of camp life past and present. A complex history of relationships among the families begins to take shape. Identities blur and the passage of time stutters as older campers see their kids and grandkids doing the same things they did when they were young. At the end of the week, this playing with time is displayed in a slide show accompanied by soulful music. Photos taken during the current meeting are merged with pictures from past meetings, creating a powerful memory pastiche blurring past and present.

A Theater of Memory

While there are sermons and stories, songs, and prayers, perhaps the most striking features of Salem Camp Meeting are built into the rhythm of sensory experiences that resonate throughout the week. These memory triggers led me to conceive of the camp meeting as a "theater of family memory" (Shore 2008).[1] The most obvious of these triggers are the hymns sung at every service in the tabernacle, accompanied by the dual pianos and sometimes by visiting choirs. A few hymns are sung repeatedly and have close associations with the camp meeting. Most popular is Doris Akers's beautiful hymn "Sweet, Sweet Spirit," which has become something of an anthem at Salem. Whenever I happen to drive by the campground now, years after I last attended the camp meeting, I inevitably hear one or another of those hymns in my head, and the song will play itself in my mind for hours.

The musical memory exercises a primal grip, carried by the tune, the rhythm, and the haunting power of the words. "The good old hymns, the hymns of the 1800s," said Becky Ramsey, one of the piano duo that has played at the campground for almost half a century, "those evangelistic hymns stay pretty much the same. They're the ones that people like to sing." Her twin, Alice Griffin, finishes the thought: "That's what people appreciate about camp meeting. When other things change, Salem stays the same. I think it's what you remember after you've left camp meeting. You go back to your regular duties. Those songs will come back to your mind and bring back the things you've heard here, the sermons, the people you've seen, the heat, the fellowship. But it's those *songs* that embody the faith."

As Alice suggests, another sensory anchor of Salem Camp Meeting is the heat of the place. July in central Georgia is notoriously hot and humid.

Though a few of the tents are air-conditioned, most are not. By discouraging air conditioners in the tents, the campers hope to encourage people to hang out on their front porches and verandas, as was the case a century ago in small towns throughout the South. Campers seemed to recognize that the intense heat of the camp meeting was a significant part of their Salem experience.

An unexpected but powerful memory trigger at the camp meeting is the pervasive sawdust that covers the floors of both the older tents and the tabernacle. Loads of wood shavings are delivered to the campground before each camp meeting, and preparing the campground includes spreading sawdust. When asked about what comes to mind when they think of Salem Camp Meeting, many campers immediately answered "sawdust." What was once actual sawdust is now more often pine shavings, but the term sawdust has stuck. Not only does sawdust provide a distinctive smell at the campground, especially pungent and evocative in the absence of air conditioning, but the shavings also get caught in campers' shoes and slippers and even find their way into clothes (figure 7.8). Several campers commented they will still find some sawdust in their shoes months after camp meeting ends and that it will always remind them of the campground.

Figure 7.8
Sawdust memories

Figure 7.9
Hotel dining room

Sawdust memories can become bookends of a lifetime. One tenter said that she brought a vial of Salem sawdust to the birthing room where her new grandchild had just been born to welcome the baby to the world. Another said that she wanted Salem sawdust placed in her coffin when she died so she could be buried with campground dust. "Months after Camp Meeting, I always have sawdust caught in the sole of my shoe," mused one of the youth leaders. "Every time I put my shoes on, I have that feeling. The sawdust reminds you. I know when I leave [camp meeting] I'll always find sawdust in my clothes. And it's like a point to remember."

The third sensory memory trigger at the campground is the smell and taste of campground cooking. Campers eagerly recited the list of regular dishes associated with the campground, essentially a litany of traditional Southern comfort foods: fried chicken, country fried steak and gravy, collard greens, butter beans, fried okra, and green beans, all accompanied by sweet tea. Food figures prominently in campers' stories of camp meeting life (figure 7.9). In my experience, there was little attempt at variation or exotic innovation in meals at Salem since the predictable repetition of familiar tastes enjoyed with extended family was a central ingredient of camp meeting life and memory cultivation.

Figure 7.10
The Jenkins clan

Family takes on a special meaning at the campground. Most tenters live in middle-class suburban houses for most of the year, living in nuclear families. The family farm is just a distant memory now for most campers. But for one week a year, campers trade their houses for rustic cabins, sleeping in dormitory-like rooms with large groups of extended family members. For one week, all the cousins become campground brothers and sisters (figure 7.10). "Family" becomes clan, often taking on the clan identity of the tent. The whole extended family is said to be bound by the spiritual power of the meeting.

All My Life

At Salem Camp Meeting, the family idiom is elastic and contagious. For many campers, family extends beyond the individual tents. Some families are related to each other, and everyone knows the connections. But campers also consider the camp meeting as one big spiritual family: "The people that stay here," noted one tenter, "are family. And I don't know how to explain that." For families that have relocated frequently or have dispersed around the country, Salem Campground is a reliable permanent home, an anchor for their identities. For a society where economic mobility is commonly measured by changing homes and moving from place to place, the camp meeting is a recurring homecoming, a centripetal forcefield, counteracting the effects of the dispersal of family in modern life. Here is how one camper characterized the effect of camp meeting on her peripatetic life:

> My dad was a chaplain in the Airforce. And we moved around. I went to ten different schools. We lived all over the United States. But [Dad] would always try to get vacation time so we could come back for Camp Meeting. No matter where we were, we'd try to get back—from California twice, from Albany, Georgia, Illinois, California, Japan. And living in so many different homes and belonging to different chapels and churches, this was home. It was the only thing that was always permanent. That in itself was such a blessing. To see life continuing on. There's a healing feeling that you're not alone and no matter what happens during the year, you are loved and accepted, and God's going to love you and you're going to make it through.

Campers were eager to attest how long they had been coming to Salem, and continuity of attendance is a badge of honor at Salem. A young woman put it like this: "Well, I've been coming all my life. And my mom and her family and her mother and her family have been coming all their lives." Another said, "Well, I've been going to Salem for all my life, since I was a little baby, and my mom's been going since she was a little baby, and her mom's been going since she was a little baby. And so I've been going forever." Her identity at Salem is extended to her matrilineage. Here the emphasis is on how the camp meeting can define both an individual lifetime and the continuity of a chain family links, most commonly of mothers and daughters. It becomes the idiom of a "forever" identity.

For those marrying into the camp meeting, adapting to Salem presents unique challenges. Though the leadership of Salem is primarily male, recruitment into the campground often is through mothers. Adopting traditional domestic gender roles, women almost always cook, so any woman marrying into a family of tenters will likely solidify her camp meeting identity through her work in the kitchen. "The women who marry into it," said one lifelong tenter, "have to become a part of it because of what it is. The cooking and everything. It's expected of you. But I'm not sure that all the women who marry into it are very happy with it."

Men have a much more diffuse role at the campground, and other than helping to set up and close up the tent each year, they have less clearly marked functions. Some men who marry into Salem families don't take off from work during the meeting week, and they stay in their homes while their wives and children are at Salem. These men will often show up on "big Sunday," the last full day of the meeting, but otherwise remain relatively alienated from the camp meeting. One woman, a lifelong camper, admitted that "[my husband] didn't know what he was in for. He doesn't stay out here with me. He stays home. He comes out for Sunday lunch, and that's it. He never sleeps up here. Never. No. He likes his easy chair and the air conditioning and to sleep in his bed." Her sister echoed these tensions: "Neither did mine. As my husband said, 'You're going to take my asthmatic child into this barn?' This barn, this old hot barn. It's fun, though."

We filmed an interview with a young couple, Kristin and George, who were recently engaged. With some awkwardness, they discussed their different experiences of camp meeting. Kristin was a lifelong camper with a passionate attachment to Salem. Her fiancé, George, a relative newcomer, was more ambivalent.

K: Most of the people out here have known me since I was born. I've lived in Conyers my entire life. I've been out here my entire life. People here have known me forever. Every time I introduce George to someone here, they'll say "Oh, I've known Kristin since she was two years old." Or "I remember when she cried in the nursery." So it's real familiar. [to George] I mean, do you feel that? I guess you don't feel as comfortable as I do.

G: Probably not. Ummm. But I do feel very comfortable though. Ummm. I can just walk in there and take a nap. And then we'll just go and walk around and go into somebody else's tent.

K: I would love to raise a family out here. It's been such a big part of my life and of my memory that I want my kids to know the people who have had such a big effect on me and who I look up to.

G: [laughing nervously] I haven't heard about this before. . . . I'm just brought into this family, and, umm, I feel out of place at times. But everyone's so welcoming. It's hard to explain. Like, sleeping in the tent with all the other guys. I know I'm welcome there, but I really don't feel that comfortable sleeping with guys I don't know. They've all grown up together so they're like brothers.

K: But you're going to get like that. Twenty years down the road you'll be able to say, "I've known those kids since they were this high."

As a religious revival tradition, camp meetings allow campers to share and renew their faith with fellow Christians. As a ritual of social revitalization and reconnection, camp meeting exploits the power of the family idiom to emphasize extended family identity over nuclear family and to reinforce a kind of spiritual kinship among all campers. Psychologically, the camp meeting can be thought of as a kind of identity updating. Here you can compare yourself and your kids to photos of relatives and ancestors. You can look in the mirror to see yourself now and then look at the photos of yourself from years back. People can examine handprints or height markers on the walls they made decades ago. Sitting on the porch, you can see your grandchildren doing precisely what you did when you were their age.

Camp meeting plays tricks with your sense of time. The unchanging look and feel of the place and the stability of the events blunt the perception of passing time. At the same time, it offers a framework of changing roles to help campers update their identities, realizing who they are now. In other words, identity is updated at the same time as it is blurred. This paradox of passing time is central to the power of camp meeting.

Race Relations

One dimension of camp meeting remains to be discussed: the issue of race. Salem Camp Meeting developed as a ritual in the heart of the Bible Belt. The counties from which it draws its members are also in the heart of the Cotton Belt, where, before emancipation, slave labor was central to the local economy. The racial composition of Newton County is currently 40 percent black and 53 percent white. Neighboring Rockdale County's black population makes up 45 percent of the total, 5 percent more than its white population. The complex, tragic history of race relations has always been a central factor in the life of these counties, though it is now largely hidden from view. Many black families in these counties are descendants of slaves who, until emancipation, were owned by local white families. While both counties have experienced dramatic population growth, as newcomers have moved in from the Atlanta metropolitan area, this history of slavery is never far from the surface of race relations despite almost two centuries of emancipation. One cannot discuss any institution in Georgia without taking race relations into account.

After the Civil War, black churches, particularly in the Carolinas, initiated revival meetings for their members modeled on the camp meeting tradition. But like most religious institutions in the South, the camp meeting tradition reproduced the historic racial divide. It is hard not to notice that Salem Camp Meeting is an almost exclusively white institution. In the modern South, black visitors and speakers occasionally participate in religious gatherings and are welcomed to all services. But none of the regular campers are black, Hispanic, or Asian. The "family feeling" that campers comment on is in part a product of its class and racial homogeneity.

Traditionally, black people did participate in the camp meeting, but as workmen, maids, and cooks. One camper reminisced about the years when she didn't have to cook at Salem, saying that "we used to have a lady that would cook for us, and I don't know how she did it. When my sister's children were little, mother's lady Elizabeth that helped her, she would come and cook for us. But she's getting up in her seventies, and it's too hot for her to be back here. But it used to be a big tradition that there would be women who would come and cook." Even today, when most families no longer bring black domestic workers to help them during the camp meeting, a few black cooks who have worked for the families for generations will come to help prepare meals, especially on Big Sunday just before the camp meeting ends.

At the time of our research, the Salem Hotel employed a black cook named Ruth, who had worked there for over fifty years. When we interviewed her, she droned through the long list of all white men she worked for over the years at the hotel. "Then Mr. Jane came; I worked for him," she said. "Mr. Dimone came, I worked for him. Carbin (?) came, I worked for him. The Hamptons came; I worked for them. The Lewises came I worked for them, and then Hicks came, I worked for him." Then, turning to the food, she mused in a memorable slow drawl, "All we cook are string beans, butter beans, peas, okra—and chicken. We have chicken at every meal but breakfast." The only time I saw Ruth outside the hotel kitchen was when she performed in her church choir at one tabernacle prayer service.

Commemoration in a Major Key

Remembering together is as much a state of feeling as a state of mind. Like a symphony, commemorations unfold in a unique emotional key. As the photos throughout the chapter suggest, Salem Camp Meeting is played out in an unrelenting upbeat key. Upon entering the charmed circle of the campground, one is immediately struck by a pervasive sense of joy, calm, and nostalgia. This feeling, warm and welcoming, is really what the camp meeting is all about. Coming from a secular New York Jewish background, I didn't know what to expect when I first stepped onto the campground, camera and notebooks in hand. What would I discover here in the heart of the Bible Belt? Would I be accepted and welcomed, or would I be viewed as an unwelcome intruder?

While campers were used to having journalists visit the campground, an anthropologist was something different. I came to stay awhile, and camped out with them. They must have wondered what I was up to and what I would be writing about them. When, in 2005, the last year we attended the camp meeting, our just-completed documentary film about Salem was shown in the tabernacle one evening, the reception was very positive. I was relieved when campers asked how, as outsiders, we had managed to capture so well the feeling and the meaning of Salem. "That's our job, to capture the facts and the spirit of the meeting," I had answered.

Now, as I prepared to leave Salem for the last time, I walked over to the Kelly tent to say goodbye to Mary, one of the women with whom I had become friendly over the years. "Well," she said with a big smile, "Are you comin' back next year? Are you converted?" I was taken aback by the question. In all the time I spent at Salem, no one had ever even hinted at any intention to convert me until that moment. I replied that conversion was not part of my project, though I had come away from Salem with respect for the power of the campers' faith and gratitude for the way they had welcomed me into their community.

This one foot in, one foot out stance was how it always was for the anthropologist. My job was to discover the spirit of the camp meeting as it unfolded at Salem and reflect on what it means and does to its members. As is always the case, along the way, we had uncovered a number of tensions there, small cracks in the smooth surface of the place. While we explored these issues just as we explored the positive aspects of the gathering, we aimed to tell Salem's story accurately and account for the intense devotion of so many campers to the place. I think we did that.

During the many days I spent at Salem, I witnessed no family fights, saw no couples giving each other the cold shoulder, and heard no families badmouth each other. One got the feeling that, here at Salem, the Hatfields and the McCoys would have enthusiastically welcomed each other onto their porches. Whatever there was that might have challenged the spirit of good feeling at Salem was left to "out there" beyond the campground, or at least to the privacy of the tents' back rooms. The perfect performance of family fellowship for one week was the goal of Salem Camp Meeting, and from what I could tell, it worked. A nostalgic, if imaginary, vision of family revival was beautifully performed at Salem. The smooth enacting of family values is hardly surprising considering that camp meeting families have had almost two centuries of practice behind their ritual. That is why the camp meeting endures as an annual ritual and also why each performance cannot last for more than its allotted week. Like Disney World's nostalgic Main Street USA, the campground welcomes campers to a kind of Christian Magic Kingdom. And then, after a week, it ends until the next year.

The magic of Salem Camp Meeting is due, in significant part, to the fact that its membership is largely limited to "people like us." While the annual gathering is officially interdenominational, it nonetheless draws its members from a relatively homogeneous population: middle-class white Protestants (mostly Methodist and Presbyterian) originating in two counties in central Georgia. Family is its theme, and many campers were related to one another. But inevitably, life in Georgia gets more complicated when you factor in social difference, especially racial difference. And so, in the next chapter, we turn to a different kind of commemoration in the same part of Georgia. This commemoration unfolds in a minor key, involving the violent history of race relations not far from Salem. We turn to a form of ritual commemoration that speaks of history, not as nostalgia but as unresolved trauma.

8 Unforgettable: The Moore's Ford Lynching Reenactment

Death, be not proud, though some have called thee
Mighty and dreadful, for thou art not so;
For those whom thou think'st thou dost overthrow
Die not, poor Death, nor yet canst thou kill me.
—John Donne

Some people closest to a murder are anxious to forget it. But not everyone.
Consider the notorious case of the lynching of two young black couples at
the Moore's Ford Bridge in Georgia's Walton County back on a hot July day
in 1946. Some white residents of the prosperous town of Monroe, friends,
relatives, and descendants of the shooters, would have been relieved if
everyone would simply forget that the crime had ever happened. Some
might have even argued that, back then, it was not considered a crime for
a white man to kill black folks, especially if they had done something to
deserve it.

But not everybody is willing to forget. For over seventy years, many members of the county's black community, descendants, relatives, and friends of
the four victims, along with civil rights advocates across the United States,
have tried hard to make that lynching unforgettable. In this rural setting,
the long struggle for civil rights for the descendants of enslaved people
became a contest between forgetting and remembering the grim history of
lynching in America. In Georgia, the problem at hand was *this* lynching of
two young couples in their twenties, perhaps the most notorious case of
mass lynching in American history.

On July 25, 1946, at Moore's Ford Bridge, Roger Malcolm and his
common-law wife Dorothy Dorsey Malcolm, along with George Dorsey

and his wife Mae Murray (Roger's sister), were forced out of the car in which they were riding. They were shot to death by a volley of some sixty bullets by a mob of white men, near where the rickety bridge crossed the Apalachee River, some fifty miles east of Atlanta. Now, seventy-five years later, well-publicized cases of racially motivated killings, many recorded by ubiquitous cell phone cameras, suggest that the story of lynching in America is far from finished. In the case of the Moore's Ford lynching, it looks like the story will never be put to rest. Despite years of investigation by local police, the Federal Bureau of Investigation (FBI), and the state of Georgia, the men who shot the two couples have never been officially identified despite being unmasked at the time of the shooting. The murders created a sensation throughout the country. All the major newspapers featured the killings in their headlines, much to the embarrassment of white Georgians, especially those from Walton and neighboring Oconee counties. Georgia Governor Ellis Arnall had offered a $10,000 reward for information leading to the arrest of the shooters.

Despite the FBI's interviewing more than three thousand people over six months, no one confessed to participating in the shooting, and no witness was willing to come forward to identify the shooters. In December of 1946, a federal grand jury was convened to interview potential perpetrators and witnesses. Still, after three intense weeks of interviewing, the jury could not name any names with certainty. No one, black or white, would talk.

Despite the conspiracy of silence fueled by fear of reprisal by the perpetrators, the case has refused to die even though all the killers are now presumed dead. In 2001, Governor Roy Barnes reopened the Moore's Ford case for investigation by the Georgia Bureau of Investigation (GBI). Five years later, the FBI reopened their own case. But in 2015, the FBI once again closed it, unable to identify the perpetrators and convinced that, after sixty-nine years, none of the shooters were still alive to be prosecuted. The GBI gave up on its investigation in 2018, officially declaring the seventy-year-old mass lynching an unsolved crime. But the public has refused to forget. In 1997 Richard Rusk, the son of former Secretary of State Dean Rusk, along with a group of black and white citizens of Georgia, established the Moore's Ford Memorial Committee to seek ways to commemorate the lynching and work for racial justice in the state.

Funerals for George Dorsey and his sister Dorothy Dorsey Malcolm were held at the Mount Perry Baptist Church on July 28, 1946. Because of his military service, George's casket was draped with an American flag. They were both buried in unmarked graves at the cemetery adjoining the church. The funeral of Mae Murray Dorsey, George Dorsey's "wife" (some claimed they were never legally married), took place the same day at Tabernacle Baptist Church in Monroe, and she was buried in an unmarked grave next to her parents in Zion Hill Cemetery. Roger Malcolm, the original target of the lynching, was buried the day after the others in an unmarked grave next to the tiny Chestnut Grove Baptist Church near Hestertown where he had lived. Roger's funeral service was attended by just a handful of people.

Since the graves of all four lynching victims were unmarked, the committee's first project was to give the victims a clear identity, locating and marking with tombstones the graves where they were buried. Scholarships were created in the names of the victims in the hope that no one would ever forget their names. In 1999, on the fifty-third anniversary of the shootings, the committee worked with the Georgia Historical Society to place a historical marker commemorating the lynching on a prominent spot two-and-a-half miles from the shootings on State Highway 78, the main highway between Atlanta and Athens. Even though some four thousand lynchings have been documented for the United States, this was the first historical marker ever to acknowledge a lynching site. In 1999, the committee also organized a memorial service to honor George Dorsey, who had served in World War II.

In 2005 the Moore's Ford Memorial Committee organized the first of what would become an annual reenactment of the Moore's Ford lynching. The event was initiated by Tyrone Brooks, a member of the Georgia legislature and a well-known civil rights activist (figure 8.1). On July 24, 2021, I attended the seventeenth annual Moore's Ford reenactment accompanied by Mark Auslander, an anthropologist who has studied the Moore's Ford lynching and the history of black families in middle Georgia for over twenty years. I was prepared for a kind of elaborate street theater performance threading its way throughout Walton County, only thirty minutes from my home.

What I was not prepared for, however, was the emotional power of experiencing the reenactment up close. Behind every reenactment lies a story. Before describing the reenactment in detail, it is essential to clarify the events being reenacted and the social and political context of the lynchings.

Figure 8.1
Tyrone Brooks

The Backstory[1]

Just before 6 p.m. on July 25, 1946, at the Moore's Ford Bridge, twenty-nine-year-old Roger Malcolm, his common-law wife Dorothy, and another young couple, Mae Dorsey and her husband George, were all forced from a car driven by a wealthy white farmer named Loy Harrison. At this spot in central Georgia, where the rickety bridge spanned the Apalachee River at the line separating Walton and Oconee Counties, the couples found themselves face-to-face with twenty white men armed with revolvers and shotguns. Within minutes, all four of them would be tied up and shot to death at point-blank range on a field near the bridge. As previously mentioned, seventy-five years later, the identity of the lynching party remains a mystery even though the killers were all local men and none were masked. The Moore's Ford lynching, among the last and worst mass lynching in American history, has survived both as an almost mythical story and as an annual ritual reenactment.

The events leading up to the lynching start two weeks before the shooting when, on July 11, Roger had stabbed Barnette Hester, a white farmer, during a fight over Roger's wife, Dorothy. Roger and Barnette had grown up together as agemates and playfellows on the Hester family farm in Hesterville, where the Malcolms had lived as tenant farmers. A year earlier, Roger's family had been moved off the farm by Barnette's older brother Weldon, who no longer needed their labor. But Barnette needed help on his farm down the road from his brother, and he let Roger and Dorothy move into a tenant house on his property.

Roger worked as a day laborer in the fields, while Dorothy helped Barnette and his wife with cooking, house cleaning, and childcare. Though they had grown up as playmates, there was no missing the wide social gap between the two young men. The Hesters were white landowners, while the Malcolms were poor black tenant farmers, the Hesters' tenants and employees.

The relationship between Roger and his old playmate Barnette had become strained. Roger had left his legal wife Mattie Louise (Mack) and taken up with Dorothy, with whom he now lived in a common-law marriage. Though Roger was still legally wed to Mattie, Dorothy called herself Mrs. Roger Malcolm. Some in the county said that Dorothy was a "fast girl" who flirted with both white and black men. Roger had heard gossip that Dorothy was sleeping with one of the Hester brothers. He had grown increasingly suspicious of Dorothy, and the couple fought frequently. On July 11, Roger and Dorothy were at each other once again. Having had enough of what he assumed was Dorothy's fooling around, Roger planned to leave town and head north to Chicago, alone. Some say that Dorothy was pregnant, though the evidence is unclear. Still, in the reenactment, she is always portrayed as very pregnant.

On the morning of July 11, Roger had stormed out of the house and gone to buy a bottle of bootleg liquor, which he took to the home of a friend, Alleen Brown. The more he drank, the angrier he became, accusing Dorothy of sleeping around with a white man. Eventually, fueled in part by the alcohol, he worked himself into such a frenzy of anger that he grabbed a knife, saying he was going after Dorothy. Alleen tried to stop him, but Roger was determined. Returning to his house, Roger lunged at Dorothy with a pocketknife. Dorothy was quick on her feet and managed to evade the knife blade, fleeing the house, followed by Roger wielding his knife.

Hearing the commotion, Barnette came out of his house. Seeing what was going on, Barnette placed himself between Roger and Dorothy just in time for Roger's knife to pierce his chest just below the heart. Gravely hurt, Barnette stumbled into his house where his father Bob and his wife had been looking on. Initially, neither Barnette's wife nor his father realized that Barnette had been stabbed until he fell to the floor and they caught sight of his bloody wound. With the help of Barnette's older brother Weldon, the Hesters carried Barnette to their car and set out for the local hospital in Monroe.

As the car pulled out, Barnette's father called out the car window to one of his nephews who had arrived at the scene, telling him to get Roger, who had fled into a nearby cornfield, explaining that Roger had stabbed Barnette. Confronted in the cornfield by the Hesters, Roger dropped his knife and gave himself up. The Hesters bound Roger's hands and feet and waited for the arrival of the two Walton County deputy sheriffs. Roger was untied, handcuffed, and taken to the local jail in Monroe's courthouse, where he awaited trial. His bail was set at $600.

Roger had never before been in jail, but he knew enough to fear that he would not get out alive. In those days, a black man stabbing his white boss and landlord was considered by some a lynching crime. Roger was rightly scared for his life. The Hesters feared that Barnette would not survive the attack. Though seriously wounded, Barnette did slowly recover from the stabbing. He was eventually released from the hospital and sent home. Though he survived, Barnette would suffer the effects of the stab wound for the rest of his life.

On July 25, two weeks after the stabbing, Roger was released from jail on bail. The $600 bond was paid by Loy Harrison, a local wealthy cotton farmer. A big, powerfully built man at six feet tall and 275 pounds, Loy had a notoriously bad temper. People knew better than to get in his way. Loy had become rich mainly through selling the bootleg liquor produced by several stills on his farm. He was always in need of extra farmhands, and bailing out prisoners like Roger was a common means of recruiting free labor since freed prisoners would work to pay off their debt.

But something did not make sense about Loy's offer of bail. When Loy had first been approached by Roger's wife Dorothy and her brother George, he had refused to bail Roger out of jail, claiming that he just wasn't a reliable worker. The Malcolms had tried to borrow the bail money from another wealthy white landowner in the county, but he had also refused. So, days later, out of options, they went back to Loy and asked him a second time. Surprisingly, this time he accepted and paid Roger's $600 bail bond. Roger was relieved since he believed he would be safe from lynching on Loy's farm. Loy was an intimidating man, and no one would dare step on his land without permission. Still, people wondered why Loy had changed his mind about paying the bond. Though it has never been proven, some are convinced he was in on the lynching to this day.

Loy headed for Monroe to pay Roger's bond and take him back to his farm. In the car were Roger's sister Mae Malcolm Dorsey, her husband George, and Roger's common-law wife, Dorothy. He stopped at the sheriff's office to pay the bond. They all drove over to the jail to pick up Roger at around 5:00 p.m., and by 5:30, they were all heading back to Loy's farm across the Apalachee River in Oconee County. As Loy's car approached the Moore's Ford Bridge, they noticed a vehicle following them. Then they saw three cars parked on the far side of the bridge.

A group of four or five white men stepped out from behind the parked cars and blocked the road across the bridge. Then another more extensive group of armed white men appeared. When Loy's car had come to a stop, the mob called for Roger to get out of the vehicle. They opened the back door, pulled Roger out onto the road, and tied him up. Seeing George in the front seat, they decided they would take him as well. George and Roger were tied up together and taken to a field just off the road and down a hill.

Roger's wife Dorothy, still in the car's back seat, started screaming. When she yelled that she recognized one of the men, they decided to take her along with George's wife, Mae. There was no point leaving any witnesses who could identify the killers. All four were eventually bound together with rope and shot dead by a barrage of more than sixty bullets in the field near the bridge. Loy was left untouched. The bodies of the four victims were left on the field. Quickly, the mob got back in the cars and sped off.

Political Ramifications

The events described above occurred just one day before a crucial Democratic gubernatorial primary election in Georgia. The two events were closely linked. The leading contenders for the Democratic nomination for governor were James V. Carmichael, an Atlanta attorney, a businessman, and a political moderate, and Eugene Talmadge, who had been governor for two consecutive terms from 1933 to 1937 and a third term from 1941 to 1944. Now he was seeking a fourth term in the governor's mansion. Talmadge, a populist who campaigned on supporting rural white farmers, was an ardent racist and white supremacist who had bragged about reading Hitler's *Mein Kampf* seven times. Though a Democrat, Talmadge hated President Franklin Roosevelt and his New Deal policies that sought to raise wages in the South. Talmadge had argued that this would destroy the South's reputation as a low-wage state and discourage employers from moving to Georgia.

Even though Georgia had ratified the Fifteenth Amendment to the Constitution in 1870 that prohibited denying the vote to citizens "on the basis of race or color," the black vote continued to be suppressed in Georgia by various forms of intimidation and by a long tradition of white-only primary elections by Georgia's Democratic Party. Since Georgia was effectively a one-party state, Republican candidates having little chance of winning statewide office, the Democratic primaries effectively decided the winners of statewide elections. In 1942, former Georgia attorney general Ellis Arnall had run against Eugene Talmadge with the slogan "Eliminate the Dictator" and had won the governorship. Taking office in 1943, Arnall proved to be a reformer and, for a Georgia governor, something of a liberal, abolishing the poll tax and revoking the charter of the Ku Klux Klan.

Most significant for expanding voting rights was the 1945 court case *King v. Chapman*. On July 4, 1944, Primus E. King, a registered black voter, attempted to cast his vote at the Columbus, Georgia, courthouse in the state's Democratic Party's primary election. When he was turned away by the police, who claimed it was a white-only election, King filed a lawsuit in federal court. A landmark ruling found in Mr. King's favor, ruling that the denial of black voters' right to cast their ballots was unconstitutional. The US Court of Appeals affirmed the decision, and when, on April 4, 1946, the US Supreme Court refused to hear J. E. Chapman's appeal, the white primary in Georgia was officially outlawed. The upcoming gubernatorial primary election would be the first real test of the black voter's right to participate in a primary.

Eugene Talmadge was a skilled orator and a savvy campaigner. For example, he hired a man who looked like his main competition, James Carmichael, to tour the state accompanied by two well-dressed cigar-smoking black men, reminding white Georgians that a vote for Carmichael was a vote for empowering black politicians. There was nothing subtle about his white supremacist message. On June 28, Talmadge and his entourage visited Monroe where he spoke from a platform on the courthouse steps: "My opponents say it is the law—that you have to let the Negroes vote. They say I've stirred up the issue. But I ask you, who brought forth that Supreme Court decision making it possible for Negroes to ride by the side of white people on buses?"[2]

Talmadge's entire campaign appealed to white fears that racial equality would inevitably mean a loss of white supremacy in Georgia. While it was never proven, it was rumored that Talmadge had a role in planning the Moore's Ford lynching, a chilling possibility that had the effect of intimidating black voters. The lynching took place the day before the primary election in an atmosphere of intense anxiety among many white farmers in Georgia about the potential rise of black political power. Though the Supreme Court had guaranteed the black population of Walton County the right to vote in a primary election, hardly any black votes were cast in the county the day after the biggest mass lynching in Georgia history. Local fear and intimidation had proven more potent than federal law.

Talmadge eventually lost the popular vote to Carmichael by around sixteen thousand votes. Nonetheless, he still won the primary since he had won the majority of counties in Georgia, including Walton County. Traditional voter suppression techniques meant that an estimated fifty thousand black votes had gone uncounted. Georgia's Democratic primary was governed by a "county unit" voting system modeled on the federal Electoral College. Each county was allocated a certain number of county unit votes, which went to the top vote-getter in a primary election. While the unit votes were allocated based on population, they did not come close to reflecting the actual population differences between counties. This meant that each vote in the heavily populated urban counties was ultimately worth much less than each vote in Georgia's rural counties. For example, while Atlanta's Fulton County had sixteen times the population of Walton County, it had only three times as many county unit votes.[3] Effectively, one vote in Walton County was worth more than five votes in Fulton County. The voting system was clearly rigged to favor rural counties in the same way that the Electoral College favors rural states. So despite losing the popular vote, Eugene Talmadge was able to handily beat his liberal rival in the decisive county unit votes. He won the primary and eventually went on to win another term as governor.[4]

Ritual Reenactment

Since 2005, due in significant part to the efforts of civil rights leader Tyrone Brooks, the Moore's Ford lynching has been commemorated by an annual reenactment of the murders performed on or close to the anniversary of the original lynching. I attended the seventeenth annual reenactment on July 24, 2021, and photographed the entire event. Some of these photos will accompany my account of the reenactment. I have laid out the story behind the reenactment in some detail to provide readers with a historical context for it and to help readers see how a ritual reenactment differs from the history it is supposed to stage. While reenactment rituals present themselves as historical recreations, they have their own constraints and goals, which are often somewhat different from those of a historian.

Famous battles and events have been subject to reenactment since at least the time of the Romans, who staged reenactment battles as public spectacles in amphitheaters. Christian religious pageants have featured reenactments of famous scenes from the Bible, such as the famous tradition in Oberammergau, Germany of reenacting the crucifixion of Christ in a passion play every ten years since 1684. Most popular since the nineteenth century have been reenactments of scenes from famous battles. It is interesting to note that reenactments seem to favor recreations of famous scenes involving violence and death, which raises the question of whether reenactments serve as a way for performers and audience to simultaneously experience violence and death and "tame" it as a performance. In the late nineteenth century in the United States, Civil War veterans started to stage reenactments of famous battles. Most notable, perhaps, was the reenactment of scenes from the Battle of Gettysburg by both Union and Confederate veterans on the fiftieth anniversary of the battle in 1913. A new wave of Civil War reenactments followed from the Civil War Centenary celebrations starting in 1961 and have remained popular to this day.

During the early years of the Moore's Ford reenactment, the organizers placed ads on Facebook to recruit actors. At first, they could not locate any white actors willing to take the roles of the lynching mob. In the early years, black actors donned white masks to play the parts. Eventually, white actors were recruited for the roles, but they often reported feeling extreme discomfort at the idea of playing the role of lynchers. In addition to recruiting local actors for the reenactment, a professional director is in charge of the performance. Cassandra Greene has directed the Moore's Ford reenactment for over a decade.

There is a script for the reenactment, and rehearsals start every year in June. With a script, actors, and a director, reenactments seem to be more of a theatrical performance than a ritual and represent a challenge to precise classification. The line between theater and ritual is often thin, and in the case of reenactments, it is permeable. As a scripted dramatic performance, the reenactment is a kind of theater, in this case movable street theater, following the path of the events it attempts to recreate. But in its intentions to powerfully transform the consciousness of both actors and onlookers, annually commemorate the victims and the events of the lynching, and cultivate social memory of events with contemporary significance, the Moore's Ford reenactment is also very much a ritual of remembrance.

As movable theater, the Moore's Ford reenactment unfolds as several distinct acts in different places. Here is how the 2021 reenactment was organized.

I. Organizers' Welcome at the First African Baptist Church in Monroe

Organizers first welcomed guests to the seventeenth annual More's Ford reenactment. There were only about sixty in attendance this year because of the pandemic. In past years the reenactment could attract hundreds of viewers. While most of the audience were black, it included a handful of white viewers, including several reporters and photographers. While guests were being welcomed, a final rehearsal by performers was taking place inside the church hall.

II. Pilgrimage to the Burial Sites of the Four Victims

This was the longest part of the reenactment ritual. A motorcade of cars traveled to the three rural cemeteries where the victims were buried. Though the graves had been previously unmarked, the Moore's Ford Memorial Committee had located the likely gravesites and erected headstones for each victim. The tombstones of George Dorsey and his sister Dorothy are next to each other at the cemetery at Mount Perry Baptist Church (figure 8.2). A special plaque honoring George Dorsey's military service was placed near his grave. Roger Malcolm was buried at a small cemetery next to the Chestnut Grove Church in Hestertown. George's wife Mae Dorsey was buried at Zion Hill Cemetery. At each site, a relative or descendant of the deceased victim addressed the crowd of onlookers, expressing appreciation

Figure 8.2
The tombstones of George Dorsey and his sister Dorothy

for the long-overdue acknowledgment of their relative and discussing their relationship to the lynching victim.

III.   Stabbing of Barnette Hester by Roger Malcolm

This scene was performed outside the Monroe County Courthouse rather than on Barnette Hester's farm in Hestertown. In the reenactment, Barnette is played by a burly older man, while historically, he was a slim man of twenty-nine, the same age as Roger. Barnette is depicted as attacking Roger, while historically, he was stabbed while trying to protect Dorothy from Roger's knife (figure 8.3). Dorothy is played as in the late stages of pregnancy. Some earlier versions of the reenactment had the killers cutting her baby from her body. While there is no decisive evidence that Dorothy was pregnant at the time of the lynching, her pregnancy and the death of her baby have become an important part of the reenactment story.

IV.   Eugene Talmadge's Speech on the Courthouse Steps

Talmadge is accurately portrayed as a powerful speaker, warning white farmers that a vote for his Democratic rival would be a vote to empower black voters and end white supremacy.

Figure 8.3
Reenactment of the stabbing of Barnette Hester

V. Black Voters Attempt to Vote at Monroe Courthouse on Primary Election Day

This scene depicts several black voters being intimidated by white citizens as they attempt to enter Monroe Courthouse to vote. While it effectively high- lights the challenges that black voters faced, it does not reveal that numerous black voters actually voted for Eugene Talmadge because of fear of reprisals if they voted against him. Voter suppression took many forms in Georgia.

VI. Bailing Roger Malcolm Out of Jail

Roger exits the jail at the back of the courthouse, comes down the stairs, and gets in Loy Harrison's car. In the 2021 reenactment, the stress was on the authenticity of props, and they had found a 1947 Mercury that was in working condition. For many years the reenactment used a 1955 Lincoln Town Car belonging to a local man. That vehicle was not in reliable run- ning condition, but the owner was able to get the engine going for the reenactment. Eventually, they had to find another car, so they opted for a closer match to the original vehicle. Dorothy, George, and Mae climb into the car with Roger and Loy, and they drive off, headed toward Loy's farm.

VII. Loy Harrison's Car Arrives at Moore's Ford

As Loy's car heads out of Monroe toward the Moore's Ford Bridge, some ten miles away, the audience heads for the bridge in a motorcade, accompanied

Figure 8.4
Loy Harrison's car arriving at Moore's Ford Bridge

by a local police car. It is hardly surprising that the reenactment is not universally welcomed by the white population in the county as it serves as a reminder of an event many of them would rather forget. The motorcade will pass several farms of families who have a history of open hostility to the reenactment. So since the first reenactment, local police have accompanied the motorcade as it travels throughout the county, which sometimes produces ironic smiles from the audience.

The car carrying the two couples does not go straight to the bridge since they will await the audience's arrival before making their entrance at the scene of the shootings. Arriving at the bridge, onlookers see a car parked at the far end of the bridge and a group of white reenactors milling about, waiting for their cue to start the confrontation scene. As the car approaches the bridge, the white mob lines up to block it from crossing the bridge (figure 8.4).

Roger is pulled from the car, and a rope is placed around his neck. Then the mob decides to take George as well, and he is also tied up. When Dorothy screams that she recognizes one of the mob leaders, the two women are also pulled from the car screaming (figure 8.5). Bound together with rope,

Figure 8.5
The two couples being pulled from the car and tied up

the two couples now realize what will happen. The audience, milling about chatting with each other as they awaited the arrival of the car, grows tense and grim as they face the "reality" of what they are witnessing.

VIII.   The Shootings in the Field

The four captives are taken down to a field near the bridge, where the mob shoots them (figure 8.6). Standing at a distance from the events is a black woman in a brightly colored long dress and bearing a walking stick. She represents the griot, the traveling poet and storyteller figure from West African tradition and the keeper of local history (figure 8.7). She sings Billie Holliday's heartbreaking song "Strange Fruit," recalling the tragic history of lynchings in America.

IX.   Postmortem: The Reenactors Mingle with the Audience

One of the strangest moments of the reenactment ritual, what I call the "postmortem," occurs as the reenactors slowly emerge from their roles when the performance ends (figure 8.8). The white actors who play the parts of the lynch mob relax their performing posture and start to chat

Figure 8.6
The shootings in the field

with the audience. The black actors who were just "dead" on the field open their eyes and slowly stand up, dazed from the intensity of their experience and slowly return to life as actors rather than characters. The experience of emerging from their roles must be quite different for white and black performers. For the white actors playing the lynchers, their everyday identities as committed opponents of racism are deeply opposed to the roles they played. For several hours they have lived in the skin of the black man's other, on the same site where white men had committed a famous atrocity. But, emerging from their despised "white man roles," they remain white men.

Coming out of role is inevitably different for the black actors since the historical event they have just enacted is still with us (figure 8.9). No longer known as lynching, it has been reborn as police brutality and killings that have produced Black Lives Matter. Assuming their ordinary lives as black folks must present a performer's paradox in which the "reality" to which they return is not so different from the one they have just lived (and died) through. Though they have theoretically left behind their characters, all the reenactors remain in their costumes. The clothes of the four black

Figure 8.7
Bearing witness

Figure 8.8
Back from the dead

Figure 8.9
Coming out of role

victims are still covered with blood, and the white actors are still carrying their guns. The effect is a strange blend of fiction and fact, past and present. It is a disturbing experience.

X.   Return to the Church in Monroe for a Meal and Fellowship

Some of the audience and most of the reenactors return to the fellowship hall of the First African Baptist Church in Monroe for refreshments and conversation.

Discussion

The ritual of reenactment is not precisely the same as the reenactment itself. The *reenactment ritual* includes several events (I, II, and IX) not within the reenactment. While the reenactment purports to be a kind of enacted history, the scenes are not entirely faithful to the chronology or the setting of the events they dramatize. For instance, the tour of the burial sites precedes the dramatization of the killings. Moreover, the voting in the election dramatization preceding the massacre scene actually took place the day after the lynching. And finally, Roger Malcolm's stabbing of Barnette Hester that is represented as occurring outside the Monroe Courthouse actually occurred on the Hester farm in Hestertown, about six miles from Monroe. Roger Malcolm's stabbing of Barnette Hester is presented as a direct attack on Hester rather than as an accidental stabbing of the man while he was trying to intercede in Roger's attack on wife. Theatrical effectiveness sometimes trumps historical accuracy in the ritual.

We have an adaptation of a history at once theatrical and political, not an attempt to present a perfectly accurate replay of that history. Some of these liberties with historical accuracy are convenient ways to compress a complex stream of events in both time and space. Less interested in the accuracy of the details, the director of the reenactment emphasized important moral or political points that are to be remembered by those participating in and watching the ritual.

A lot of the historical detail and context is left out so that attention can be focused on key themes: the key events leading up to the lynching, the identities of the victims, the vulnerability of black people in small-town Georgia at the time to arbitrary white violence, the reality of race-based voter suppression, the status differences between white and black people, the constant intimidation and humiliation suffered by black people at the hands of their white employers and landlords, and the continuing relevance of the lynching in the contemporary US. This is how myth differs from history, focusing instead on essential truths, often at the expense of historical detail. Ritual theater can take a complex history and produce a powerful and enduring myth.

Whereas we usually think of theatrical dramas as entertainment, no one who acts in or observes reenactments would consider reenactment as entertainment. The performances rarely achieve the skill level of professional theater and often include amateur actors. Moreover, the attitude of all participants is one of solemn reflection rather than aesthetic enjoyment. A reenactment may be based on history, but it is not always intended as an historically accurate account. Reenactments are rituals, a way of remembering and experiencing the past. Rituals have a life of their own.

The Moore's Ford lynching reenactment creates a uniquely powerful experience for the participants, but the experience is inevitably a bit different depending on the role one plays. The actors are not only playing their roles for the audience. Some might well choose to perform the reenactment even if no audience showed up since they are playing their parts to understand better what it must have felt like to be a black victim of the lynching or a white member of the lynching mob back in 1946. Indeed, in the early years of the reenactment, when no white actors could be found to play the lynch mob roles, some of the black actors playing the parts of the white men reported feeling temporarily charged up by the feeling of power that their guns and white masks had lent them. In an excellent essay discussing the role of contact with objects from the past in reenactment dramas, Mark Auslander quotes one black reenactor's vivid experience of empowerment when he donned the white mask in a Moore's Ford reenactment.

> To this day, a number of the African American performers shudder as they recall the experience of wearing the white mask and "becoming" Klansmen. Jerome states, "All my life I wondered how anyone could do something so ungodly, so terrible, as participate in a lynching. . . . Well, when I put on that mask, something strange happened, something terrible I could say, that taught me something. Something I wish I'd never learned. . . . You know, it is a terrible thing to say but being a Klan . . . it was kind of a rush. A thrill . . . we were shouting and screaming and beating on them all together, and there was a part of me that felt

excited, felt so angry, felt like I could do anything . . . never knew I had that in me." (Auslander 2013, p. 175)

In this reaction of a black actor assuming the role of the oppressor, we see a variation on what's known as Stockholm syndrome, where captives come to identify with their captors. None of the white actors reported experiencing the same rush, and if they did, none were willing to acknowledge it. Still, assuming the role of a member of the lynching party would inevitably create a complex and paradoxical experience for the white actors being forced to take a role appropriate to their appearance. No one could play such a role without being deeply affected by the experience.

For the black actors playing the black victims, the experience would be quite different. Here they would be forced to "play" a role for which they had been prepared not just by their appearance but also by their own experience of life in a society where racism is still very much in play. There was no role contradiction but only a chance to experience the extreme intensification of a set of feelings that had likely been with them their entire lives. Look at the faces in figures 8.8 and 8.9. Here the black actors playing the victims are just coming out of their roles after the performance. One can see their dazed and confused expressions as the actors, who minutes before had been "dead on the ground," attempt to reclaim their "real" selves and figure out what that means.

Finally, there is the audience. We could view the action up close since there is no stage or curtain, no fourth wall to separate the audience from the action. There is little of the usual symbolic apparatus of theater to assure us that this is "just play." This absence of framing devices creates an ambiguous space for what I call *marginal play*—performances where the boundaries between the real and the unreal are blurred to powerful effect (Shore 1996, chapter 4). After all, this is the actual place, the ground where the killings had occurred. Though you can't see it, there's black blood on that ground. And while no one would want to interfere with the performance, you could come up close to the action and step into the scene.

I could easily step into the scene. I had no problem photographing the action from in close. Nor was I kept from standing over the "dead" bodies after the shooting.[5] The effect on the audience was palpable, especially once the violence began. But once again, it must have been a somewhat different experience for black viewers and white audience members. For black observers, the reenactment must have brought home some terrifying truths with a rare intensity. For our part, we white audience members could not escape the awareness that, whatever our politics, we were in a world where skin color matters, watching an image of ourselves as the oppressor. It was a shattering experience on every level. It was no play that we were watching, but, like Hamlet's play *The Mousetrap*, we found ourselves caught unexpectedly in a powerful ritual of remembrance in which we were all implicated (Shore 2022, chapter 1). The reenactment ritual was not just memorable. It was unforgettable.

9 Ritual Baseball

Performance Frames

By now it should be clear that ritual is an unsteady category, a kind of behavior that is often on the verge of slipping off into something else. Consider how actions become rituals. Ordinary behavior can gain weight, gradually taking on the feel of a ritual through repetition and the addition of new layers of meaning. In this way, we get "quasi rituals," acts that are "sort of" rituals, ritual in the making. In other cases, the ambiguity is a matter of perspective. A ritual can look like theater to an audience while it is experienced as a ritual by the participants. For observers, a reenactment such as the performance at Moore's Ford described in the last chapter might be considered street theater since it is scripted, rehearsed, and there's an audience. Still, experiencing the reenactment is more than just a theatrical performance. It is also ritual remembrance. Ambiguities like these are inherent in all performances.

In this chapter, we explore a different categorization problem: when games—in this case, baseball—reveal a hidden ritual dimension.[1] We will consider the ritual possibilities in the performance of team sports. But before we head to the ballpark, we need to consider what makes something "a performance." Performances are "framed behavior," constrained and intensified behavior patterns rising above ordinary action. As we noted, performance is a sequence of behavior that "pops." Performances come in many forms, and we can usually tell them apart. For example, we have no problem distinguishing a birthday party from a wedding or a play from a basketball game even though they are all performances.

But performances can easily produce category confusion. While there are fundamental distinctions between different kinds of performances, performance genres like ritual, theater, and games are rarely neatly separated, and performances often turn out to be a mix of genres. Performance artists often exploit these ambiguities, as when a theater group does street theater or breaks the theater's fourth wall to bring the audience into the performance. Sports promoters enhance the entertainment value of a sporting event like the Super Bowl by introducing a musical performance or a theatrical spectacle into the halftime break. Any given performance will fall somewhere along a spectrum of genres, emphasizing different aspects of performance. More often than we realize, distinct performance genres can overlap, producing hybrid performances.

To announce itself, a performance usually employs boundary markers to signal its beginning and end. The markers define "a performance frame," announcing that we are no longer experiencing ordinary behavior. For example, theatrical performances use stages, curtains, the dimming of lights, and exaggerated "theatrical" speech and action to signal the start of a play. Curtain closure or the brightening of lights will often mark its end. We usually recognize these cues, and they alert us that the framed action is to be understood as "a play." Public rituals also declare themselves by special markers of space, time, dress, and language. For instance, in the context of a courtroom, the judge's black robes would not usually be interpreted as a theatrical prop but as ritual dress (unless the courtroom scene were taking place on a theater stage). Spectator sports are also framed by special frame markers. Unique spaces, uniforms, the sound of a whistle, or the playing of a national anthem all signal that the ensuing behavior is within a "game frame." Until the officials or the clock signal the end of play, conduct on the field is governed, not by everyday behavioral norms but by "the rules of the game."

Humans are skilled at reading these frame cues to distinguish different kinds of behavior and prepare appropriate responses. A courtroom becomes a ritual space when the bailiff utters the ritual words, "All rise. The court is now in session, presided over by the Honorable [name]." Everyone stands up as a judge in black robes enters and sits on a raised platform. An American wedding ceremony will usually be marked by the playing of special music and a procession rhythmically "processing" down the aisle. As the music signals the start of the ceremony, the audience quiets down and prepares to stand at the bride's entrance. No one would question the fact that the wedding has now begun. Despite the many variations on the wedding ritual in contemporary culture, these markers are almost always present. Wedding guests usually know that they have entered the wedding frame. Another example of framed behavior is the classroom. In many cultures, a class at school will begin when the teacher enters the classroom, and the students stand and greet the teacher in unison with a ritual greeting. This ceremony marks the beginning of classroom behavior. Members of a community are expected to understand and respond appropriately to these frame markers.[2]

Because performance frames always exist along a sliding scale of types, performance is often ambiguous. To keep things simple, we usually ignore the ambiguities and choose a conventional frame to label a hybrid performance. A wedding is a ritual, we assure ourselves, not a theatrical performance. But some weddings feel more theatrical than others. Since it is a kind of performance, ritual is inherently a spectrum phenomenon, differing only in degree from its cousins.[3] How we choose to label it is often a matter of convention and emphasis.

Fortunately, we can look for cues to decide what kind of performance frame we are in. For example, we think of *theater* when behavior is organized by a script and includes performance conventions that stress the separation of players (on stage), technical personnel (backstage), and an audience. While watching a play, we also assume the goal is to make us forget that the action is scripted and pretend that we are watching a slice of real life. In its reliance on scripted action, theater is similar to *ritual*. But while modern theater strives to make this "scriptedness" disappear, ritual stresses the script as a script, foregrounding the weightiness of the actions as a sign of their sacredness.[4]

In theater, actors are trained to reembody their roles with their interpretations, using their acting skills to convince the audience that they are not acting. Moreover, while rituals often strive for perfect repetition, every performance of the same play can be different, bringing an old script new life. In theater, the script is backgrounded in favor of the illusion of authentic events, convincing the audience to "suspend disbelief," pretending that the staged action is really happening. There is always room for improvisation. Directors can play with the script, and each production offers a new possibility of producing a unique theatrical event. This suspension of disbelief central to theater is why Shakespeare can playfully begin *Romeo and Juliet* with an apparent "spoiler" sonnet giving away the play's plot. Of course,

Shakespeare is not intending to spoil the play for the audience. He is challenging gifted actors and directors to convince the audience to forget that they know the ending and enter the space of the play with heart and hope.

Like ritual and theater, games are also performance frames. But they use the rules of the game to produce unpredictable events. A fully scripted game is considered "fixed" (think of the scandal of a fixed boxing match or horse race) and is usually illegal. But even here, there are ambiguities of genre. Wrestling promotors can get away with "fixing" matches by claiming that matches are not really sports but a kind of theater.

When spectators watch a game, they usually take the rules for granted. Fans want action. They are not interested in how the rules produce runs, touchdowns, pass plays, three-pointers, goals, aces, winners, and losers. Unless the rules are violated and the violation influences the outcome, fans are generally less interested in the rules and more focused on *strategies* of play—how players and teams orchestrate those rules to their advantage. Games are all about the events they produce, winners and losers, offense and defense, the home team, and the away team. They unite people by dividing people. Thriving on the unpredictable, games produce strong emotions of hope and disappointment, loyalty, and opposition in players and fans alike.

How do games differ from rituals?[5] Like games, ritual is governed by rules of behavior. Every ritual has a script, just like a play. But the goal of a ritual is to produce a predictable outcome, not an unforeseen event. With ritual, attention is on the script's predictability and its meanings. Control and predictability are paramount. Rituals generally seek to avoid uncertain outcomes. Whereas games are organized to divide us, rituals seek to unite people in a comforting sense of repetition and stable order (Lévi-Strauss 1966). The sacred script is the heart of the ritual, not just a backdrop.

Baseball as Ritual

This chapter is an unusual look at baseball viewed as a ritual expressing fundamental American values (figure 9.1). People usually think of baseball as a game rather than a ritual. We know that a baseball game is full of minor rituals. Some players wear their lucky socks or special underwear for luck. Some batters kiss a crucifix before stepping up to the plate to bat. We've all seen pitchers who kiss the ball for good luck before throwing a pitch. We may dismiss these compulsive acts as superstitions, but they are genuine

Figure 9.1
Baseball nostalgia: America's national pastime. "Baseball at Night" by Moris Kantor by clankcycles is licensed under CC BY-NC-SA 2.0.

personal rituals intended to bring the player luck.[6] Baseball games also produce collective rituals. The game starts with a ritual singing of the national anthem, followed by the traditional call "play ball!" The opening of the baseball season, known as opening day, is celebrated by baseball fans as a holiday. In Cincinnati, where the Cincinnati Red Stockings played the first professional baseball game in 1889, opening day is celebrated by the Findlay Market Parade. The Cincinnati Reds always (re)play their opening day game at home to honor their history as the oldest professional team. Fans have created their own baseball rituals. Some arrive at the park sporting their team's uniform, bringing gloves to the game to try and catch a ball hit into the stands. The game even has its ritual snacks like hotdogs, nachos, Cracker Jacks, and beer consumed in the stands by spectators.[7]

Baseball fans love to try and participate in the game from the stands. They have their own ritual "wave" that periodically circles the stands, just as the players attempt to circle the bases. The wave allows fans to mimic the game on the field as they try to get it to complete the circuit of the stadium. It is no secret that baseball games have their fair share of ritual moments. But the action on the field is still the main event. This play produces winner and losers, altering team standings, shifting batters' batting averages and pitchers' ERA (earned run average) statistics. As a game, baseball is all about the action.

But suppose we become anthropologists of baseball for a moment. In that case, we can refocus our attention from the particular events of a baseball game to its more general forms and observe how baseball patterns time, space, and action. When we step back from the game's action and examine its more general forms, we realize that the game of baseball can also be understood as a ritual performance. We can see our national pastime in a new way, as *ritual baseball*. Viewed as ritual, baseball in its American form enacts important values and contradictions in American culture. Ritual baseball does not have winners and losers and lacks the thrill of play. Instead, in its rules and its handling of time and space, it stages a drama of profound cultural significance every time the game is played.

Admittedly, this deep dive into baseball's secret soul is not how we usually understand the sport. We are generally too interested in the "who does what" of the sport to consider the less obvious inner contours of the game. The ritual elements of baseball are built into the sport, silently shadowing the play. While most of us are not aware of the ritual shadows projected by the game, they have a powerful effect on how we respond to it. Ritual baseball is everywhere in the "feel" of the sport. It has shaped how baseball enters our larger cultural imagination.

Baseball Space

Take a close look at figure 9.2 below. The ritual spirit of baseball shines through in the very shape of its field. Comparing the baseball park to almost any other sports field suggests there is something very different about baseball. First, baseball is usually played in a field, giving the game a mythical pastoral setting. Almost every other playing field (e.g., football, basketball, table tennis, tennis, rugby) is rectangular and identical, with a line down the middle bisecting the rectangle into two halves. However, the baseball field is asymmetrical. And every field is different. This leads to

Figure 9.2
Oriole Park at Camden Yards. "Beautiful Night of Baseball at Oriole Park at Camden
Yards, LA Angels of Anaheim 11, Baltimore Orioles 6, Baltimore, Maryland" by Ken
Lund is licensed under CC BY-SA-2.0.

asymmetrically shaped baseball parks, closed and precisely measured out at
one end ("home") but open to the city and effectively unbounded at the
outfield end. While the infield begins at home plate, the outfield has no
designated boundary and is often designed to showcase the city beyond
the field as in the picture of Baltimore's Camden Yards in figure 9.2. This is
because the batter's goal is to hit a ball as far as possible, ideally out of the
park. This orchestration of space contrasts with other field sports, which
tend to feature closed symmetrical spaces with goals at either end of the
field.

The open-ended field of the ballpark gives baseball fields a distinctive
individuality. Angel's Stadium, Fenway Park, and Citi Field all have their
own dimensions and character. Measured along the foul lines from home
plate, a professional field must measure at least 250 feet, a distance that was
extended to 350 feet for fields built after 1958. Centerfield must extend at
least 400 feet on a line drawn from home plate through second base. But

those are minimums. There are no maximum distances, allowing teams to occasionally reconfigure their fields as a strategy favoring their pitching and batting talent. The irregular open-ended field gives baseball parks an individual personality and, as writer Tom Boswell put it, encourages "marrying your park to your team" (Boswell 1984, p. 65). We shall see that his metaphor of marriage is far from arbitrary in reference to baseball.

This asymmetrical and idiosyncratic playing field is not the only lopsided aspect of baseball. The game is structured from start to finish by odd numbers. Baseball is an odd sport in many ways. With an infield of three bases, an at bat lasting three strikes, a team of nine players, a normal game duration of nine innings, baseball might well have been named "oddball." The framing of game time is also uneven, replacing the quarters or halftimes of other sports with a seventh-inning stretch. You cannot have halftime in a game whose ending time cannot be predicted. While the game has a precise start, marked by the singing of the national anthem and the call "play ball," baseball's end, like the outfield itself, is left open, controlled not by a clock but by the play of events. The game ends only when the play produces an asymmetry in runs after nine innings.

With no guaranteed ending, baseball, host to "old-timer's day," has a way of stretching time. History's longest professional baseball game was played in 1981 between the Pawtucket Red Sox and the Rochester Red Wings, from the Triple-A International League. The marathon lasted thirty-three innings and took eight hours and twenty-five minutes to complete. The game was so long that the teams were forced to adjourn after thirty-two innings of play on April 18 and 19, 1981, completing the thirty-third inning more than two months later, on June 23, when the team schedules permitted resuming play. Pawtucket ultimately won 3 to 2. Along with timed conclusions, tie scores are not part of American baseball.

The most significant asymmetry in baseball, which seems to underlie the sport's pervasive oddness, is that the game never faces opposing teams directly against each other. Of all our major sports, only in baseball is the contest is framed as a lone individual at home plate, facing a team in the field.[8] Indeed, when a team is at bat, the other players, who have temporarily become batters, are seated out of sight in a dugout, leaving the player up at bat alone at the plate. This continuous alternation of players as fielders and batters creates a distinctive rhythm to baseball, in which individual effort is in constant alternation with team cooperation in the field. While fielding skill is essential in baseball, most players earn their statistics by batting rather than by fielding. While a real achievement, the Golden Glove Award for fielding does not compete with batting records for baseball glory. The pitcher is an exception, whose ERA is earned through his work as a fielder. We will shortly consider this anomaly more closely.

The significance of this distinction between batting and fielding is reinforced by how our language treats the two roles. Fielders are generally referred to as "playing" their positions, while "playing" never applies to the batter. One *is* at bat; the batter is the authentic baseball player. To ask who is "playing the batter" sounds ludicrous. The shift from "playing" to "being" seems to be linked to proximity to home since the only fielders who "are" what they do are the pitcher and the catcher, those who play close to home plate. The closer to home plate a player stands, the more natural it sounds to say he is his position rather than playing it. Note, for instance, that saying that a player "is a shortstop" sits more easily on the tongue than saying that someone "is a right fielder." One never asks, "who plays pitcher?" The verb naturally shifts from *playing* to *being* the closer the player is to home.

The center of gravity for authentic baseball is home plate, the source of "agency" in the game. Agency here implies initiating action rather than collective reaction. The trio of pitcher, catcher, and batter each share in producing the agency of play. The pitcher controls the pitch to the batter, attempting to strike him out. The catcher has his own hidden agency by signaling to the pitcher the pitch he prefers. The batter controls the bat with the ultimate intention of overtaking the agency of the pitch and hitting the ball out of the park beyond the field of play. At home plate, the issue is "who's in charge?"

Significantly, game playing is the language we use about our social roles. In sociology, role-*playing* is about how people play the game of social life, while psychology, a favored social science for Americans, is about who we (really) *are*. Writers like Shakespeare and scholars like Erving Goffman and Kenneth Burke have often reminded us that we are all role-players as members of society. We have come to see social life as a kind of theater. But to Americans, role-playing is always a secondary kind of action, subordinate to the ideal of personal authenticity, to having an authentic self.

This American emphasis on self and personal agency is far from universal. While the tension between individual and social self is found everywhere, many Asian societies privilege social identity over a focus on self. But cultures are not easily reduced to these simple values. More commonly, they are characterized by how they handle their contradictions as they attempt to resolve the tensions produced by their dominant values. For Americans, a central tension has been between community values versus individual freedom and initiative. And this tension is perfectly reflected in their national pastime. This value tension in American life was recognized as early as Alexis de Tocqueville's 1835 classic study of American national character in *Democracy in America*. While noting the fondness of Americans for civic and other voluntary associations, de Tocqueville saw in American democracy a powerful pull of individualism: "[N]ot only does democracy make each man forget his ancestors, but it hides his descendants from him and separates him from his contemporaries; it constantly leads him back toward himself alone and threatens finally to confine him wholly in the solitude of his own heart" (de Tocqueville 2000, p. 887). The tension between communitarian and individualistic values runs deep in American culture and character.

Baseball Metaphor

Ritual baseball serves as a model for other activities in American life. Consider the way baseball shapes business relationships. When we try to sell an idea or a product to someone, we "make a pitch." A particularly tough competitor or negotiator is said to be "playing hardball." The most elaborated use of baseball metaphor in American English is how young men use baseball to structure male dating behavior. A boy who dates many girls might be said to be "playing the field." But a more determined aspiring lover adopts the metaphorical persona of the batter rather than the fielder, imagining his dating game as a trip around the bases. "I couldn't get to first base" suggests that the hopeful lover has "struck out." Amorous success might be phrased as "a good catch," "going all the way," "hitting a home run," or simply as "scoring." Significantly, these baseball metaphors are appropriate only for a certain kind of romantic activity. For instance, no one would say, "I couldn't get to first base with my wife" since the relationship is already domesticated. Nor would it be appropriate for a male to say that "I went all the way with the prostitute" since that is a purely commercial

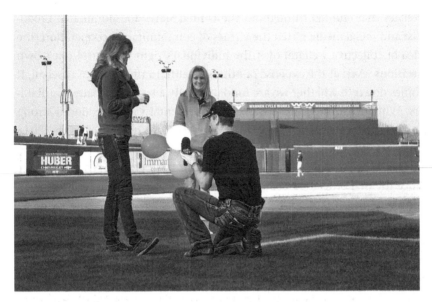

Figure 9.3
Marriage proposal at the baseball park. "The Balloon Bust Turned into a Marriage Proposal" by Minda Haas Kuhlmann is licensed under CC BY 2.0.

relationship. The baseball metaphor for sex works only when the hopeful lover entertains the possibility of finding a girl he can conceivably "bring home." In other words, the baseball metaphor governs not simply sex but serious dating.

The subtlety of these metaphors suggests that while we are not fully aware of ritual baseball, it is not far from consciousness. Indeed, these associations between baseball and the domestication of romance are suggested by the tradition of using baseball games as the site for marriage proposals, either announced on the jumbotron screen or done in person on the field (figure 9.3).

An Enduring Problem, an Enduring Game

In 2019, as the COVID-19 pandemic tightened its grip on the world, this tension in American values produced a fierce political divide over the right of the government to enforce mask and vaccination mandates. The heated

debates that erupted throughout the United States and dominated broadcast and social media pitted the virtues of communitarian cooperation (the
idea of collective welfare) over the individual's right to control one's own
decisions, even at the expense of others' health. In the idiom of baseball, it
comes down to whether we are fundamentally a society of batters or fielders. While this American tension in fundamental values produced strong
and sometimes violent political disagreement during and after the 2016
elections, it is nothing new. The complex relationship between contending
images of what makes Americans American has been played out ritually
since the first official baseball game took place in Hoboken, New Jersey, in
June of 1846.

American baseball's dramatization of the tension between social cooperation and individual enterprise has always favored the individual over
the team, batting over fielding. Baseball's heroes have most often been its
sluggers; its Barry Bonds, Babe Ruths, Alex Hernandezes, Ted Williamses,
and Joe DiMaggios. As mythic heroes of baseball go, "Casey at the bat" resonates far more with Americans than "Casey out in left field" ever could.[9]
But baseball players and fans will remind us that you can't win a baseball
game by sticking to home plate. To win, you also need teamwork. Periodically, you need to take to the field, which is why the tension hidden in the
shadows of baseball play is not finally resolvable and why baseball, game
and ritual, endures.

Conclusion

In this chapter, we have taken an odd look at baseball. Rather than viewing
it as a game, we stepped back to see the ritual aspects of the game in how it
deals with space, time, and action. Viewed as rituals, sports have a lot to tell
us about the communities that play them. Again and again, they act out a
community's vision of life's challenges and possibilities. Sometimes called
America's pastime, baseball might also be said to represent America's past
time. It is a profoundly nostalgic game for many Americans whose affection
for the game is linked to its pastoral and agricultural mythology. Baseball's
authentic home is the park or field, the country planted in the heart of the
big city. The ideal rookie is "the natural," a "hayseed" coming up from the
farm teams to play in the big city. Baseball has long been at the center of
the American imagination. It has been called "the literary sport," stoking

the imagination and inspiring more novels, movies, short stories, and films than any other game.

While baseball may represent America's pastime, it does not appear to be the sport for America's future. That honor now belongs to football. In a 2018 Gallup poll surveying fan interest in major sports, football dominated, with 37 percent of those polled naming football as their favorite sport. The same poll had basketball as the second most popular sport (11 percent), with baseball coming in third, at just 9 percent.

One of the reasons for the emergence of football as America's preferred spectator sport is that collegiate baseball has never caught on in the United States as a televised sport, whereas, in both football and basketball, college games compete for viewer popularity with the professional leagues. Viewers get a double dose of those sports. There are other reasons why professional football has overtaken baseball in popularity and revenue. Perhaps the least recognized cause of this change in taste for sport is related to the difference between the ritual character of baseball and football. Somehow, football feels like the present, while baseball feels like the past.

Like baseball, a shadow ritual organization to football powerfully shapes its ethos. Football lacks both the pastoral qualities of baseball and its endearing asymmetries. While baseball is a relatively leisurely game, with long periods of slow activity punctuated by bursts of action, football is all action, nonstop excitement, and nonstop violence. It is sort of like the evening news. Rather than the ballpark, football takes place on the gridiron, a rectangular field of fixed size, with precise yard and ten-yard markings.

Like many of our most popular video games, football is modeled on war. Its play orchestrates skirmishes aimed at moving an offensive team (think platoon) further and further into an opponent's territory until the enemy's side of the field is occupied completely. A separate defensive team attempts to thwart the forward thrust of their opponent's attack. When the offensive team fails to overrun their opponent's territory in four attempts (downs), the ball "turns over" to the other team, and the direction of attack reverses. The successful total occupation of the enemy's territory is called a touchdown.

The fact that American sports fans have increasingly traded the pastoral qualities of baseball for football's glorification of violently colonizing an opponent's territory is not a coincidence. Just check the evening news. Rituals are responsive to culture and history. Our changing taste for our sports suggests sobering changes in American life and our sense of who we are. Contemplating the ritual that lies just beneath the play of sport gives us a glimpse of the serious side of ourselves at play. The historical changes in the popularity of different sports offer us some surprising insights into how we are changing. Stepping back from the heat of the game to view sport as ritual may not seem as exciting as focusing on the action on the field. But seeing a sport from the ritual viewpoint can pack some surprises of its own.

10 Family Zoom: Virtual Rituals in the Age of the Internet

I am writing this book in 2022, in the midst of the worldwide COVID-19 pandemic. An unexpected and unwelcome guest, the virus now seems to have settled in for the long run, and we have all been forced to adapt. While the pandemic has been a truly universal experience, uniting the world in shared anxiety and suffering, it has also driven us physically apart. Increasingly, face-to-face encounters in the classroom and the workplace have become mask-to-mask or screen-to-screen meetings. To an unprecedented extent, the world has gone online, propelled by the development of synchronous streaming video programs like Skype, Duo, Hangout, Zoom, and Facetime. With in-person classes replaced by online learning, school time merged with screen time. Covid has taught us new habits and new ways of engaging with each other. No one is sure how many of the changes will become permanent even as the pandemic subsides, but there is no question that Covid has significantly virtualized our world.

The social distancing brought on by the pandemic has drawn many common face-to-face rituals onto the internet. Take the case of my own family. Over the past two years, I have been meeting my siblings online in a weekly meeting we have come to call Family Zoom. Scattered between California, New York, New Jersey, and Atlanta, my siblings and I have not all met face-to-face since the pandemic started in 2020. Before then, we would usually meet several times a year to celebrate landmark birthdays, bar mitzvahs, weddings, funerals, and other occasions. In our mother's later years, we would gather to celebrate her landmark birthdays, including a massive party at my brother's house in New Jersey on the occasion of her hundredth birthday. Our family is close-knit, and she reigned at its heart as the family matriarch. My mother's often-stated desire was that her children should remain close after her death, a wish that has proven easy to honor and that the internet has made possible even during lockdowns.

My sister Rima who lives in New York City first proposed Family Zoom during the initial period of lockdown back in 2020. We negotiated a time on Friday afternoons that generally suited all of our schedules, and we have been gathering online every Friday since then. The fact that Zoom worked on desktops, laptops, tablets, and phones meant that our family time could be portable, and when the situation has warranted our being away from home, we have generally been able to join in the gathering from a car, a train, an airport, a hotel room, and even, once, from a hospital emergency room. It turned out that our family ritual was a movable feast. We could be together from virtually anywhere there was an internet connection.

In addition to myself, my siblings attending Family Zoom include my sister Rima in New York, a writer focusing on biography and retired professor from the Bank Street School in New York, my sister Barbara who runs a college application counseling service in Northern California, and my brother Ken who (semi) retired several years ago as the head psychologist for a school district in New Jersey and has authored several books and videos on preventing bullying in school settings. Family Zoom also includes our two honorary siblings, our sister-in-law Elaine who was married to my older brother (who died in 1982) but who has remained very close to our family, and her current husband Howard, with whom we all have been close for decades. Over the years, they have both become part of our family. Elaine and Howard are both very talented and successful artists, Elaine as a sculptor and Howard as a photographer and painter.

Every Friday at 4 p.m., Family Zoom is online for about an hour and a half. Over the past two years, the gathering has gradually assumed the character of a family ritual. Without consciously planning it, our online interactions have found a comfortable rhythm that is repeated predictably every week. Rima will send out a Zoom invitation about an hour before the 4 p.m. meeting, and even though we all know her Zoom login, we all wait for the weekly email announcing the session. The relatively small number of participants means that we can all fit on a single screen of a desktop, which enhances the feeling of being "together" (figure 10.1). While we are physically far apart and brought together only in cyberspace, the computer screen has become a convincing and effective analog to shared gathering space. When the image of one of us periodically freezes on screen or the

Figure 10.1
Family Zoom

audio stops working, we're reminded of the virtual nature of our "togeth-erness," but when it all works smoothly, as it usually does, the sense of us being together is pretty convincing.

While Family Zoom has no explicit agenda or rules of engagement, we have developed some predictable interaction patterns that have begun to feel like a family ritual. To inspire joint activity other than chatting, we devised some online events in which everyone can participate. On several of our birthdays, we produced and read some lighthearted but flattering limericks dedicated to the birthday sibling. Everyone was brought into the act of composing. We also each compiled a list of our top five nostalgic pop songs and took turns playing well-known recordings of the songs for every-one. It was a lot of fun. Barbara, who is eight years younger than her next oldest sibling, chose some music I didn't know, reflecting significant gener-ational gaps. Some of our choices turned out to be surprising and revealing.

Our spouses, partners, children, and grandchildren who are not regular participants in Family Zoom make periodic appearances, but for the most part, it is just the six of us. Reasonable turn-taking is an important aspect of group conversations, and we quickly negotiated a conversational pat-tern where everyone has a roughly equal chance to talk. While the rules of turn-taking are never made explicit, the family group tries to live by a tacit agreement about equal airtime. Since conversations don't always abide by the rules of equal time, we have figured out some tactful ways to create a rough balance, bringing everyone into the conversation. If one of us does not volunteer an update on our life, someone will make sure to ask them what's going on with them, bringing them into the conversation. When we notice that the conversation has focused for a long time on one of us, that person will often tactfully steer the conversation to someone else. In that way, we have managed to maintain a sense of inclusiveness in the focus of our gathering and have largely avoided the common problem of a dominating talker taking over a conversation. Our gatherings follow the usual rules of conversational interaction in the United States but doing them online has added a significant dimension to the usual ritual of family talk.

Since Zoom allows screen sharing, we have been able to share videos and photos with our siblings. For those of us with grandchildren, these shared pictures have allowed us to keep up with the development of our grand nieces and nephews and do a bit of bragging about the accomplishments of our own grandchildren. Elaine and Howard and Ken's artist wife Maxine have been able to share photos of their latest paintings and sculptures and of their exhibitions. Without consciously planning it, we have managed to provide equal time for talking about each one of us separately and for more general topics that engage the whole group.

A fair amount of talk has been reminiscences, often very funny stories, about our missing sibling, Ricky, an artist, and colorful personality, who died at the age of thirty-eight in 1982. We also love to share stories about our mother, Flo Shore, a remarkable woman who was the center of our mutual family life until her death several years ago. When Elaine's brother, who many of us did not know well, passed away, we asked her to talk about him, and a good part of that chat was stories of her childhood with her siblings. Like Salem Camp Meeting, both the living and the dead are present at our online gatherings.

Despite busy schedules, we have managed to maintain our Family Zoom ritual for over two years. It is still going strong. No matter where we are and what we are doing, connecting to Family Zoom every week has become a priority in our lives. It has taken on the compulsive character common to ritualized events. Our attempt to keep in touch during the pandemic has produced something unexpected, a sense of continual family togetherness that, despite the physical distance between us, had brought us all closer together than we had been before the pandemic. The internet and the development of streaming video chat rooms have provided us with a powerful sense of family time that, despite the limitations of virtual communication, has effectively undercut the very idea of social distancing.

From Radio to Television to the Internet

While the pandemic has enhanced the role of the internet as a ritual space, ritual events have had a significant online presence since the earliest days of the internet. Presidential inaugurations, Independence Day celebrations, and New Year's Eve are among the many ritualized events that we have learned to "participate in" through television or on the internet. The last fifty years have seen a dramatic expansion of the communicative power of digital communication, increasing the variety of available digital platforms and enhancing our power to simulate reality.

Consider the relatively brief timeline of the evolution of the modern internet. The first host-to-host computer connection was the US Department of Defense's Advanced Research Projects Agency Network, which went online in October of 1969 to allow time-sharing by the military's computer network. Local digital networks proliferated in the 1970s, mostly focused on military or academic communication. In the 1980s, the National Science Foundation began funding the development of the National Science Foundation Network in order to connect a handful of supercomputer research centers at major American universities.

The early 1990s saw the commercial development of the modern internet. The earliest web browser, named World Wide Web, was developed in 1991 by an English computer scientist Tim Berners-Lee using Steve Jobs' NeXT computer to write the program. The program was later renamed Nexus, when the name World Wide Web had come to be used as a general term for the internet. Several other browser programs followed. But it was the development of the browser Mosaic at the National Center for Supercomputing at the University of Illinois in Champaign-Urbana in 1972 that facilitated the combination of text and graphics. Mosaic, later renamed Netscape Navigator, became the first widely available internet browser and made the World Wide Web into the "everything-everywhere" communications medium we know today.

Digital broadcasting has changed dramatically as communication technology has improved. In the early 1990s, at the dawn of the modern internet, online ritual was effectively limited to text-based accounts or evocations of rituals found on bulletin boards, chat rooms, discussion forums, and blogs. Accompanying photos or drawings only became possible once graphical interfaces were made possible by more sophisticated software and hardware, often aimed at enhancing the realism of computer games.

Significant increases in computing power, memory storage, and graphics processing have enhanced the power of computers to simulate visual and aural experiences. Today, along with text, the internet hosts detailed visual images and streaming video, along with immersive stereo and quadraphonic sound. Online translators allow almost instant translation of both written and spoken text into dozens of languages. With the help of Hollywood animators and video game developers, it is becoming increasingly hard to tell a simulated animation from a photographic image.

Online Religion

The most obvious impact of the digital revolution on ritual has been in the broadcasting of religious worship. People tend to be of two minds when they think about religious experience in the context of artificial intelligence (AI). There are those who see these domains as inherently incompatible since machine intelligence is assumed to be unfeeling and not conducive to spiritual experience. In this view, computer-mediated experience is the antithesis of religion. But some computer scientists like the futurist Ray Kurzweil take the opposite view and see in AI an inherent spirituality. A perennial digital optimist in a world full of skeptics, Kurzweil envisions AI moving human experience closer to the sort of transcendent spirituality we find in most religions. In his book *The Age of Spiritual Machines: When Computers Exceed Human Intelligence*, Kurzweil characterizes AI as inherently spiritual. AI, he argues, promotes "a feeling of transcending one's everyday physical and mortal bounds to a sense of deeper reality" (Kurzweil 2000, p. 151). He predicts that advanced AIs will soon emerge that approach and eventually transcend human self-awareness and that such advanced machines will "claim to be conscious and thus to be spiritual entities. They will believe that they have spiritual experiences" (p. 152).[1] This ambivalence in the speculations about religion and AI is also characteristic of users' experience of online religious rituals. For some, virtual space and VR hold enormous promise for facilitating and even enhancing the experience of religious worship. For others, the disembodied character of virtual space and on-screen reality drastically limit the possibilities of online ritual experience.

Before the computer age, religious programming had already been widely broadcast via radio and television. In the United States, the first radio broadcast of a religious service was from the Calvary Episcopal Church in Pittsburgh in January of 1921. The first radio sermon in Britain was broadcast a year later. The first use of satellite radio to broadcast religious services was by the Moody Bible Institute. For Catholics, papal ceremonies were first broadcast in Europe in 1954. Around the same time in the United States, Bishop Fulton J. Sheen began his televised sermon broadcasts. Since the 1990s, television broadcasts of religious services have become ubiquitous. In the United States alone there are over 1,600 stations broadcasting Christian religious programming. The most popular use of the airwaves for religious programming is by Evangelical churches. However, on-air religious programming is not limited to Christian denominations. All the major world religions have taken advantage of the chance to broadcast their religious services including their rituals on radio and television.

With the explosive growth of the internet over the last three decades, many religious organizations have developed websites allowing worshippers to practice their faith online. The internet offers some advantages over traditional radio and television programming for hosting religious rituals, allowing programming to be stored and accessed at any time by users rather than limited to viewing at a preset schedule. While remote participation in live services and other rituals requires participants to abide by set time schedules, personal rituals like online prayer, Buddhist meditation, Hindu puja, or pilgrimage to holy sites are not necessarily limited by the calendar or clock but can be accessed by worshippers at any convenient time. Synchronous internet programs permit two-way communication, allowing online worshippers to respond to online content and to contribute actively to the ritual.

In an interesting essay about Korean Buddhist online rituals, Han-Rai Woo draws a significant distinction between "ritual online" and "online ritual" (Woo 2013, p. 2). Ritual online is simply the posting of a ritual text or a video recording of a ritual performance on a website to be accessed at any time by online users. Here, the internet is simply a delivery mechanism for recordings of a ritual rather than a stage for the active performance of a ritual. By contrast, an "online ritual" is actively performed or simulated online by one or more participants, using the virtual capabilities of the internet. Woo contends that Korean Christian websites, focused as they are on "the Word," generally use the internet to post text or video recordings of church services for people to access passively, while Korean Buddhists are more likely to create an interactive space for interactive cyber ritual. As we will see below, most of the online religious rituals sponsored by the world's major religions fall into the first category of ritual online, serving as archives or delivery platforms for text or video performances rather than exploiting the possibilities of the internet for virtual interactive ritual. That will probably change in the future as users learn to use the internet's virtual capabilities.

This tendency to treat the internet as a delivery platform rather than as a performance stage was clear from the earliest days of internet religion. Early versions of internet religious ritual were relatively static. In a 2006 article on cyber ritual, Cheryl Casey describes a virtual Episcopalian church service available for online worshippers twenty-four hours a day seven days a week. On this site, entering the church is accomplished by clicking a link that brings up a photograph of the inside of an empty church, followed by the text of a church service that appears against the backdrop of the seal of the Communion of Evangelical Episcopal Churches, certifying the fore-grounded text. Here is how Casey describes the church service:

> Before beginning the service, the participant reads the following instructions: "The words printed in 'bold' type are the words spoken by Father Brown, and the words in 'regular' type are the words for you, the people, to speak, either aloud, or silently, as you worship at St. John's Internet Church." At this point, the participant is free to scroll through the text of the service, which is punctuated by headings that indicate the different parts of the liturgy, and by textual cues for silence, response, or song. The service otherwise follows the traditional format and content. (Casey 2006, p. 81)

The website advertises itself as an online church service, yet what we actually get is a posting of the text of an ordinary church service and a set of instructions guiding worshippers through the service. This text-based approach to online ritual exploits relatively few potential advantages of internet communication for simulating the experience of ritual. The only visual cues the worshipper gets are a photograph of an empty church and a script to read. Experiencing this online service as a ritual requires an extraordinary act of imagination by the reader, who must mentally picture Father Brown leading the service while he or she takes on the part of the congregation.

The major world religions have all embraced the internet, offering, among other resources, access to online worship. Contemporary religious websites tend to take advantage of the internet's enhanced multimedia capacities, offering resources in the form of texts, pictures, sound recordings, and videos. Today, the most common use of the internet for religious organizations is online access to worship services via streaming video. Online religious services have become increasingly common during the current pandemic when many in-person religious services have been (temporarily) replaced by online versions. It remains to be seen how many worshippers will continue their virtual attendance once the pandemic ebbs. While streaming video differs in some ways from live television broadcasts, these internet broadcasts are not the most radical use of internet worship but are really an updated extension of the venerable radio and television religious broadcasts of the last fifty years.

To convey an idea of the current state of online worship, we can sample a few of the websites currently featuring religious rituals for the major world religions. I have organized these snapshots by religion. There are thousands of religious websites broadcast from around the world, so it is important to remember that this sample is just a small slice of the vast and diverse online world of religious worship.

Christian Sites

Protestant churches were the earliest religious groups to take advantage of mass broadcasting and have been on the air since the 1920s. Most active are the many nondenominational Evangelical churches, which, early on, recognized the potential power and reach of the airwaves for attracting converts to their churches. These web-based networks call themselves "churches" and usually have a home base where the church was founded plus numerous physical "campuses." With only half of American adults reporting regular church attendance, and a tendency for them to switch churches, internet churches have provided a new option for church membership, especially for families who do not have easy physical access to a church.[2]

The largest online Protestant church is Life Church based in Edmond, Oklahoma, whose broadcasts reach an average of seventy thousand worshippers a week. Started in 1996 by senior pastor Craig Groeschel and his wife Amy, the church now boasts local branch churches in twelve states and dozens of countries worldwide, offering worshippers the choice of joining online or at a local church "campus." Describing itself as "one church in multiple locations," the church effectively emphasizes its dual character as both ubiquitous and locally grounded. Life Church broadcasts ninety streaming services a week on five different platforms but also emphasizes its local churches and their activities. The broadcasts emphasize slickly produced gospel music, alternating with sermons, online prayer, and appeals for contributions. Close-ups of the performers on stage alternate with shots of enraptured worshippers in the audience.

The website is packed with resources for the online congregant, offering dozens of videos featuring spiritual guidance and personal stories of salvation, a book club, links to reading material, and a Bible app called YouVersion for phones and tablets that presents videos of scenes where the Bible is used to make sense of everyday challenges and situations. Since the church is family oriented, there are links for teenagers and a special Bible app for young children. And, as always, there is the link for making contributions. The church features a link to an area called "Local Groups" where worshippers can find, organize, or join a small "LifeGroup" that becomes a support group and a source of local discussion. Here is how the website describes the LifeGroup: "You were designed to live in community. Find or lead a group of people you can belong to, be real with, and grow alongside—in person or completely online. Search by location, shared interest, or Life.Church Online service time to find the perfect group for your schedule and season of life." While the church exalts the size and diversity of its membership, the LifeGroup provides a human-scaled space for being with people of similar interests or from the same locale.

Aspiring to be both global and local, evangelical virtual churches such as Life Church have found effective ways to reconcile the abstractness and unlimited scale of church in cyberspace with a sense of personalized connection anchored in concrete relationships and a local sense of place. The virtual campus has no physical dimensions and has an outreach capacity limited only by the span of the World Wide Web, while the ever-multiplying local campuses provide a physical dimension to the church community but retain the church's "everywhere" character by not limiting the number or the geographical reach of the campuses. This tendency to pair unlimited virtual outreach with small-scale group activities is common in virtual Evangelical churches.

The Catholic Church has been more reserved than the Protestant Evangelical churches about the religious use of the internet. But cautiously, the Catholic Church has come to accept the inevitable religious role of the internet. In December of 1961, Pope John XXIII convened the Second Vatican Council to institute a number of reforms in the church. Among the most influential of these reforms was proposed in a document called Sacrosanctum Concilium (Constitution on the Sacred Liturgy) dealing with public worship and the conduct of Catholic liturgy (Turner 2019). The document was drafted with the aim of encouraging a more direct active engagement by ordinary worshippers in the performance of the liturgy. The hierarchical emphasis of the church had so emphasized the active role of the priests in performing church ritual that the ordinary worshippers—the laity—had tended to worship by passively following the directions of the priests. The Vatican was committed to encouraging in all worshippers a more engaged attitude toward church liturgy. The emergence of the internet two decades later would present serious challenges to this commitment of the Vatican to a more active form of worship. However, so powerful was the reach of the internet that the church could not afford to ignore its presence. But the contradictions between Catholic conceptions of sacramental worship and the inherent constraints of virtual ritual could only produce an ambivalent response of the Vatican to internet worship.

In 2015 Pope Francis told a young girl that he was embarrassed to admit being "a disaster" when it comes to modern technology, acknowledging that he did not even know how to use a computer (Turner 2019). While advising parents to ban cell phones from the family dinner and to keep personal computers away from children's bedrooms, Pope Francis has come to recognize the inevitable power and potential of the internet in religious life, concluding that the internet had to be viewed as "a gift of God." The same ambivalence is clear in the 2003 Vatican letter from the Pontifical Council for Social Communications, titled "The Church and the Internet" (Foley 2002). The letter begins on a positive note:

The Church's interest in the internet is a particular expression of her longstanding interest in the media of social communication. Seeing the media as an outcome of the historical scientific process by which humankind "advances further and further in the discovery of the resources and values contained in the whole of creation," the Church often has declared her conviction that they are, in the words of the Second Vatican Council, "marvelous technical inventions" that already do much to meet human needs and may yet do even more.

Thus the Church has taken a fundamentally positive approach to the media. Even when condemning serious abuses, documents of this Pontifical Council for Social Communications have been at pains to make it clear that "a merely censorious attitude on the part of the Church . . . is neither sufficient nor appropriate." (Foley 2002)

The letter recognizes the potential of the internet for expanding the reach of the church and for furthering the church's role in Catholic education. But it also recognizes the many dangers the internet poses, especially for children, and urges parents to become educated users of the internet to guide the young in healthy uses of online communication. Acknowledging the way in which the internet frees users from top-down control of information, the Vatican still recommends that the church needs to retain some control over what is put online under its name. The letter is especially wary of "unofficial websites" that claim to be Catholic while deviating from orthodox church teachings.

The letter's most direct reference to the internet's relation to church liturgy comes at the end of part two of the letter that stresses the limitations of virtual religion:

[T]he virtual reality of cyberspace has some worrisome implications for religion as well as for other areas of life. Virtual reality is no substitute for the Real Presence of Christ in the Eucharist, the sacramental reality of the other sacraments, and shared worship in a flesh-and-blood human community. There are no sacraments on the Internet; and even the religious experiences possible there by the grace of God are insufficient apart from real-world interaction with other persons of faith. Here is another aspect of the Internet that calls for study and reflection. At the same time, pastoral planning should consider how to lead people from cyberspace to true community and how, through teaching and catechesis, the Internet might subsequently be used to sustain and enrich them in their Christian commitment. (Foley 2002)

Compared with the more "symbolic" Protestant theology, Catholic liturgy has a "realist" bias, emphasizing the physical presence of Christ in the Eucharist and the literalness of ritual practice. Catholic ritual is heavily dependent on the embodied sensory qualities of ritual practice, including touch, taste, and smell, and so recognizes the limitations of virtual space for religious experience. In an essay discussing the problematical status of the internet for Catholic liturgy, Jack Turner notes the importance of direct physical presence in Catholic worship:

> For Christian churches that have an essentially sacramental understanding of the church and the liturgy . . . physical action and physical contact with the elements of worship and life are an essential part of encountering God. The sacraments especially are uniquely associated with a specific physical expression: one is baptized in water, hands are imposed on the heads of those ordained to ministry, and oil is traced on the brow in chrismation/confirmation and during unction. In so many ways, this sacramental theology is bound up with the redemption of creation through the use of physical objects, especially those that are transformed from their ordinary purpose and function through the power of the Holy Spirit through the prayer of the church. (Turner 2019, p. 224)

Catholic websites tend to offer online access to broadcasts of the Holy Mass. The Catholic website "Massonline.org" broadcasts live performances of the Catholic Mass in real time rather than archives of recorded masses. While online viewers are not attending in person, they are at least attending a real mass in progress in real time, one that conforms to an actual ritual cycle at a church somewhere in the world. This limitation grounds the ritual in a stable ritual cycle of a particular church in a particular place. Online users can "move" from place to place to find a mass taking place at set times.

The website offers the Holy Mass in a wide variety of languages, including Spanish, Persian, Mandarin, and Tamil and Malayalam (South Indian languages), in addition to an extensive calendar of live broadcasts of English masses. But a mass must conform to a traditional schedule for a particular church. An online viewer can attend a new mass broadcast from somewhere in the world every half hour. These broadcasts are streamed live from churches around the world rather than retrieved from an archive of recorded masses that can be streamed at any time. Despite its allowing online presence at the service, this live-streaming of the Holy Mass reinforces the Catholic emphasis on actual rather than virtual church attendance, forcing viewers to conform to some extent to the practices of a real church.

The Catholic TV Network has video recordings of masses in English broadcast from Massachusetts.[3] The mass I watched featured a priest and a young woman assisting him; otherwise, the church seemed to be empty.

The priest performed the traditional mass as if there were a congregation present. The major deviation came when it was time for Holy Communion, when the priest blessed the wine and the host but rather than offering them to congregants, he consumed them himself. In contrast to most Protestant services, the Catholic Holy Mass can never be fully realized in a virtual format. The rite of Holy Communion requires direct physical engagement by communicants, and the website acknowledges and attempts to accommodate this limitation. While the priest was performing the communion, the following text was scrolled on the screen.

> My Jesus,
> I truly believe that
> you are present in the
> Sacrament of the
> Holy Eucharist.
>
> I love You above all things,
> and I desire to receive You.
>
> Since I cannot
> at this moment
> receive you sacramentally
> come at least spiritually into my heart
> I embrace You as if
> You were already there
> And unite myself wholly to You.
>
> Never let me
> Be parted from You.
>
> Amen

Catholic teaching emphasizes the importance of regular physical attendance at Holy Mass. Physical presence with others is considered an essential aspect of church worship. While solitary prayer is recognized as an important component of Catholic religious practice, the church has always emphasized the social character of its liturgy, something that cannot be fully experienced by the inherent physical isolation of online devotion. Moreover, the central sacrament of the faith, the Eucharist, the ritual reenactment of Jesus's last supper with his apostles, is, for Catholics, always a physical act of consuming the wafer and the wine, which are understood to "transubstantiate" during the sacramental rite into the actual body and blood of Christ. So for Catholics, virtual ritual can never take the place of the "real" thing. This means that "attending" mass online is inevitably a second-best option, recommended only for those who cannot make it to the church.

Here is how the website puts it: "This website was created for the sick, home bound and for those who, due to other important reasons, could not go to Mass; or those who, due to their locations, do not have Churches to go to. We hope that our website will help our sisters and brothers in faith to celebrate the Holy Mass live online wherever they are." The website has a section for user comments, and these comments will often state the reason why online worshippers cannot make it to a church: old age, illness, pandemic isolation, remoteness from a church, or scheduling issues.

Online Jewish Worship

Jewish worship is well represented on the internet. As with Christian churches, many synagogues now make their Friday night and Saturday morning services available for online attendance. For example, Congregation Beth Shalom, a relatively traditional temple in Northbrook, Illinois, hosts a website with many resources for worshippers, including a schedule of online broadcasts of services and PDF files with prayerbook and Torah texts.[4] While the temple features a program for congregants interested in participating in reading Torah portions during the services, online reading does not appear to be an option.

Orthodox Jewish custom forbids any kind of work or the operation of machines during the Sabbath. While the issue of allowing online viewers to operate their computers to attend services is not addressed by the website, it does note that no staff will be available during services to help with any technical glitches that may come up. Internet worship is thus something of a problem for the most orthodox Jewish congregations. One of the best known of the Orthodox Jewish movements is the Chabad-Lubavitch worldwide movement that promotes traditional Jewish religious practice and cultural traditions (see https://chabad.org). One local Chabad community in New York City hosts an active website that advertises daily and Sabbath in-person worship.[5] Faced with challenges limiting in-person gatherings during the Covid pandemic, the Uptown Chabad could not offer online Sabbath services because of the prohibition on the use of machines and equipment on Shabbat (Sabbath). The best they could do was to arrange socially distanced outdoor in-person services in several backyards. For those unable or unwilling to attend in person, daily non-Shabbat services were broadcast on Zoom, but Shabbat services could only be attended in person.

The less traditional Reform congregations face no restrictions on broadcasting and, not surprisingly, are the most frequently represented branch of Judaism on the internet. Many of the online Jewish sites are Reformed temples, some are overtly politically progressive, and many feature women rabbis. One prominent online Reform temple is Central Synagogue in New York City, whose congregation currently numbers 2,600 families.[6] Housed in a beautiful old synagogue on E. 55th Street in Manhattan that was completed in 1872 and has seating for 1,400 worshippers, Central Synagogue traces its roots to two smaller synagogues founded in Manhattan's Lower East Side in 1836 and 1849 by German-speaking immigrants from Eastern Europe. All services are live-streamed and can be accessed on YouTube or on the temple's Facebook site. The temple's website offers digital downloads of the order of the service and the *Mishkan T'filah*, a digitized version of the Reform prayerbook, so online worshippers can participate actively in the service.

One website called Ritualwell is dedicated to "reconstructing Judaism" by making it "boldly relevant."[7] The site is basically an archive providing access to a broad spectrum of Jewish rituals. Dividing its offerings into six ritual themes: life cycles, healing and hard times, everyday holiness, holidays, and Shabbat (sabbath), each theme contains links to more specific ritual occasions. In addition to the traditional Jewish ritual themes (i.e., death and mourning, raising children, growing older, Sabbath prayers), the offerings include many updated prayers devoted to progressive women's issues and matters dealing with gender identity and sexuality. An examination of the actual rituals offered by the site reveals that the "rituals" offered online are neither video nor live-streamed ritual enactments. Online readers are not even given descriptions of ritual actions. The available rituals are limited to prayer texts sometimes accompanied by a few photographs. This raises the question of what these religious internet sites consider ritual, an issue to be addressed below.

A more interactive version of online Jewish ritual is found at Nava Tehila, a Jerusalem-based nongovernmental organization that sponsors online performances of Sabbath ritual on a Zoom site that permits participants to join in prayer and song. The recorded service I watched, live-streamed on April 24, 2020, included both Israeli and American worshippers and an Israeli rabbi.[8] The rabbi's Hebrew sermon alternated with her English translations, and the songs were all in Hebrew. Because the service was streamed live, participants in the United States were in a much earlier time zone than those in Jerusalem. In Jerusalem, the service was taking place at the appropriate sunset hour on Friday, but time differences meant that participants in other time zones were celebrating the Sabbath at the wrong hour. In greeting the rabbi, the Americans all noted that they were celebrating the Sabbath very early. The rabbi acknowledged this issue but concluded that "there is no early or late in the Torah, so if you're, say, six hours later, you're not late. You're right on time."

Addressing the experiential limitations of online ritual, Rabbi Ruth urged all online participants to enter the "davening" (recitation of prayers) viscerally, with their bodies. "We're going to let it settle in our body," she said, "and it makes sense to us when we are in our body. I'd like to invite us—and this is like a new thing we learn, since sitting idly and watching the computer doesn't work for everybody. It's visceral, it's in the body. So we want to invite you to stand up, to be silent, to cook, to do needlepoint, to do what you need to be doing, to feel comfortable, so we are building a community of davening together—with a body. We don't want to leave the body behind, because with all our bodies we like to say, we're here, we're here."

The rabbi's intense sermon alternated with songs by two groups of singers, who, accompanied by a guitar, sang Hebrew songs of worship. Everyone on screen joined in the singing, ecstatically swaying their bodies to the music. Rabbi Ruth invited congregants to express their feelings as they worshipped on the chat forum so their feelings could be shared and the group could develop a community of intense engagement. At one point, she invited the audience to "stand up and in your own way—it could be call and response—you are master of your own davening—experience eruption in all its power."

After one-and-a-half hours, the service concluded with the traditional reading of the mourners' prayer for the dead—the Kaddish. This time it was read by a visiting rabbi. The Kaddish was followed by a joyful song. Finally, Ruth wished each "window" of the broadcast (Chicago, Jerusalem, and Boulder, Colorado) "Shabbat Shalom," the traditional Hebrew greeting and farewell for the Sabbath, and each participant returned the greeting.

Islam's Cyber Mosques

The various branches of Islam have found a home on hundreds of internet sites devoted to information, history, prayer, pilgrimage, and other aspects of Muslim worship. The Shiite sect alone offers worshippers an exhaustive guide to online worship through the Iran-based website www.shiasearch .com that contains links to hundreds of websites on various aspects of Islam in Persian (Farsi), French, Arabic, Hindi, Urdu, and English. The index for the site's vast resources includes such topics as the Koran, religious places, religious ceremonies, images, movies, pilgrimage, prayer, women, religious figures, mosques, and ethics. There is also a Q&A section. Most of the sites are relatively static information banks rather than interactive, dynamic sites of religious practice. The links to pilgrimage or prayer contain detailed descriptions of various prayers and pilgrimages, with detailed texts of relevant prayers. The links to ceremonies also contain detailed descriptions of various Muslim rituals, but these are supplemented by numerous photos as well as audio and video recordings.

As with the other religious websites we have described, online participation affords easy access to an almost unlimited source of detailed information on religious practice and history. Moreover, watching or listening to these recordings can convey powerful impressions of the experience of religious worship. However, it is clear that online participation like this cannot reproduce the embodied experience and the powerful social context of in-person worship. Online worship is inherently different from traditional religious practice.

Despite the limitations of online ritual worship, Muslim websites offer a number of advantages. In Iran, worshippers can gain ready online access to local clerics or their representatives for advice or policy clarification. Most websites have extensive Q&A sites where commonly asked questions are answered but also allow comments or messages for messages to be left by online visitors. The exchange of messages on these sites allows men and women to communicate with each other on religious matters in a way that is not generally available face-to-face (Kalinock 2006). While these sites do not emphasize online ritual practice, they offer visitors a wealth of information and opportunities to communicate with coreligionists in a relatively free and informal way:

In addition to reading the Quran and catching up on news from the Islamic world, Muslims can also use the new media technology to check prayer schedules, converse with other Muslims from around the world, and spread their beliefs. . . . Online communities take the form of cybermosques, online prayers, virtual pilgrimages, and email fatwa services . . . and extend to social media platforms like blogs, YouTube and Twitter. . . . Participation in such online communities has been seen to make participants less shy, more flexible in their thinking, more aware of the diverse nature of people within their society, less inhibited about the opposite gender, and more self-confident. (Ejaz 2019, p. 696)

While the internet has provided a powerful source of information for Muslim worshippers, and opened a virtual window onto a seemingly unlimited stream of video sermons and prayers, it has also loosened the grip of religious authorities on their followers' experience of Islam. The ease with which Muslims can access online information from competing sects, exchange experiences with members of the opposite sex, and access the vast range of sometimes conflicting opinions and perspectives on religious belief and practice available online represents a potential challenge to Muslim authorities and orthodoxy.

Virtual Puja: Hinduism in the Internet Age

Hinduism, with its five major sects (Vaishnavism, Shaivism, Shaktism, Ganapatism, and Saurism), is the world's third largest religion and is often considered the world's oldest major religious tradition. Though historically based on the Indian subcontinent, Hinduism has found the internet to be a powerful way to extend its reach to the Hindu diaspora and globalize the faith. The many websites devoted to Hindu traditions and practices provide a convenient way to connect the many communities of the Indian diaspora and provide the far-flung population of Hindu devotees with a way to participate in a common ceremonial tradition. As a polytheistic religion, Hinduism recognizes a pantheon of deities responsible for different aspects of life such as fire, education, health, and wealth. Foremost are the five supreme deities, *Vishnu, Shiva, Adi Parashakti, Ganesha,* and *Surya,* but ancient texts often mention thirty-three deities (devas).

Hindu temples are dedicated to specific deities, and Hindu worship often consists of special prayers, *puja*—ritual offerings to specific deities to celebrate notable events or to specific blessings, merit, and other benefits.

Homam puja are sacrificial offerings to a consecrated fire made to Lord Agni (the god of fire) as a way of gaining merit and success in life or to increase the harmony of a family by removing obstacles and negative energies. Puja rituals are common to Hindu, Jain, and Buddhist traditions. While Christian, Jewish, and Muslim worship is ideally done collectively by organized groups, Hindu religious worship is often done by individuals who make offerings and chant prayers to an altar at home or in a temple that is dedicated to a particular deity. The altar contains a statue or picture of the deity, which is understood to be a *murti* (a form or manifestation) of the deity. God is understood to be everywhere but can be locally manifested by a sacred two- or three-dimensional murti to whom the offerings are made.

Pujas can be simple or elaborate. A typical one will include a long sequence of specific rites including the setting up of an altar, rites of purification, chants to specific deities accompanied by specific hand gestures, rites involving breath control, focused meditation, the ringing of a bell to invite the deity to dispel negative energy, and various rites invoking gods and gurus. Specific instructions for these pujas are spelled out in the vedas and other sacred Hindu writings. A traditional elaborated puja called *Shodashopachara puja* comprises sixteen steps that can be carried out relatively quickly as an everyday form of worship or can be elaborated on special occasions into a ceremony lasting several hours.

In many ways, Hindu liturgy is more compatible with virtualized religious practice than Christian, Jewish, or Muslim rituals. Online ritual is often done by individuals rather than by groups, and this is no problem for Hindu worshippers. Moreover, the "virtual" character of worship does not present the same challenges for Hindu worshippers that it does for Catholics for whom the physical presence of sacraments and copresence with a priest are crucial. Hindu belief recognizes the Divine as present everywhere and acknowledges that the worshipped *murti* are ultimately an aspect of *maya*—the illusory nature of the experienced world. From this point of view, VR can be understood as the equivalent of or even more real than the world of physical appearance, giving the online world a credibility lacking in other traditions.

More challenging for online Hindu worshippers is the question of whether a computer that has been used for other purposes can be considered as a purified site for a virtual altar. Online worshippers undertaking puja to a *murti* at a temple on their computer screen will often attempt to clean the computer literally and figuratively and make sure it has not been used for unholy surfing, such as contacting pornographic sites.[9]

Another distinctive feature of Hindu websites is the proliferation of online puja service sites, such as saranam.com. These web services act as agents connecting patrons seeking a ritual performance and "franchisees" associated with particular temples in India who are available for hire to carry out pujas at their temples on behalf of the online clients. For a price, often between $5–$12, a surrogate will perform a puja at a particular temple, for a particular deity, with a specified emphasis (e.g., wealth, fertility, relationship harmony, peace, or spiritual elevation) in the name of the client. Because a puja may be done by a surrogate in someone's name, virtual ritual presents no problem for the worshipper. A "real" ritual offering is being made at a specific place and a specified time in the client's name, and the clients are sent a series of emails by the agent reminding the client when the puja will be done, letting the client know that the puja is being carried out and certifying that the rite has been completed as requested. Moreover, once the puja is done, the franchisee is obliged to send the *prasad*—the returned and consecrated offering of food and water—to the web service, which will then ship it to the client. What is striking about this practice is the way it seamlessly combines virtual and physical aspects of the ritual.

Buddhism Goes Virtual

Buddhism, also known as Buddha Dharma, is the fourth largest religion in the world.[10] Founded in India 2,500 years ago, Buddhism currently has about 520 million followers who observe the faith in numerous branches found throughout Asia and increasingly the West. The different branches of Buddhism all focus in different ways on life practices that lead to the transcendence of desire and the state of Nirvana by which an individual gains merit and is able to end the cycle of death and rebirth. Theravada Buddhism is widely practiced in Sri Lanka and throughout Southeast Asia. The numerous schools of Mahayana Buddhism are found in Malaysia, Nepal, mainland China, Taiwan, Korea, Japan, and Vietnam, while Tibetan Buddhism is practiced in the Himalayan region including Tibet (traditionally), Kalmykia in the Russian North Caucasus, and Mongolia.

All the branches of Buddhism host websites where worshippers can find information, video broadcasts of meditation sessions, lectures on Buddhist practices and traditions, and the chanting of sutras. One Tibetan Buddhist sites sponsored by the Rangjung Yeshe Institute is primarily oriented to Buddhist education.[11] Founded by Chokyi Nyima Rinpoche, the institute offers online courses at the bachelor's and master's levels in Buddhist studies and training in the translation of Buddhist texts. The website says that the institute is affiliated with Kathmandu University in Nepal and offers both degree and nondegree online courses in Buddhist philosophy and history as well as training in Sanskrit, Classical Tibetan, Colloquial Tibetan, and Nepali languages. Online offerings are limited to course materials, videos, and access to online courses rather than virtual ritual.

While most Buddhist websites are used as traditional storage and broadcasting sites for what we have called "ritual online," I want to highlight some more ambitious uses of digital technology by Buddhists in South Korea and China in attempting to simulate ritual in a more complex way. In a short but provocative conference paper, Hai-Ran Woo sketches a fascinating picture of attempts to develop genuinely interactive online Buddhist ritual in South Korea. Noting the country's highly developed digital culture and technology, Woo sees South Korean Buddhists as culturally and religiously predisposed to embrace the possibilities of genuine "online ritual": "Korean Buddhists have neither strong spirit of community nor put special value on collective ritual. Besides, they are used to the presence of statues and paintings of Buddhas, Bodhisattvas and other enlightened beings in their ritual places. Therefore, it is no wonder that most Korean Buddhists have no strong aversion about doing online-ritual which is full of visual content and performed on a personal basis" (Woo 2013, p. 3).

According to Woo, many Korean Buddhist websites provide opportunities for online worshippers to perform Buddhist rituals on performance sites often called Cyber Buddha Halls that provide visual, aural, and text components for participants to access in performing their rituals. These websites attempt to simulate the various spaces of real Buddhist temples. Most important is the Main Buddha Hall (대웅전 in Korean), where in actual temples Shakyamuni Buddha is enshrined and where the most important rites are performed. For the participants, the emphasis of the site is on making ritual offerings and chanting sutras. Some sites provide an avatar of a childlike monk to guide the worshippers through the temple. Worshippers are presented with a variety of virtual objects they can use in their rituals:

flowers to use as offerings, incense to burn, and candles to light as they chant. While Buddhist ritual is generally quite rigid in the order and nature of its prescribed actions, the online version allows worshippers to choose which acts they wish to perform and in what order they choose to do them. A ritual can be abbreviated by skipping particular rites or shortening them, or it can be elaborated depending on individual desires and needs. In this sense, the temple ritual becomes somewhat more highly individualized than it would be when done in a real temple setting.

Not surprisingly, Chinese Buddhism has made great strides in taking advantage of digital technology (Travagnin 2020). The Nanputuo Temple's online temple is called the Online Buddha Hall (Zaixian Fotang 在线佛堂). The site is designed to allow online visitors to perform six important Buddhist rites.

> Visitors to the Online Buddha Hall can virtually open the doors of five "halls" and have access to the main daily liturgy; in so doing, they can perform a total of six different ritual practices. Specifically, the homepage is split into a Buddha Recitation Hall for the recitation of the name of a buddha or bodhisattva; an Offering Hall (Lifo Tang 礼佛堂) for giving virtual offerings to buddhas and bodhisattvas; a Sutra Chanting Hall (Songjing Tang 诵经堂); a Sutra Copying Hall (Chaojing Tang 抄经堂), for copying—or, more accurately, typing—Buddhist scriptures; and a Repentance Hall (Chanhui Tang 忏悔堂). Finally, there is access to videos of the morning and evening devotions that the sangha of Nanputuo perform daily (*zhaomu ke* 朝暮课). The Online Memorial Worship Site provides visitors with the possibility to venerate previous important monks (*xianzu dade* 先祖大德) who distinguished themselves in the history of Nanputuo and to create and worship tablets of family ancestors. The worship consists of offerings of traditional offline goods such as flowers, candles, and dedication messages in digital form. (Travagnin 2020, p. 203–204)

While the virtual temple makes it possible for worshippers to perform many traditional prayers, the translation to online performance has necessitated many changes to the traditional modalities of worship. In the Sutra Copying Hall, the practice of copying sutra texts becomes an act of typing rather than writing the texts. The traditional practice of carefully tracing a character from a sutra is very different from typing a character on a computer keyboard. This transformed copying process is in line with the more general shift from handwriting characters to typing them, a shift from analog to digital modes of representation. In the online version of giving offerings, the traditional chanting and bodily movements that accompany offerings in the classical in-person practices are replaced by a simply click in the online translation, in which the embodied qualities of the original rite are lost. The virtual hall appears to have a major effect on which ritual practices are most commonly performed.

By far, the most common online practices are the making of offerings, while chanting sutras, copying sutras, and chanting the name of the Buddha are much less frequent. The central Buddhist rite of repentance is very rarely practiced online. Stefania Travagnin argues that the translation from in-person to virtual ritual creates a much more convenient form of worship but also involves a major set of trade-offs in the worshipper's experience:

> Online activity also alters the paradigms that are the bases of the offline local Buddhist community and entails a different way for the temple's visitors to relate to the sacred site of the temple and its resident sangha. The offline community relies on monks and nuns who reside in the temple and who answer questions, resolve doubts, listen to concerns, and guide practice, and in this process, devotees build a personal and unique relationship with the resident sangha. Online, those relations are homogenized and their individual character nullified.[12]

While the older generations of Chinese Buddhists clearly prefer the more familiar traditional forms of in-person worship, the younger generation is increasingly taking advantage of the new online forms of worship not only because of its convenience but also because its on-screen modalities are familiar forms of everyday communication for them.

Virtual Pilgrimage

Pilgrimage is a distinctive form of religious ritual found in all the major religious traditions (Turner 1973; Turner and Turner 1995). Pilgrimages are journeys to sacred religious sites, places where major events happened in the history of the religion, or places associated with the lives and deaths of sacred religious figures. While the decision to undertake a pilgrimage is usually a personal choice, pilgrimages are often viewed as a religious obligation for the devout. For example, Muslims (who are physically and financially able) are all expected at least once in their life to undertake the hajj, a pilgrimage to Mecca to touch the sacred black stone near the Kaaba, regarded by Muslims as "the navel of the world." Some pilgrimage sites like Lourdes in France, Compostela in Spain, Guadalupe in Mexico, or Mecca in

Saudi Arabia are major national and transnational religious centers, famous throughout the world and attracting millions of pilgrims. Others are more local and involve smaller communities of believers.

The pilgrimage often involves a long and sometimes arduous journey. This journey is often used as a kind of metaphor for moving the heart and mind in new directions and changing the pilgrim's view of life. Therefore the physical experience of moving from place to place toward a sacred goal is an essential aspect of a pilgrimage. One of the most famous pilgrimage sites, known as El Camino de Santiago (the Way of St. James), comprises an ancient network of pilgrim routes across Europe, all leading to the tomb of St. James in Santiago de Compostela in northwest Spain. There are many routes in this network, but about 60 percent of the Santiago pilgrims take a pilgrimage route known as the *Camino Francés* (French Road) that stretches nearly five hundred miles from Saint-Jean-Pied-du-Port near Biarritz in France to Santiago. The long and often arduous walk (the pilgrims all walk) will take an experienced hiker around a month to complete. While guided tours are available, the journey is often taken alone or in small groups. There are inns and places to eat all along the route, which is marked by route markers displaying an oyster shell logo.

In this case, the pilgrimage is not just a metaphorical journey but a real endurance challenge for the hikers. The spiritual journey is paralleled by a physical challenge so that the pilgrimage is imprinted on both the pilgrim's body and soul. Victor Turner describes the complex path characteristic of a traditional pilgrimage as a potent mix of spiritual and secular experiences: "I wish briefly to indicate, too, that as the pilgrim moves away from his structural involvements at home his route becomes increasingly sacralized at one level and increasingly secularized at another. He meets with more shrines and sacred objects as he advances, but he also encounters more real dangers such as bandits and robbers; he has to pay attention to the need to survive and often to earn money for transportation; and he comes across markets and fairs, especially at the end of his quest, where the shrine is flanked by the bazaar and by the fun fair" (Turner 1973, p. 204–205).

The worldwide pandemic starting in 2020 led to the mass cancellation of many pilgrimages, forcing many pilgrimage sites to produce online versions of their pilgrimage experiences. Since a physical trip was no longer possible, web sponsors had to rely on the metaphorical meanings of the travel theme in attempting to virtualize pilgrimage online. The simplest solution was to replace the pilgrimage with a website filled with photos and videos that allowed viewers to "experience" a pilgrimage through the eyes of someone else.

One example of this simple version of virtual pilgrimage appears on a website sponsored by Notre Dame University that contains photos, videos, and text accounts of a pilgrimage to Jerusalem.[13] The website opens with a general invitation for online viewers to experience a pilgrimage to the Holy Land in "a new way": "Make an online pilgrimage to the Holy Land! This virtual pilgrimage will take you to the Church of the Nativity in Bethlehem, where Jesus was born, and to the Church of the Holy Sepulcher in Jerusalem, where Jesus was crucified, killed, buried, and raised from the dead. These are the holiest sites of our Christian faith, and they invite us to linger with the history and mystery of what happened there. This 'virtual pilgrimage' is a way for FaithND readers to encounter the central mysteries of our faith in a new way."

The metaphorical sense of traveling is used so that moving through the various pages of the website becomes a form of spiritual journey: "People traveling to the Holy Land use a maxim to guide their way: 'Tourists pass through the sites; pilgrims let the sites pass through them.' We will adopt this idea as a guiding principle for this virtual pilgrimage. . . . We invite you to wander through these places as a "virtual pilgrim" so that these mysteries of our faith might also wander through you." The text also offers the online pilgrim a guided tour for an imaginary journey, aided by the photos and videos. Viewers are encouraged to use their memories of their own experiences to create a hybrid image of themselves at the places in the photos: "Think of a good friend you've known for years. Then think of the first time you visited their home and met their family. A visit like this yields a deeper understanding of your friend from encountering the source of their values and history and experience. Such an encounter deepens knowledge and love, and this is what pilgrims seek in their journeys: intimacy with the person of Jesus Christ."[14]

The virtual pilgrimage has four stages: 1) "Introduction: The Holy Land as the 'Fifth Gospel'"; 2) "Church of the Nativity: Place of Jesus' Birth"; 3) "Church of the Holy Sepulcher: Place of Death and Resurrection"; and 4) "Conclusion: The Places that Anchor Faith, Hope, and Love." The pilgrimage is set up as a chronology of the important events in Jesus's life, each anchored at a sacred place. The website offers photos and detailed descriptions of each place and gives the historical and theological setting. Each visit is followed by a video of pilgrims entering the sacred site. The text describes the journey as if the reader were actually entering the holy place:

> As pilgrims enter the Church of the Holy Sepulcher, they ascend a staircase to go up one story to the chapel that encloses the rock outcropping upon which Jesus was crucified. The limestone where the two thieves were crucified is encased in glass (as in this photo), and the place in the center that would have held Jesus' cross is covered by an altar.
>
> To reverence this place, pilgrims may approach and kneel before the place of the cross. Like the place of the Nativity, there is a marble slab with a metal plate covering a small opening. You can place your hand inside this opening and reach down more than a foot to touch the rock that held the cross.

The combination of photographs, videos, background information, and vivid descriptions of what it is like to enter these sacred spaces all work to provide a feeling for the online pilgrim of participating in the actual pilgrimage.

Currently, the most radical use of digital technology for simulating a religious pilgrimage has been the creation by the government of Saudi Arabia of a VR program allowing Muslim pilgrims to make the hajj to Mecca via the metaverse in a VR simulation. The program is a project of Saudi Arabia's Exhibitions and Museums Affairs Agency, working with Umm al-Qura University. With the outbreak of Covid, the annual number of pilgrims to Mecca fell from 2,500,000 to around 60,000 between 2019 and 2022, leading the Saudi government to turn to AI to provide an alternative to the traditional hajj. The Virtual Black Stone Initiative, as the program is known, focuses on the Hajar Aswad, the sacred black stone now found in the southwest corner of the Kaaba, the sacred house representing the house of God, located at the center of Masjid al-Haram in Mecca, Islam's most important mosque. The stone is believed to have fallen from heaven at the time Adam and Eve were created.

Seeing the Hajar Aswad is a major goal of every pilgrim making the hajj. Because they wanted the stone to be viewed in as much detail as possible by virtual pilgrims, the developers had 1,050 photographs of the stone taken, each with a resolution of 49,000 pixels. So detailed are the pictures that they took fifty hours to process. The developers are determined to simulate the actual experience of entering the mosque grounds and interacting with the sacred stone. Hinting at what is in store the future of simulated ritual experience, the computer scientists developing the VR hajj experience hope to find ways to reproduce not only three-dimensional space but also simulations of touch and smell.

Not surprisingly, the idea of a VR hajj has been greeted with considerable controversy by Muslims. Some worshippers are wildly enthusiastic about the prospect of such a realistic simulation of the pilgrimage, while others view the program as tampering with God's holy law and attempting to replace the sacred obligation for pilgrims to touch the ground of the holy mosque with their own feet with a fake trip through a plastic viewer. Even the entrepreneurs who are developing VR hajj simulations recognize its limitations: "I don't think this will ever replace the real experience, and this comes from someone who's done the real experience. This is something that is life changing," said Muhammad Chbib, a seasoned entrepreneur based in Dubai, who is in charge of business development for Muslim 3D (Maghribi 2021). While ultimately VR pilgrimage is just a simulation, VR technology holds great promise for overcoming many of the current limitations in virtualizing the actual experience of ritual.

Other Internet Rituals

Religious worship is probably the most common form of traditional ritual that has found its way to the internet. But religious rites are not the only ritual forms found online. Even before the pandemic of 2020 sent many of us online, the internet has been hosting a variety of traditional celebrations including birthday parties, funerals, memorial services, and weddings. Most of these online celebrations fall into the category of "rituals online," using the internet to simply broadcast live a ritual event to online viewers. These events make relatively little use of the potential of digital technology for simulating an interactive ritual involving active participation and interaction among participants. A step closer to virtual participation would be a wedding in which the bride and groom were both online in different places and performing the ritual exchanges of the marriage ceremony virtually.

While current internet meeting programs make online marriages relatively simple matters technologically, the legal issues are much more challenging. In the United States, virtual marriages have created considerable legal ambiguity and confusion since the laws regulating online weddings are variously controlled by both states and local counties. Different laws regulate whether a couple can apply online for a wedding license, whether an officiant can perform a wedding ceremony virtually, and whether the officiant, the bride, and the groom can be in different places during the license application and the ceremony. Since many of these laws were enacted as emergency measures during the pandemic, they have changed quickly as the Covid pandemic has grown and waned.

In the United States the legal landscape of virtual marriage regulations is both unstable and confusing. On the permissive end of the spectrum, most counties in Illinois permit both online marriage licenses and virtual marriage ceremonies. Utah is particularly open to virtual weddings, allowing considerable flexibility in the wedding arrangements. Here's how the website the "American Wedding Blog" summarizes Utah's virtual marriage laws:

> In Utah County, Utah, marriage licenses can be applied for, signed (by both the couple and the officiant), and recorded with the county all online—thanks to a fully digital and secure online system. After filing, a Certified Copy of the license is sent to the couple via email, with a paper copy sent by mail the following day. The officiant, couple, and two adult witnesses must attend the ceremony (all can attend virtually from different locations) and participate in real time, and the ceremony must be hosted from a physical location within the state.
>
> Anyone getting married in the state can get their marriage license from any county, according to state law, and state residency is not required to apply for or file a marriage license in Utah County.[15]

In Tennessee, officiants are required to be in the same physical room as the bride and groom to perform the wedding ceremony. Note that this does not prevent the ceremony from being broadcast online to virtual wedding guests. While some counties in Pennsylvania permit couples to apply online for their marriage license, the city of Philadelphia specifies that couples must appear together physically in the office of the register of wills to obtain a license. In Ohio some counties permit online application for marriage licenses but not online wedding ceremonies since the ceremony requires both in-person proof of identity for all participants and that the marriage license forms are paper forms that must be signed directly. Colorado state law currently allows couples to apply for marriage licenses remotely but specifies that at the time of the application, both members of the couple must be together in the same physical space.

A truly virtual form of marriage is made possible by the computer program *Second Life*, which allows users to enter a massively multiuser virtual universe where they can create a complete online identity (avatar) and develop a virtual "second life." Developed in 1998, *Second Life* is highly immersive and engaging. Its detailed graphics and endless menu of options for meeting others, staging events, and morphing one's virtual identity afford users the experience of a world in which they can exercise control over all aspects of their lives including their own avatar identities. *Second Life* offers the user a chance to participate in genuine "online rituals" in which players' avatars can perform ritual acts as participants rather than simply as online viewers. The *Second Life* universe includes many institutions that players can join and allows them to participate in communal activities. An example of a virtual religious community is the Ruach Ministry, which includes twenty churches as well as detailed instructions for both communal and private prayer. Alternatively, users (through their avatars) can meditate and light candles at Drolma Lhakhang Tibetan Temple or pray at a Muslin mosque (Radde-Antweiler 2007, p. 187).

Second Life also provides many options for the staging of virtual weddings. Using virtual money as payment, users have access to many wedding planners, wedding services, and diverse wedding venues. Preparation for virtual weddings is similar to that in the "first life," and those planning the event must contend with purchases of such items as wedding clothes, jewelry, makeup, flowers, and catering. In an essay analyzing *Second Life* weddings, Kerstin Radde-Antweiler views them as a form of "transfer ritual" in which the ritual elements are transferred from the real world to *Second Life*'s virtual universe in a specific context that shapes their form. She notes the flexibility in structure and form of these virtual weddings, which allows the user considerable latitude in designing the ritual:

> The structure and form of the weddings are relatively flexible, depending on what kind of wedding or ceremony the couple prefer. Mostly it includes the questioning, the vows, the exchange of rings and a long mostly self-written statement about their love and commitment to each other. The explicit and reflexive reproduction of religious traditions are rather the exception than the norm, but it is possible to identify implicit processes of reception and combination of elements from different traditions, like parts of Anglican liturgy mixed with elements of modern handfasting ritual. (Radde-Antweiler 2007, p. 190)

The flexibility Radde-Antweiler describes is in keeping with the modern taste for idiosyncratic wedding rituals. The detail and time that *Second Life* users put into planning and executing their *Second Life* weddings suggest that the virtual events are viewed as authentic rituals and are taken seriously by the participants. While they obviously cannot produce legal first-life marriages, these virtual weddings seem to come close to simulating the experience of actual marriage rites and wedding festivities.

The other online ritual genre that has been well studied is online funerals and memorials for the dead. *Second Life* provides resources for virtual funerals and memorial services just as it does for weddings. These virtual funerals include not only the actual funeral rites and burial but also virtual mourning and grief counseling. The internet has also been adapted as a site for funerals and candle-lighting ceremonies for first-life individuals and also for pets. "Online hospice" sites such as Caring Bridge provide ways for friends and family of the terminally ill to communicate with the patient during the last stages of their life and virtual portals for commemoration and mutual comfort after the patient's death. Social network services like Facebook, WeChat, Twitter, Weibo, and Instagram have been used effectively as sites for memorialization of the deceased, while video streaming services like Facetime, Skype, WhatsApp, and Zoom can stream both real and virtual funerals.

Virtual funerals became a big business during the years of the Covid pandemic, which dramatically increased the number of deaths and prevented mourners from gathering in physical spaces. Online memorials for victims of Covid often replaced actual burial services. Web services like Lighten, SympathyNet, and Willowise offer professional planning and execution for virtual funeral services and memorials.[16] In some virtual funerals, all the mourners and speakers appear in windows on the screen. In others, viewers are presented clips of mourners' remembrances of the deceased along with photos highlighting their lives and relationships.

Robots and Ritual

The internet is not the only way digital technology is reinventing rituals. Robots have also been developed to carry out rituals traditionally performed by humans. At the Buddhist Longquan Temple in Beijing, China, a miniature robot monk named Xian'er (贤二 in Chinese), looking like a cute mobile toy, was created by the temple's lead cartoonist in 2015 to provide information and answer questions for temple visitors. In 2017, in the German town of Wittenberg, the very place where, four hundred years ago, Luther sparked the Protestant Reformation by nailing his ninety-five theses to a church door, the anniversary of the religious revolution was celebrated by the introduction of a blessing robot named BlessU-2. Offering a choice of blessings in five languages, the robot communicates through both voice and a video touchscreen on its body. The user indicates the desired language and gender of the blessing voice, and the robot does the rest.

While BlessU-2 is rather crudely mechanical in appearance, more like the Tin Man of *The Wizard of Oz* than a real human, its arms and fingers are extended, and the hands light up during the blessing in imitation of human blessing gestures. Church authorities feel that the blessing robot will challenge worshippers to contemplate the relationship between religious worship and AI. Stephen Krebs of the Protestant Church in Hesse and Nassau, which initiated the project, commented that "we wanted people to consider if it is possible to be blessed by a machine, or if a human being is needed" (Sherwood 2017).

In Japan, Softbank's robot Pepper, which has been designed to read and respond appropriately to human vocal and facial emotion expressions, has been modified to conduct Buddhist funerals for mourners. Funeral services in Japan can cost tens of thousands of dollars, and the rental of a robot priest can help bring down the costs. While the cost of hiring a human priest is around $2,000, renting Pepper runs around $420. Theoretically, Pepper can be used either as a kind of backup aid to a human priest or as a replacement for the priest for those who are financially strapped. The robot can be programmed to chant sutras and beat a drum during the Buddhist funeral ceremony, but Buddhist priests are evaluating Pepper to determine whether it can deliver an emotionally satisfying ritual performance.

Not surprisingly, the idea of a robot-led funeral service has been greeted with some skepticism by many Japanese people, and only time will tell whether robotic funeral rites will eventually take hold. As with virtual marriage ceremonies, using robots to conduct rituals will produce legal challenges as well as cultural and technological ones. Government and religious authorities will have to decide whether a rite carried out by a robot will count as a legal or an official practice. The very concept of ordination will have to be rethought as intelligent machines are increasingly tasked with ritual work.

Online Interaction Ritual

So far, we have looked at in-person rituals broadcasted via the internet as well as attempts to create genuine internet rituals, virtual simulations of traditional ceremonies. The final kind of internet ritual we will consider is perhaps the most pervasive way in which the internet reshapes ritual. It is also the least obvious kind of internet ritual precisely because it is so intimately tied to our online behavior. I am referring to the rituals involved in simply navigating our computer devices.

If a ritual is a repeatable pattern of action that takes on symbolic weight, then our desktop computers, laptops, tablets, and cell phones all can be seen as almost perfect generators of ritual behavior. Whether the action patterns are texting, typing on a keyboard, manipulating a mouse or trackball, or navigating through a familiar program's commands, the physical and sensory interactions involved in our digital lives are all ritualized actions. The fact that we rarely think of digital navigation as ritual behavior only means that it falls into the category of tacit ritual, rhythmic action sets so finely integrated into our behavior that they go unlabeled and unnoticed until something goes wrong with our equipment or we have a power outage while online and experience the kind of deep disorientation we experience when the normal rhythm of our lives in disrupted.

Our online world is made up of not just operating systems, programs, and websites but also the layers of physical routines that our bodies and minds have mastered as we navigate the digital world. I have one set of physical routines I use for Microsoft Word, another set for PowerPoint, a third for navigating my Chrome browser, and so on. I have also developed familiar routines for surfing the internet and navigating familiar websites like Gmail, Facebook, Amazon, Twitter, and Instagram.

The most familiar sites I visit are my internet neighborhood, whose terrain I can usually navigate with the same ease that I commute to work every day. Using my Android cell phone is a different neighborhood and calls on a different set of routines. But, normally, I quickly switch action modes without thinking about it. Unless I get a new program or upgrade to a new version of my operating system, my physical and mental reflexes feel "at home" in my familiar digital world. Users of Apple technology develop alternate sets of routines to navigate their devices, and since I am a member of the PC/Android family, if I try to use a Mac computer, an iPad, or an iPhone, I initially feel disoriented and lost. My old routines don't work anymore. Something essential is missing in my life, and I come to realize that my interactions with my devices are not just routines but instead have become personal rituals and an aspect of my identity. Somehow, my sense of being "me" has become tied up with my interaction routines that drive my technology.

Because we take them with us everywhere we go, our cell phones have become our most intimate ritual companions. In fact, using them has become neurotically ritualized. Increasingly, we notice compulsive cell phone checking by ourselves and others. Just look around you. We seem to have created a new kind of "checking compulsion," one of the behaviors used to diagnose OCD.

The ritualization of user–computer interactions partly explains the attraction of computer gaming, where developing skill means both mastering a repertory of physical manipulation skills and developing an effective set of strategic responses. This distinction between basic interaction skills and strategic competence takes us back to the chapter on baseball games and baseball ritual and the discussion of how a game can also be viewed as a ritual. The strategic responses represent the "game" aspect of play, where the ability to respond quickly and effectively to novel events is a key to winning. But the more basic interactive skills all players share in simply playing the game represent the "ritual" aspect of play—the shared framework of interactions, knowledge, and skills that enables a player to enter into the game in the first place. This is why skilled competition in sports produces at one and the same time a gap between winners and losers and a united community of players. The same is true of computer gaming.

Players of Minecraft and those of League of Legends represent genuine online communities as well as competitors. Members of a community not only compete with one another, but they also share the knowledge, vocabulary, lore, and embodied interaction rituals that constitute their game's "social contract." Admittedly, calling our digital interaction skills *rituals* seems to stretch the traditional meaning of ritual quite a bit. But it also underscores the pervasiveness of ritualization in human life and the arbitrariness of the point along the spectrum of ritualized behavior where each culture chooses to label patterned activities as "rituals."

Conclusion. Is "Virtual Ritual" Really Ritual?

In this chapter, we have traced the many profound ways that the digital revolution has reshaped ritual performance. While the emergence of the internet was bound to reshape our ritual life, the emergence of the worldwide Covid pandemic and its persistence in the second decade of the century has dramatically intensified the use of the internet as a vehicle for broadcasting many traditional rituals, both sacred and secular. In many cases, the internet has been used largely as a delivery vehicle for recorded or live-streamed rituals in churches, temples, mosques, and other institutional settings.

However, this use of ritual online is really just an extension of older broadcasting technologies like radio and television and does not represent a radical transformation of ritual performance or exploit the possibilities of AI for creating "deep simulation." The current development of the metaverse relies on developing really powerful VR applications. We have noted the development of impressive 3D simulations of the Muslim hajj. However, impressive as they may seem, today's VR applications can be seen as the equivalent of Nintendo's 1980s *Mario Brothers* games when compared with what is to come. Harnessing the power of AI to simulate reality in many of its modalities will be the key to enhancing the experience of cyber ritual.

How ritual is experienced is the central problem faced by today's virtualization of rituals. There is nothing stopping us from simply declaring online ritual or ritual online to be genuine rituals since the definition of a ritual has always been elastic enough to accommodate a lot of variation. What we agree to call "ritual" is subject to cultural and personal variation since it is inherently a spectrum phenomenon, always threatening to shade off into something else. The real question is about experience and the way in which changes in the mode of representation constrain human experience in profound ways.

The cognitive implications of different communication media was brilliantly theorized by Walter Ong, a Jesuit philosopher and professor of literature, in his 1967 book *The Presence of the Word* and, most influentially, in his 1982 monograph *Orality and Literacy*. In these and other publications, Ong argues that the development of writing represented a watershed for humanity, forever changing the way that reality would be viewed and remembered (Ong 1967, 1982). More generally, Ong postulates that oral cultures without writing technology produced a very different kind of mindset from those in which experiences could be written down. Fundamental to oral cultures, Ong argues, were ritual as a mode of communication and memory exploiting all of the human senses in articulating its worldview. At the beginning of his 1982 book, Ong comments, almost parenthetically, on how the electronic media of the time—radio and television—were producing yet another transformation in how reality was being understood.

> Literacy began with writing but, at a later stage of course, also involves print. This book thus attends somewhat to print as well as to writing. It also makes some passing mention of the electronic processing of the word and of thought, as on radio and television and via satellite. Our understanding of the differences between orality and literacy developed only in the electronic age, not earlier. Contrasts between electronic media and print have sensitized us to the earlier contrast between writing and orality. The electronic age is also an age of 'secondary orality', the orality of telephones, radio, and television, which depends on writing and print for its existence. (Ong 1982, p. 2)

In a groundbreaking paper on religious experience in the digital age, Steven O'Leary extends the significance of Ong's notion of "secondary orality" to the development of internet technology.

> The term "secondary orality" refers to the fact that in the new electronic media the divorce between word and image begun by print is reversed, so that the total sensorium again includes sight and voice, image, and music. This stage "has striking resemblance to [primary oral cultures] in its participatory mystique, its fostering of a communal sense, its concentration on the present moment and even its use of formulas," it differs from the old in that "it generates a sense for groups immeasurably larger than those of primary oral culture—McLuhan's 'global village.'" (O'Leary 1996, p. 795–786)

While the secondary orality of the internet has allowed for the worldwide broadcast of information that can be seen and heard as well as read, several key aspects of traditional ritual cognition are still missing: bodily sensation, touch, taste, and smell. Current VR technology has yet to simulate these embodied dimensions of human experience, and until they do, the virtual experience of ritual can only be characterized as partial and incomplete. It is not enough to simply relabel virtual ceremonies as "rituals" and to claim that they are thus equivalent to in-person rituals. Rituals are inherently embodied experiences, which is why it is difficult to describe them in words. Watch any ritual and you will see bodies in rhythmic motion, the human sensorium in flight. And watching a ritual is a very different experience from doing it. Not only do rituals require bodily movement, but they also orchestrate powerful sensory experiences that include feelings (emotions), touch, and smell. Until VR technology finds a way to credibly simulate these sensory experiences, virtual ritual can never be a full replication of the ritual experience.

Ritual in its virtual forms will, of course, continue to flood the internet as it morphs into the metaverse. And we will surely continue to call these virtualized performances "ritual." But from the crucial perspective of embodied experience, we can only conclude that our current technology cannot completely simulate in-person real ritual, at least not yet. However, given the astonishing speed at which AI is developing, it would be naïve to claim that we will never have an adequate experiential simulation of human ritual. As the virtual universe—our electronic metalife—continues to unfold at our fingertips, only fools would think they can predict the limits of where AI will take us. We are not there yet. But we are virtually there.

11 Does a Ritual Always Have a Meaning?

At this late stage of our journey through the kingdom of ritual, it might seem odd to be asking whether a ritual has meaning. So far, we have simply assumed that it does. On the face of it, ritual would seem to be all about meaning. But here, at the end of our journey, we can consider this question in a thoughtful way. Ask yourself to describe the meaning of the following rituals: a traditional Hindu wedding ceremony, the Catholic Mass, Salem Camp Meeting, your morning shower, my bar mitzvah, family dinner on Sundays, Thanksgiving, a quinceañera celebrating a Mexican girl's fifteenth birthday, Independence Day fireworks, and morning meditation. It is likely that you have an intuition that each of these rituals is meaningful. But you might also have trouble articulating just what that meaning is or deciding which meaning or whose meaning is the real one. As we will see, the ability to articulate the meaning of an experience is not the same thing as experiencing it as meaningful.

I am an anthropologist trained in the analysis of symbol systems. For a decade, I directed a Sloan Foundation research center at Emory University studying American family rituals. I have spent much of my career studying rituals, searching for their meaning, and some of my interpretations of rituals appear in this book. While I am confident that these interpretations shed some light on the rituals' meanings, I also know that, ultimately, none of my interpretations can be a complete account of their meaning.

Our assumption that a ritual has meaning is reinforced by the experience of watching a ritual. Experiencing ritual seems to ignite what the renowned Cambridge psychologist Frederic Bartlett called the "effort after meaning," an effort that Bartlett believed was the ultimate goal of remembering (Bartlett 1932). But with ritual, we face a paradox. The closer we get to a ritual, the further we seem to be from distilling its meaning. We experience the effort, but the goal seems elusive. I think this is because a ritual does not have *a meaning*; it can only have *meanings*. This chapter takes up the thorny question of the meaning of ritual and attempts to dispose of the disconcerting claims of some scholars that, with ritual, meaning is beside the point and rituals are inherently empty actions. In the following pages, I will explain why I think they are wrong. But first things first. Before confronting the problem of meaning, we have to deal with the question of symbols. Any discussion of ritual symbols must start with the brilliant work of the distinguished anthropologist Victor Turner.

Victor Turner's "Planes of Classification"

Turner was trained in the British tradition of social anthropology, where scholars focused on understanding the structures and functions of the institutions that made up the social structure of tribal societies. Turner's research was carried out in Zambia among the Ndembu people, a tribe of some sixty thousand people in northwestern Zambia, also known as the Lunda. Turner was interested in Ndembu social organization, but he was equally fascinated by the Ndembu mind, especially as it revealed itself in religious beliefs and practices. He was interested in the complex relations between the symbols and the minds of those that used them. During his fieldwork, he found himself fascinated by the elaborate rituals performed by the Ndembu, and he turned his attention to discovering what their arcane and puzzling rituals were actually about and how they worked their magic on the ritualists. Over the next three decades, Turner's many publications would illuminate a brilliant new path for understanding not just particular Ndembu rituals but what he called, more generally, "the ritual process."

Turner's 1969 book *The Ritual Process: Structure and Anti-Structure* presents detailed analyses of the numerous rituals of the Ndembu people (Turner 1969). Complaining that many scholars in the generation of anthropologists that preceded him had approached the study of "primitive religions" with a dreary "religious unmusicality" (p. 6), Turner sought to bring new life to the study of ritual symbols by examining Ndembu rituals in great detail, without condescension and with a sympathetic eye. Consulting Ndembu ritual specialists to understand their interpretation of their rituals, and using insights from psychology and semiotics as well as anthropology, Turner brought a new level of theoretical sophistication to the study of ritual.

In the opening chapter of the book, "Planes of Classification," Turner confronts the problem of uncovering ritual meaning by acknowledging that a ritual may mean different things to an outside observer than it means to those performing it.

> It is true that almost from the beginning of my stay among the Ndembu I had, on invitation, attended the frequent performances of the girls' puberty rites (Nkang'a) and had tried to describe what I had seen as accurately as possible. But it is one thing to observe people performing the stylized gestures and singing the cryptic songs of ritual performances and quite another to reach an adequate understanding of what the movements and words mean to *them*. (Turner 1969, p. 7)

Referring to the classic distinction between *etic* and *emic* analyses, Turner suggests that what a ritual may mean for an outside observer (the etic perspective) might be different from what it means to the local group performing the ritual (the emic perspective). From the outset of his analysis, he acknowledges many paths to meaning. Ritual symbols, he claimed, were inherently polysemic. The chapter focuses on the Ndembu *Isoma* ritual, a rite performed to cure a barren woman whose fertility is thought to have been impaired by the angry ghost of a maternal ancestor. Turner seeks to uncover both the structure of ritual action in *Isoma* and the ways in which its symbols work on the experience of the performers.

"The first step in such a task," Turner says, "is to pay close attention to the way the Ndembu explain their own symbols" (1969, p. 10). His next step is to understand the network of social relationships involved in the ritual. In exploring Ndembu social organization, Turner uncovers a major contradiction. The Ndembu are matrilineal, tracing their primary descent ties through mothers. But postmarital residence is virilocal, meaning that wives generally come to live in their husband's villages.[1] The women, whose offspring continue the lineage, disperse upon marriage to live with their husbands. This produces a pervasive conflict between one's loyalties to one's descent group and loyalties to the kin with whom they live. Turner discovers that the *Isoma* rites are usually performed for women thought to have been rendered infertile by the jealous spirits of deceased maternal kin. Ghosts of maternal kin attack female descendants who, residing with their husbands' people, are said to have forgotten their obligations to their own descent groups.

> They have been caught, so Ndembu regularly say, because they have "forgotten" those shades who are not only their direct ascendants but also the immediate

progenetrices of their matrikin—who form the core membership of villages different from those of their husbands. The curative rites, including Isoma, have as one social function that of "causing them to remember" these shades, who are structural nodes of a locally residing matrilineage. The condition of barrenness these shades bring about is considered to be a temporary one, to be removed by performance of the appropriate rites. Once a woman remembers the afflicting shade, and thus her primary allegiance to matrikin, the interdiction on her fertility will cease; she can go on living with her husband but with a sharpened awareness of where her and her children's ultimate loyalties lie. (Turner 1969, p. 13)

Turner infers that *Isoma* is a ritual response to this pervasive contradiction in Ndembu social structure and the ritual symbols reflect the conflicting patterns of Ndembu social relations. "The crisis brought on by this contradiction between norms," he argues, "is resolved by rituals rich in symbolism and pregnant with meaning." (Turner 1969, p. 7). He also argues that "the structural tension between matrilineal descent and virilocal marriage seems to dominate the ritual idiom of Isoma. It is because the woman has come too closely in touch with the 'man's side' in her marriage that her dead matrikin have impaired her fertility. The right relation that should exist between descent and affinity has been upset; the marriage has come to outweigh the matrilineage" (Turner 1970, p. 18).

In trying to penetrate the dense "forest of symbols" used in *Isoma*, Turner discovers that the local meaning of many of these symbols is closely connected to the etymology of the symbol's name, giving him a place to begin his exegesis of Ndembu symbols. The Ndembu apparently have their own theory of how ritual symbols work. They conceive of ritual units—the symbols—as "landmarks" or "blazes" that guide performers on a ritual journey. "A ritual element or unit is called *chijikijilu*," he writes. "Literally, this word signifies a 'landmark' or 'blaze'. Its etymon is ku-jikijila, 'to blaze a trail'—by slashing a mark on a tree with an ax or breaking one of its branches" (p. 15). These symbolic landmarks are connectors, linking the world of ordinary human experience with the invisible world in which the afflicting ghosts reside. *Isoma*, Turner concludes, is effectively an exorcism rite whose aim is to expel both the ghost afflicting the patient and the destructive mystical forces emanating from some of the victim's living relatives.

Turner continued his analysis of Ndembu ritual in his 1970 book *The Forest of Symbols*, where he proposes that Ndembu ritual symbols share three general characteristics. The first is *condensation* whereby many different things and qualities are forced together into a single symbol, affording ritual symbols a potentially wide range of meanings. Ritual symbols are thus *multivocal*, suggesting not a single association but a fan of numerous possible meanings. The second quality is the *unification of disparate references*, where distinct things are linked by shared analogical qualities.

Turner calls the third characteristic of Ndembu symbols *polarization of meaning*. A multivocal symbol may suggest associations at both an *ideological* pole, an abstract social referent, and a *sensory pole*, linking the symbol to intimate aspects of human anatomy and physiology. By encompassing both poles, the symbol can convey a message that is at once social and intimately personal, a bridge between social and personal meanings. Thus the *mudyi* tree that exudes a white milky sap is used in Ndembu ritual because it brings together, on the one hand, symbols representing the social idea of matrilineal descent (a tree) and, on the other, the personal reference to milk flowing from the female breast.

Turner goes on to theorize how these disparate meanings interact for those undergoing the ritual: "At the sensory pole are concentrated those significata that may be expected to arouse desires and feelings; at the ideological pole one finds an arrangement of norms and values that guide and control persons in social groups and categories" (Turner 1970, p. 28). Turner shows how the symbolic properties of ritual acts can be orchestrated in a ritual performance to interact, transforming both the ritualist's experience of her body and her relation to her social world. He has brilliantly captured the sense in which ritual symbols come to life, transforming both a performer's intimate experience and creating new socially relevant meanings.

The many symbols used in *Isoma* are mostly based on metaphorical connections between a symbol and its ritual effect.

> As with all Ndembu rites, the pattern of procedure in each specific case is set by the diviner originally consulted about the patient's affliction. He is the one who establishes that the woman has lost a succession of children by miscarriage or death in infancy—misfortunes summarized in the term *lufwisha*. It is he who decrees that the rites must begin at the hole or burrow, either of a giant rat (*chituba*) or of an ant-bear (*mfuji*). Why does he make this rather odd prescription? Ndembu explain it as follows: Both these animals stop up their burrows after excavating them. Each is a symbol (*chijikijilu*) for the Isoma shade-manifestation which has hidden away the woman's fertility (*lusemu*). The doctor adepts must open the blocked entrance of the burrow, and thus symbolically give her back her fertility, and also enable her to raise her children well. (Turner 1970, p. 20–21)

The sensory characteristics of the medicines can be transmitted to the bodies of the afflicted women through metaphoric transfer.

> At one performance I attended, the senior adept went to a *kapwipu* tree (*Swarlzia madagascariensis*), which is used because its wood is hard. Hardness represents the health and strength (*wukolu*) desired for the patient. The senior adept cleared the base of the tree of weeds with his ritual hoe, then put the pieces of edible tubers representing the patient's body on the cleared space (*mukombela*) and spoke as follows: "When this woman was pregnant before, her lips, eyes, palms and the soles of her feet turned yellow [a sign of anemia]. Now she is pregnant again. This time make her strong, so that she may bear a living child, and may it grow strong." (Turner 1970, p. 24)

The medicines collected for the ritual are valued for their symbolic properties, which are believed to be transmitted to the patient during the ritual. "Some (e.g., *kapwipu, mubang'a*) are used because they have tough (hence "strengthening") wood, others (e.g., *mucha, musafwa, mufung'u, museng'u, musoli,* and *mubulu*) because they are fruit-bearing trees, representing the ritual intention of making the patient fruitful once more. However, all share the ritually important property that bark string cannot be taken from them, for this would "tie up" the fertility of the patient" (Turner 1970, p. 24). In this way, a ritual deploys the power of symbolic association and metaphorical transformation as a kind of symbolic curing process.

In *The Forest of Symbols*, Turner distinguishes between three quite different sources of information that contribute to the interpretation of ritual: (1) the empirical form and observable qualities of the ritual acts, (2) local interpretations offered by specialists and other members of the community, and (3) "significant contexts worked out by the anthropologists" (p. 20). The third source of information can be thought of as the analytical perspective of the outside observer who may recognize certain significant patterns in the ritual that are not explicitly mentioned by the local ritualists but make sense of the observed data. This suggests that a thorough interpretation of a ritual will involve a mix of local meaning and external observation, both emic and etic data. It also raises the very real possibility that an observer's interpretation might differ in significant ways from the explanations of the local actors. The result will be meanings rather than a meaning. Turner confronts the problem head on.

> [T]he anthropologist who has previously made a structural analysis of Ndembu society, isolating its organizational principles and distinguishing its groups and

relationships, has no particular bias and can observe the real interconnections and conflicts between groups and persons, in so far as these receive ritual representation. What is meaningless for an actor playing a specific role may well be highly significant for an observer and the analyst of the total system.

On these grounds I consider it legitimate to include within the total meaning of a dominant ritual symbol, aspects of behavior associated with it which the actors themselves are unable to interpret, and indeed of which they may be unaware. (Turner 1970, p. 27)

Turner's work revolutionized the study of ritual meaning by bringing empirical rigor and theoretical sophistication to the analysis of ritual symbols. Having attended Turner's seminars on ritual at the University of Chicago as a graduate student, my own view of ritual has been deeply inspired by his cognitively oriented approach to the study of ritual symbols.

Symbolic Load

Turner's work is a good place to start thinking about both symbols and meaning. However, not all ritual symbols work in the ways that Ndembu symbols operate. The Ndembu have their own theory of ritual symbols, which informs their complex ritual traditions. But while not all ritual systems work according to Ndembu principles, all ritual actions can be understood as symbolic. So it is important to understand in a more general sense just what we mean by calling something a symbol. At the beginning of this book, I asserted that our *routines* become *rituals* when they are symbolically loaded. But what makes something symbolic?

Symbols are associations. In acquiring a symbolic load, an act gains depth, attaching itself to other things: images, actions, or concepts that dwell down the road, beyond the literal acts. Sometimes those other things are clear and concrete. Christians can hold up a small cross or cross themselves on their chests to ritually communicate their connection to Jesus Christ, their crucified savior. But in other cases, the symbolic associations are abstract concepts, less vivid, perhaps, but no less important. For someone with OCD, washing her hands is not just cleaning them but a ritualized way to assure herself that the world is in order. She performs one act (literally) to accomplish another act (figuratively).

In the same way, the morning coffee routine becomes ritualized as "my morning coffee" when, in addition to providing me with caffeine, regular coffee drinking becomes my way to remind myself that I'm still me and the world is in its usual state this morning. The simple act of drinking coffee has become loaded with symbolic power. My continuing identity may seem a banal sort of meaning, but our selves are quite fragile. The reassurance of the steadiness of my identity is very important to my normal functioning. Symbolic objects work the same way as symbolic actions. When, instead of seeing just a piece of multicolored cloth, we see an American flag, it triggers for Americans a web of associations, both conceptual and emotional, and feelings: home, liberty, the United States, figures in colonial history, or, for an enemy of the United States, danger or evil. Symbols are magnets for meaning, attracting associations, and taking things far beyond themselves.

A symbol can remind us of other things in several ways. Often the connection is made through analogy, a similarity of form (Shore 1996, chapter 13). This is how a painted likeness of a person can remind us of that person, or how lowering our body in front of others can symbolize our submission to them. Reading the association straight off of the original form, this analogical transfer is metaphorical meaning. At other times, we associate a symbol with something because it is a salient part of the thing it represents. The White House symbolizes the American presidency not because it looks like a president but because the president lives there. Smoke can symbolize fire because it is produced by fire. The smell of incense can trigger an association with the religious act in which it is regularly used for religious rites. The part stands in for the whole scene in which it participates. In semiotics, this part-to-whole symbolizing creates *metonymic* or *indexical* meaning.

Finally, there are many cases where the frequent co-occurrence of a symbol with something not intrinsically associated with it leads us to mentally equate the contiguous thing with the symbol. The human mind is well equipped to produce associations between unrelated things, a connection similar to a conditioned reflex. This association is really an attenuated form of metonymy since we come to associate one experience with its frequent neighbor.

In linguistics, haphazard historical associations of specific sound patterns with specific concepts have been characterized as *arbitrary associations* characteristic of many of our word meanings.[2] However, while these associations by random contiguity start out as arbitrary, once the association is made in the mind, it is no longer experienced as arbitrary. Quite the opposite. The formerly random connection produces a kind of semantic reflex that comes to feel natural. In this way, an arbitrary combination of sounds becomes a familiar word with meaning. The word can stand in so frequently for its neighboring association that we can forget that it's just an arbitrary placeholder. We find ourselves treating the word as if it were actually the thing it represents. Consider Juliet's famous question "What's in a name?" In *Romeo and Juliet*, she asks the question to dismiss the importance of names, but her dismissal of the power of words comes back to haunt her and ultimately to kill her (Shore 2021, chapter 5).

We feel hurt if someone maliciously messes with our name. We take great care in choosing the names of our children. In the case of an inappropriate name, over time and through use, the child and the name will grow more alike. To honor the Lord, Orthodox Jews will not write the Hebrew name of God. So great is the power of symbolic association that our words become real to us. It is this stickiness of our symbolic associations that allows us to think, remember, and imagine in a world of words. We hear a word repeatedly in the presence of a thing or a pattern of actions, and eventually that word reflexively evokes the experience of that pattern. The word takes on meaning. For those who don't know our language and have not formed those associations, our words are perceived as empty sounds. What is meaningful to us is meaningless to them. This semantic stickiness of our symbols is mostly a local matter.

Asked to define a word, we often struggle to find language to summarize the associated sensory patterns it summons. Most everyday words are learned in use through action in a context, not through dictionaries. We don't generally have ready definitions for our words since we have come to know them through their use. For instance, when I hear the word "car," I don't usually think of a definition. Instead, I summon a range of associations with a kind of vehicle, such as mental images, sounds, smells, and events. While a dictionary legislates a coherent general definition of the word *car* to help coordinate shared or public meanings, the actual meanings of the word to any speaker of English is inevitably a flood of mental and sensory associations that has no clear definitional boundary.

What is true of words is also true of other kinds of symbols such as objects, sounds, colors, or smells. These various symbolic associations are the raw material from which we interpret our experiences. Our symbols are bridges to meanings. Without this ability to forge associations—metaphoric, metonymic, or contiguous—our world would lose its meaning. Each thing would be what Kant famously called *das Ding an sich* ("the thing in itself"). Everything would have essence but no depth, no meaning associations. When we understand a thing as a symbol, we come to see it as *das Ding im anderen*, "the thing in the other." It's the magical way the human mind uses its extraordinary powers of association to expand its worldview. Without symbols, our earth would be flat.

What provokes our impulse to make symbolic associations, impelling us to look beyond the symbol for "deeper meaning?" Humans depend on cues that signal to us that certain words, objects, or actions are symbolic. It's like the wink of a mischievous storyteller trying to hint to us that we should look beyond the surfaces of his tale for a hidden or ironic meaning. In the evolution of human behaviors, it is often the *formalization* of action that does the winking. We have seen how formalization generates routines out of habits and rituals out of routines. Through repetition, stereotyping, slowing down movement, exaggeration, and rhythm, chains of actions are made repeatable and are transformed into patterned action sets. A designer might say that rituals are actions designed to "pop." Formalized actions are our cues to press on for meaning, to seek associations. All performed behavior is formalized in some way, standing out from ordinary action and commanding our interpretive attention. Ritual tends to be at the far end of the scale of formalization. And so ritualized action will usually trigger in us the impulse to interpret, to assume association depth, and to cross the bridge and read meanings into the act.

Meaningless Ritual?

A common misconception is that the "meaning" of a ritual is like a dictionary definition of a word and that every ritual has a meaning that can be stated. This misconception has produced a debate among scholars of ritual as to whether a ritual really is meaningful action. While ritualized language is found in many rituals, ritual is grounded in gesture rather than in language. Ritual is a much older form of communication than language. On the other hand, our everyday sense of meaning generally assumes verbalization. Meaning tends to imply a stateable meaning. Therefore some scholars have assumed that if people are unable to state the meaning of a ritual, there must be no meaning.

In 1979, Frits Staal, a scholar of Hindu religion, published an influential article that claimed to refute the idea that ritual was symbolic behavior. His argument rested on the claim that his informants, performers of the three-thousand-year-old Vedic ritual of Agnicayana, could never state the meaning of their ritual acts.

> A widespread but erroneous assumption about ritual is that it consists in symbolic activities which refer to something else. It is characteristic of a ritual performance, however, that it is self-contained and self-absorbed. The performers are totally immersed in the proper execution of their complex tasks. Isolated in their sacred enclosure, they concentrate on correctness of act, recitation and chant. Their primary concern, if not obsession, is with rules. There are no symbolic meanings going through their minds when they are engaged in performing ritual. Such absorption, by itself, does not show that ritual cannot have a symbolic meaning. However, also when we ask a brahmin explicitly why the rituals are performed, we never receive an answer which refers to symbolic activity. There are numerous different answers, such as: we do it because our ancestors did it; because we are eligible to do it; because it is good for society; because it is good; because it is our duty; because it is said to lead to immortality; because it leads to immortality. (Staal 1979, p. 3)

Staal did not claim that rituals cannot have symbolic meaning, only that symbolic meaning is not an inherent feature of ritual since the ritual he studied does not appear to have a stateable meaning for the performers.

Staal was too quick to draw inferences from his informants' statements. The inability to verbally explicate a meaning does not prove that the ritual has no meaning. If meanings are associations, many of our deepest meanings will not be readily verbalized. In addition to listening to the patient's words, a skilled psychoanalyst will read unspeakable meanings from posture, intonation, emotional expressions, and other nonverbal signs. As scholars who often depend on interviews for understanding cultural symbols, we have to be careful not to assume that meaning does not exist because it is not verbalized. This is particularly true for the meaning of ritual, which, because it is grounded in bodily experience, is not always subject to verbalization.

Meaningful associations come in many forms other than words. Images, sounds, smells, emotions, memory traces, and bodily rhythms are the basis of many meaningful experiences that elude explication. Consider the semantics of facial recognition. We are born with the ability to recognize the pattern of a human face. As infants, we usually learn to recognize and respond to the face of our mothers or other primary caregivers. But most of us would not be able to state what allows us to recognize our mother's face or explain what it means to us. And infants have yet to acquire language. Yet no one would claim that the mother's face has no meaning for the infant. Most of us will recognize a familiar face instantly but not be able to describe that recognition to someone else.

Similarly, to claim that the performance of a ritual has no meaning because performers cannot provide a verbal explication ignores the many nonverbal ways in which ritual is experienced, including rhythmic movement, patterned sound, smell, and the sense of release from personal agency, as the ritual movement takes over one's body. To banish such profound experiences from consideration as part of a ritual's "meaning" is to ignore some of the most basic elements of ritual experience. What is true for everyday rituals is even more true for religious rites. If the goal of a religious ritual is to experience the power of divinity or transcendence, then it is quite likely that the deepest aspects of the meaning of the ritual will not be readily verbalized.

An argument similar to Staal's denial of ritual meaning is made by Caroline Humphrey and James Laidlaw in their 1994 book *The Archetypal Actions of Ritual: A Theory of Ritual Illustrated by the Jain Rite of Worship* (Humphrey and Laidlaw, 1994). In observing and interviewing their Jain informants, the authors draw the following conclusion: "For the authors' respondents, acts within the context of the puja ritual were merely empty movements." "[M]eanings," they claim, "must be put into ritual, to infuse its emptiness with spiritual significance" (p. 2). While superficially similar to Staal's observations, Humphrey and Laidlaw are actually making a different sort of claim. During puja, the Jain ritualists were attending only to the rhythm of their movements and were not aware of explicit symbolic associations. And so, in the authors' view, the actions were "empty." But the authors conclude that the ritual actions do not become spiritual acts until they are infused with meaning by the performers or observers after the fact. The performers are so busy trying to get the actions right that their attention is not on the meaning of their actions.

What the ritual produces, they argue, is a powerful sense of "ritual commitment" on the part of the performers to carry out acts that are the product of prior stipulation. What is this sense of ritual commitment if not a profound meaning produced by the ritual? This commitment underlies agency reversal, where the performers carry out an act of which they are not the authors. The ritual is performing them, and so they are not alone in this world: "it is you as yourself who actually performs these acts . . . who constitutes your action as ritualized and thus make it the case that you are no longer, for a while, author of your acts" (p. 99). They acknowledge that symbolic meaning does tend to accumulate around social rituals, but the meaning is not inherent in the actions themselves. But that is just to say that the ritual actions are symbolic actions, that the actions are magnets for meaningful associations.

Then there is the question of whether a ritual's meaning is always fully shared. In a review of the book, Jennifer Scriven questions the authors' assumption that the meaning of a ritual implies a consensus. Humphrey and Laidlaw assume that to have meaning, a ritual must have a shared meaning.

> Another flaw is Humphrey and Laidlaw's use of consensus among participants as a determinant of true meaning within a ritual. They say that "most influential anthropological studies of ritual have tended . . . to portray closed, local communities with a shared culture and symbolic code, and symbolic consensus has come to be seen as characteristic of ritual" (p. 80). This is true in many cases. The authors use a similar tactic, however, when arguing their theory. They stress throughout the work that they did not find a consensus, and that this lack indicates no underlying meaning. (Scriven 2006, p. 103)

While I largely disagree with Staal as well as with Humphrey and Laidlaw's more complex position, their critiques force us to confront the question of whether a ritual necessarily has meaning and, if so, what kind of meaning. Attempts to answer this question are hobbled by the lack of a coherent conception of meaning and meaning-making. Writers often assume a self-evident meaning of "meaning." Not finding it in the rituals they observe, they conclude that meaning is not an essential feature of ritual. But this is argument by labeling. However, by taking a careful look at the process of meaning-making, we can see how ritual always underwrites meaning-making without denying the insights of these observations about apparently empty rituals or lack of consensus.

Different Kinds of Meaning

Meaning is the result of interpreting symbols. Almost always, meaning-making produces a web of associations, not a single thread. While there are

standardized and codified "official meanings," such as dictionary definitions, spontaneous meaning-making always produces "meanings" rather
than "a meaning." It's the way our minds work. Selecting among or comparing different meanings is what we call *interpretation*, which is basic to
both social and personal meaning-making. The formalization of ritual
actions, whether personal, social, or institutional, marks them as special.
Formalization primes actions for interpretation. Whenever we see a ritual
being performed, we are impelled to ask ourselves what it means.

In semiotics, the way in which a symbol is related to its referent is called
its *motivation*. Meanings are motivated by symbols in a variety of ways.
Associations with ritual acts may be derived from the form and qualities of
the actions themselves, in which case we talk about "the meaning of the
ritual." When an interpretation is made by reading the meaning directly
from the ritual acts, we can say that the meaning is highly *empirically motivated*. This is the case with a lot of status rituals involving body postures,
elaborate dress, arcane speech forms, and so on. Without knowing the local
conventional meanings of the actions, we can make a good guess by reading analogically publicly available aspects of the ritual actions (e.g., bigger
names imply a more important person, a jeweled crown and a high seat
implies more power, a lowered body implies subordination). In this case,
the meaning can be said to be motivated by the forms of the ritual acts
themselves.

In other cases, our associations depend on conventional, traditional,
or official interpretations, often widely shared by a community. We are
informed by some authority what the meaning of a ritual is. In this case, we
can refer to "the meaning from" the authoritative source. Official meanings
like this can be said to be "conventionally motivated." Finally, when the
associations are personal and idiosyncratic, involving individual memory
associations triggered by ritual actions (e.g., my father's death, being abused
as a child, my mother's smiling face), we do not speak of the *meaning* of *the
act* but rather the *meaning for* someone. In this case, we can say that the
meaning is "subjectively motivated."

"Meaning of," "meaning from," and "meaning for" are all important
aspects of meaning-making, and they are not mutually exclusive. We are
likely to subscribe to several different kinds of meaning at the same time,
invoking different readings depending on the context. Since symbolic
meaning often involves a relationship between a particular ritual act with

empirical properties, a community of believers sharing conventions, and individual participants with their unique memories and histories, conventional, psychological, and empirical meanings are usually all in play in making meaning. The absence of conventional meaning, as when a ritual has no official interpretation, leaves the performer free to try to read the act from its empirical properties or to construct a purely subjective reading based on their experiences. Most of the time, all three kinds of meaning-making will be going on at once.

A Jewish boy going through a bar mitzvah ritual will be having an experience at once conventional (interpreting it from the perspective of the rabbi's explanations), personal (his personal history with his family, his association with the temple), and empirical (standing before the congregation, reading from the Torah, chanting his haftorah portion in Hebrew, and rocking his body to the rhythm of the chant). All these factors will affect his web of associations with his bar mitzvah. The meanings his mother and father have will partially overlap his meanings but will inevitably be somewhat different. If they all share the conventional meanings of the experience, when asked about the meaning of the ritual, they may all defer to the conventional public meaning of the bar mitzvah.

Often communities will have alternative official meanings for a ritual, producing factional splits or conflicting interpretations of the meaning of a ritual. Feminist scholars in anthropology have reanalyzed classic works on ritual to suggest that women often interpret the meaning of rituals somewhat differently from men. A noted example is the reanalysis of Bronislaw Malinowski's classic work on Trobriand Island ritual in New Guinea by Annette Weiner. In her 1983 book *Women of Value, Men of Renown: New Perspectives in Trobriand Exchange*, Weiner reanalyzed Trobriand mortuary ceremonies that Malinowski had described but this time focusing on women's wealth and their exchanges of banana leaf bundles and woven skirts. Not only did Weiner's interpretation of Trobriand mortuary rites differ from Malinowski's, but it pointed up the differences in the meaning men and women attribute to mortuary exchanges. Such gendered differences in interpretation have become standard focuses in contemporary ethnography, expanding the range of meanings a society may have for its rituals. But such differences do not suggest that rituals lack meaning, only that, in their potential for multiple meanings, rituals may be more complex than we had assumed.

Common Actions, Diverse Meanings

This potential diversity of meanings in ritual may seem troublesome in that it contradicts rituals' important functions of promoting social coordination and producing a sense of group belonging. This coordinating function of ritual is shared by humans with other social animals. Since other animals do not elaborate interpretations of their rituals, the lack of a consensual meaning for many human rituals would seem to disrupt this work of ritual in promoting social coordination.

This apparent contradiction helps us to understand one of the central features of ritual: its insistence on shared actions rather than on shared meaning. I suspect this is the aspect of ritual to which Staal, Laidlaw, and Humphrey were reacting in their claims that a ritual didn't necessarily have a meaning. Differences of interpretation of a ritual are more likely to be tolerated than differences in prescribed actions. In his remarkable book *Religion and Ritual in the Making of Humanity*, anthropologist Roy Rappaport defines ritual as "the performance of more or less invariant sequences of formal acts and utterances not entirely encoded by the performers" (Rappaport 1999, p. 24) and focuses on the stipulation of action rather than on meaning. Similarly, Humphrey and Laidlaw (1994) have suggested that, in performing rituals, the performers' attention is often on correct action rather than on the interpretation of meaning. This emphasis on shared action rather than on meaning is not a coincidence. For ritualists, correct performance tends to trump correct interpretation. Interpreting a ritual can come later or be left to experts. By focusing attention on shared action rather than on shared meaning, social, sacred, and civic rituals can convey a powerful sense of unity, without worrying about variations in meanings.[3]

While ritual, as a form of symbolic behavior, is likely to produce a proliferation of alternative meanings in both performers and the audience, the prescribed unity of ritual action presents a powerful counterforce highlighting consensus and unity, masking at the moment of performance the multiple and often heterodox meanings in play. People with very different understandings of American history can all stand and sing the national anthem in unison, creating a momentary sense of community that would not be possible if the "meaning" of the act were up for debate. We can see this unifying use of ritual action at work in sports, where the game is intended to produce an opposition of winners and losers. This is why major sporting events often begin and end with joint ritual acts, the playing of a national anthem, or a shaking of hands, conveying the unity underlying the competition and masking the very different interpretations and feelings of the winners and losers.

This use of ritual to promote the appearance of consensus is particularly salient during the Olympics, where the intense series of competitions between countries and individuals that is at the heart of the Olympics is bookended at the start and finish of the Olympics by spectacular ceremonies celebrating all the teams and the "Olympic spirit" that binds all the competing nations together. When people join together in a national celebration, they may act as one body but do not necessarily experience the ritual in a unified way. Early in the twentieth century, the legendary French sociologist Emile Durkheim proposed that religious ritual promotes social solidarity. Joint action, he proposed, has the power to create emotional bond that can transcend differences in belief. Meaning turns out to be too fragile and unreliable to guarantee perfect consensus. Durkheim believed that synchrony of action is much more effective, which is why ritual is so important in any organization that wants to promote harmony. In his 1912 monograph *The Elementary Forms of the Religious Life*, Durkheim analyzes in great detail the symbols and rituals of the Aranda people of central Australia to discover the essence of human religious belief and experience.

After critiquing the classic theories of religion of his time, Durkheim concludes that the object of religious veneration is society itself. In his view, religious practice, what he terms "the cult," is the binding force that ties a community together by transforming individuals into citizens. Through participating in religious rites, the individual self is reborn as the social self. Here is how Durkheim concludes his magisterial study:

> We have seen that this reality—which mythologies have represented in so many different forms, but which is the objective, universal, and eternal cause of those *sui generis* sensations of which religious experience is made—is society. I have shown what moral forces it develops, and how it awakens that feeling of support, safety, and protective guidance which binds a man to his cult. It is this reality that makes him rise above himself. Indeed this is the reality that makes man, for what makes man is that set of intellectual goods which is civilization, and civilization is the work of society. In this way is explained the preeminent work of the cult in all religions, whatever they are. This is so because society cannot make its influence

felt unless it is in action, and it is in action only if the individuals who comprise it are assembled and acting in common. It is through common action that society becomes conscious; society is above all an active cooperation. As I have shown, even collective ideas and feelings are possible only through overt movements that symbolize them. Thus it is action that dominates religious life, for the very reason that society is its source. (Durkheim 1995, pp. 420–421)

In an insightful discussion of Durkheim's understanding of ritual, Lorenzo D'Orsi and Fabio Dei emphasize that for Durkheim rituals do not just reflect or symbolize society. Ritual action is best understood as a generative process, producing society. For Durkheim, the authors argue,

rites do not merely "express" nor simply "reflect" collective values and socialties, but generate them. For example, when social actors perform gestures in harmony with each other, they create, through a mechanic and performative practice, the very group they are part of. The community does not pre-exist action, but is instead created by a repetition of the same acts. In order for a community to come into being, it is first necessary to perform it collectively. One does not "enter" into a group, intended as an already given entity that only has to be "renewed". We could rather say that, apart from the sequences of gestures that are actually carried out to perform a rite, there is no other social reality (D'Orsi and Dei 2018, p. 121).

While Durkheim focused on the power of joint action to produce a sense of community, he also knew that ritual could orchestrate a consensus of feeling as well as action.

Promoting a consensus of belief through ritual is possible, but requires a suppression of potential alternative meanings. To suppress non-official meaning, ritual action is accompanied by intense ideological control, what we usually think of as "brainwashing." Such "outside-in" rituals are accompanied by enforced catechisms of shared songs, stories, and slogans in the attempt to shape thought and feeling as well as action. The opportunities for focusing on personal or alternative collective meanings will be discouraged, constrained by an emphasis on the authoritative explication of ritual action by authorities and prohibiting or discouraging expression of alternative interpretations.

In "outside-in" ritual, the *meaning of* a ritual will be shaped by *meanings from* a central source. This attempt at standardizing meaning-making is characteristic of authoritarian regimes. It is also commonly part of military training, where obedience to authority is paired with an emphasis on collective action and precision marching. Restrictive ritualization is also seen in classrooms that emphasize rote recitation of a teacher's point of view by students. Here the joint action of a group moving and chanting together can promote a predisposition for consensual meaning. But it is important to emphasize that even in such restrictive ritual regimes alternative meanings can never be completely suppressed.

At the other end of the spectrum are rituals aimed at encouraging the personalization of meanings. We can think of these rituals as "inside out" performances. Rituals used in theatrical training, particularly in Method Acting promote individual improvisation, where the spontaneous performance emphasizes "meaning for" the performer.

The middle ground of ritualized performance features rituals that promote the unity of action by encouraging collective movement but allow the performers and viewers to shape a range of divergent meanings. A good example of such "balanced" rituals are meditation practices of groups that promote a common meditation frame of mind through the extreme formalization of their joint action. But contemporary meditation groups do not legislate the content or meaning of the meditation experience. Here, the synchrony produced by ritual form is deployed in the service of personalized meaning. Most of our familiar rituals operate in this way, producing an array of different kinds of meaning that resonate simultaneously.

In conclusion, I agree with the claim that a ritual cannot be said to have *a meaning*, but for reasons quite different from those proposed by those critics who view ritual as empty action. Ritual does not have *a meaning* because it attracts *multiple meanings*, layers of meaning coming from many sources. Meaning-making, in the complex sense described in this chapter, is central to ritual's power. Indeed, I have gone so far as to characterize ritual action as a magnet for meanings. As a form of symbolic behavior, ritual triggers our impulse to interpret, to spin out associations. What ritual does not guarantee is the creation of a single collective interpretation except under special circumstances. Given the promiscuous and multivocal character of meaning-making, a consensus of action could never ensure a consensus of meaning.

What the harmonizing power of ritual action can promote is a fundamental sense of common identity, a powerful feeling of fellowship for those performing together that Durkheim called "social solidarity." Joint action serves as a kind of foundational sharing, essential to social life. Where I differ from Durkheim is his view of ritual solidarity as the total incorporation of the individual into the social. Ritual is indeed an important step in the creation of social identity. But meaning-making is an equal opportunity process with room for collective, local, and personal meanings. Given the complex ways that humans spin out meanings, a ritual can never be said to mean only this or that. By their nature, ritual meanings proliferate. Their magic is mercifully messy.

Having traveled the world in our search for the powers of ritual, I want to conclude the book by bringing ritual home. Most of the rituals we have encountered in these pages are institutions I have studied or participated in personally. It has been for me the journey of a lifetime. So the book is not only a general introduction to ritual studies. It is also intended as a memoir of a life illuminated by significant ritual moments. Rather than conclude the book with a grandly abstract synthesis of ritual theory, I want to end more modestly by reflecting on some of the ways I have learned to harness the power of ritual in my everyday life. And so the book ends in a practical, do-it-yourself frame of mind.

I would not consider myself a religious person in the conventional sense of the word. Our family celebrated the major Jewish holidays, and I went through the motions of being bar mitzvahed by reading my Torah portion in transliterated Hebrew, with no idea what I was saying. This was not good preparation for either an unsteady bar mitzvah boy or for a future scholar of ritual studies. And so, relatively illiterate in the personal experience of sacred liturgy, my autobiographical reflections will focus on the modest rituals of everyday life rather than on what I have called big-R rituals that are the bread and butter of ritual theory.

That focus may turn out to be an unexpected advantage. Throughout this book, I have characterized ritual as a spectrum phenomenon. Ritualized behavior has been hard to pin down in ritual theory because ritualization produces a gradient of behavior from relatively simple, unmarked acts all the way to the most elaborated, showy ceremonies. This gradient is rarely recognized. In classifying behavior, societies generally choose a place on the elaborated end of the spectrum where they start calling acts "rituals." Only the most obvious rituals tend to get named. It is left to the animal behavior scientists and the sociologists studying interaction ritual to acknowledge that the actual spectrum of ritualization extends way beyond the obvious acts we call rituals. But I am convinced that for a deep understanding of the nature of ritual, the spectrum has to be acknowledged, and I have done so throughout this book.

To most of us, the extent of ritualization of everyday life usually comes as a surprise. But the invisibility of many of our homely rituals is one of the hidden aspects of ritual that inspired the title of this book. Perhaps the most important conclusion of my study is the realization that these invisible, second-class rituals, dressed in everyday garb, are ultimately at least as important to us as the grandly costumed productions that we label rituals. I would even argue that these less visible rituals are more important, a brazen claim with which, I suspect, the local rabbi would not agree.

Ritual is a gift for us. Most of the institutions that shape our lives—academic, political, religious, and economic—do not leave us with a great deal of choice or control. Our lives seem to be inexorably shaped by forces well beyond our reach. For better or for worse, we go with the flow. But ritual is different. Not just power, ritual is *our* power. The ability to ritualize our actions and share them with others belongs to each of us, thanks to the human nervous system. And that ability offers us an arena of our lives we can harness at will, significantly reshaping our families, our friendships, our work environments, and our inner lives. It is to this last remarkable hidden power of ritual to remake ourselves that I want to turn here in the home stretch of our journey through the landscape of ritual.

For those readers who are devout practitioners of organized religion in one form or another, you already know how important ritual is for your spiritual life. You probably can do without my recommendations. But for the rest of us, I want to reflect on how we can all harness the powers of ritual to significantly enhance our quality of everyday life, especially in these stressful times. Drawing on the many ways I have learned to find comfort and contentment from rituals in my life, I want to offer a few suggestions. And I can think of no better place to start my reflections, than with lunch.

Lunch

Twenty-five years ago, my colleague Frank Manley retired from Emory University, where he had been, many years apart, both an undergraduate student and a distinguished member of the English faculty. Frank and I had cotaught a Ritual in Shakespeare course for some twenty years and had developed a close friendship. Frank was a gifted playwright and short-story writer, as well as a formidable scholar (an expert on John Donne and St. Thomas More). He was also the founding director of Emory's Creative Writing Program that eventually became one of the country's best. As the day of his retirement approached, Frank and I had lunch to discuss his retirement plans. "I'd like to make sure I keep seeing my close Emory friends," he said. Frank was, by nature, a loner, and fearing he would become isolated, he proposed that we start a small lunch group to meet every couple of weeks at a local restaurant. It was, as it turned out, a modest suggestion with far-reaching consequences.

Frank suggested inviting into the lunch group three other friends of his: his oldest Emory friend the distinguished Kipling scholar Bill Dillingham, the gifted young Chinese novelist Shufei Jin (better known by his pen name Ha Jin) from the English department, and Vinnie Murphy, professor of theater studies and gifted director of Theater Emory. I knew them all and was happy to be included in such a lively group of lunch comrades. A traditionalist, Frank suggested that we keep it a boys' club, and that tradition stuck. At one of our early lunches, Vinnie presented each of us with a small medal with an engraving of Chairman Mao. As a result, and in honor of our friend Shufei, we gave ourselves a name. And so, as the millennium ended, the Gang of Four was born.

Though academics are all members of departments and interact with a constant flow of students, a career in academia can be an isolating experience. Social relationships within the department can be complicated by factionalism, driven by disputes over department growth, hiring, and tenure decisions. And unless you are a laboratory scientist, scholars tend to work alone in their studies, buried in books and hunched over computer keyboards when we are not teaching or attending department meetings. Though there are all sorts of people in the professoriate, I would guess that many of us fall along the introvert end of the personality scale. Indeed, Frank was like this, as am I.

Aware of his tendency to withdraw, Frank saw our lunch group as a way to maintain those friendships he treasured. So, as the twentieth century drew to a close, we started having regular lunches together. Now, a quarter century later, the lunch tradition continues, though the COVID-19 pandemic has placed a temporary hold on our fortnightly gatherings. As life would have it, this extended period has left its mark on our group. Shufei's novel *Waiting* won the National Book Award in 1999 and the Pen/ Faulkner Award for Fiction in 2000, and he became an overnight celebrity. In 2002 he accepted a job in Boston University's Creative Writing Program, where he had studied nine years earlier and where he still teaches. And so we lost the first of our gang members.

We tried out a few new members at our table, but they did not last long. But when we invited Don Saliers, a distinguished and beloved professor of liturgy at the Candler School of Theology and a gifted musician, to join us, the fit was perfect. Once again, we were the gang of four. I proposed that we invite to our table one of my Emory friends, John A. Lennon, an accomplished composer and professor of composition and theory in the music department. And so John became the fifth member of our lunch gang and stayed with the group until he took early retirement from Emory around 2010 and moved to California to focus on his composing (figure 12.1).

In 2009, we lost Frank. Just shy of his eightieth birthday, Frank died unexpectedly from a heart attack. He was found unconscious at home by

Figure 12.1
The Black Hand

his wife Caroline in his favorite chair, book in hand. Each of us spoke at his funeral service. Frank's unexpected death left a big hole in our lives and an empty seat at our lunch table. Deprived of our friend and founding figure, the gang was back to four. Heartbroken, we decided to keep on meeting for lunch, now partly to honor the memory of Frank.

In 2012, Don proposed that his close friend Brooks Holifield, a renowned scholar of American church history who recently retired from Candler School of Theology, would be a perfect addition. Fortunately, Brooks accepted the invitation and quickly became a warm and lively presence at our lunches. Finally, several years later, I proposed adding one more seat to the table. We invited Gary Hauk, formerly secretary to the university at Emory, the president's chief speechwriter and university historian, and an avid marathon runner. Since most of us were "history" at Emory, Gary knew all of us by now. He proved to be a perfect addition to our lunches, witty, erudite, and good fun at the table.

We were now six, and we felt the need to mark the development with a new name. I think it was Vinnie who proposed that we call ourselves "the Black Hand," a name given to a lawless secret society famed for its black deeds (figure 12.2). And so our lunch tradition, having survived for fifteen

Figure 12.2
Frank, John, Don, and Vinnie at an early gathering of the Black Hand

years, became "the Black Hand" or, as we came to call it, "the Hand." We were fond of noting that this particular hand had six fingers. It still does.

As the years have passed, we have grown close and developed an intense loyalty to our group and its lunches. Several of our oldest members have commented how important our lunch group has become in their lives as they have grown older. Our most senior member, Bill, now in his nineties, refers to us as his brothers and has requested that we serve as his pallbearers at his funeral. We agreed but insisted that he delay the event as long as possible, a request that he has generously honored.

Our lunches gradually solidified into a ritual occasion with a few of its own traditions. We always insist on a common bill for our lunch and divide the cost of the meal equally, with no thought as to who ordered what. While this is a relatively minor thing, our tradition of sharing the bill has become an important symbol of our commitment to each other. Whenever waiters forget to give us a single check, we insist that they redo it as a collective bill. Another tradition of our lunch is the rotation of restaurants. While we frequent several eateries in Atlanta, we have a few that have become group favorites, and we keep circling back to these three or four home bases. Our lunch has become a culinary walkabout.

Conversation has never been a problem at gatherings of the Black Hand. We all "profess" for a living, so there are few silences. Our conversations have gradually developed a rhythm born of long familiarity. Collectively, the group possesses a wide range of interests and an impressive fund of knowledge. No one voice dominates at the table, and everyone is curious to learn from each other. The conversation usually sparkles, punctuated by humor. Heady ideas alternate with personal anecdotes and, of course, some good food. We have never had to discuss our rules of engagement, and conversation happens as a matter of course. Ritual intercourse evolves its own rhythms and is never legislated.

We all enjoy the play of ideas, and our lunch talk includes politics, music, art, literature, theater, religion, and philosophy. We also share what's going on in our lives. And there is no gossip. If, as is often the case, one of us is currently working on a project—a book or a play or a musical composition—we are sure to want to hear about it. We are all supportive of each other, reading each other's work and attending each other's talks and performances whenever possible. While an undercurrent of status competition can accompany relationships among academics, we have gotten past all of that. On the whole, our time together is remarkably free of tension or anxiety. We have never had a significant disagreement or unpleasant conversation in twenty-five years of lunches. We leave our lunches filled with the good cheer and stimulation that old friendship and affection can nurture. As the years have passed and age has started to show its hand, lunch talk has increasingly included discussing medical issues, symptoms, and treatments. This is hardly surprising. We are not oblivious to the passage of time, and our ritual lunch has kept pace with our lives as it should, as it must.

Ad Hoc Ritual Groups

No one other than I has ever called our lunches a ritual. These informal or personal rituals may not carry the same symbolic weight as official collective rituals like Thanksgiving dinner, wedding ceremonies, or church service. Nonetheless, the Black Hand is undoubtedly a ritual group, one that was deliberately created a quarter century ago as a way to forestall isolation in retirement. And it has worked better than anyone could have hoped. You can always plan to get together for lunch. But nothing can guarantee the meeting will solidify into a tradition with its own name and that the tradition will endure for a quarter century. This ritual has worked and will continue to work until it no longer serves a good purpose, and then it will sputter out. That's the way of these temporary rituals. They are ad hoc affairs.

Despite the wonders of modern technology and the benefits we derive from scientific medicine, the pressures and pace of contemporary life seem to produce considerable anxiety and endemic loneliness. The arrival of the Covid pandemic in 2020 as an unwelcome guest that has shown no interest in leaving town has only exacerbated these challenges. We all seek the comforts of friendship and community, but they seem out of reach for many. Ritual can come to the rescue if only we choose to harness it. Because they are created informally by individuals and often have a limited run, I call these gatherings *ad hoc ritual groups*. Ad hoc rituals like our Black Hand lunches can nurture the very community that we have been missing. And as we discovered with our lunch gatherings, ad hoc rituals can have a significant positive impact on those involved in them. While we may lament the lack of community and intimate friendship in our lives, it is remarkably easy to tap into the social power of ritual by nurturing such ad hoc ritual groups.

Ad hoc ritual groups require some planning and effort to organize and maintain. Someone has to take the initiative to propose an initial gathering and invite congenial friends to join them. But once established, a ritual that serves a genuine need has a way of taking over and providing a familiar framework for regular engagement. In relation to such informal rituals, we are all expert ritualists. The first few meetings are just unique events requiring initiative and planning. But if it finds the right soil and takes root, an event can become a routine and before long begin to flower as a self-perpetuating ritual, needing only slight management. Agency reversal has already started to work its magic. We now "belong to" the group that we created.

The character and ethos of the Black Hand were shaped significantly by the fact that we were all academic colleagues and our interests gravitated around art, music, religion, and the humanities. But groups will be as varied as the temperaments and interests of their members. Regular lunch is always a suitable frame for social bonding, but there are a lot of other possibilities. Many in the United States, primarily women, do this through book clubs. My wife Linda belongs to a group that meets monthly to discuss a book they've all read. The women (it's a girls' club, like most book groups) take turns hosting dinner at their house, followed by a couple of hours of talk. It's been going on for three decades. Discussing the book is only a small part of the monthly gathering.

My son, an avid joiner, belongs to a coed book club in Washington, DC whose theme is dinner and a Washington-themed book. He also attends a separate dinner club that meets every few weeks and whose members rotate hosting dinner. When my wife and I first moved to our current home in a town east of Atlanta about fifteen years ago, we were invited to join a dinner club hosted by one of its members each month. This local ad hoc group allowed us to meet many of our first friends in our new hometown. It has since withered away, having served its purpose admirably.

Community Dinner: Orchestrating Diversity

Many ad hoc ritual groups like our Black Hand bring together like-minded people who share common interests and backgrounds. The members of the

Figure 12.3
Eating together

Black Hand are all older white male intellectuals with interests in the arts and humanities. It was not planned that way, but people with shared backgrounds and interests tend to gravitate toward each other. Such groups of similar people are relatively easy to create. But what such shared interest groups gain in easy intimacy they may lose in their lack of diversity.
Poster advertising Carrboro's Community Dinner

Fortunately, ad hoc rituals can also help bring together people who don't have much in common. An excellent example of such a ritual tradition bringing together diverse people is the annual community dinner in Carrboro, North Carolina, just next door to Chapel Hill (figure 12.3). It's a collective event based on difference rather than similarity. In 2003 I visited Carrboro to see an old friend, Bob Levy, a distinguished anthropologist and psychiatrist. Recently retired from the Department of Anthropology at the University of California, San Diego, Bob had moved to North Carolina with his wife Nerys, an accomplished artist. Nerys and Bob had invited me to visit them during the sixth annual Carrboro Community Dinner, with which Nerys was closely connected.[1] The community dinner was the brainchild of local restaurant owner Mildred Dip, known affectionately in the community as Mama Dip, the name associated with her soul food restaurant Mama Dip's Kitchen. After she died in 2018, the Carrboro Community Dinner was renamed the Mildred Council Community Dinner in her honor.

Figure 12.4
Poster advertising Carrboro's Community Dinner

The goal of the dinner is to encourage members of all the various ethnic communities and economic strata in Carrboro to come together for a meal jointly catered by Mama Dip's Kitchen and the Carolina Inn. The community of Carrboro is diverse, made up of white southerners, northern transplants, and black, Native American, Hispanic, and several Asian communities. Concerned that these different communities rarely got together and knew little about each other, a small group of local citizens decided to create an annual dinner where everyone could rub shoulders and eat together and give some weight to the notion that Carrboro was a community. What emerged from these discussions was the community dinner. This celebration of community takes place every spring in the cafeteria of a local school, and over the past quarter century it has become integral to life in Carrboro.

In addition to eating together, the community dinner is intended to showcase talent from all of the various communities in the town (figure 12.5). While people are eating, they are treated to singing, dancing, orchestral music, puppetry, and whatever other performances members of the community choose to present. Art projects from local schools are displayed on the walls so that every culture and age group in the community has a part.

The Carrboro Community Dinner depends heavily on volunteer organizers and labor. Attendees are charged an entrance fee, but dinner is kept affordable and does not cover the actual costs. The organization subsidizes people with disabilities and the economically disadvantaged to allow everyone to attend. Over the years, it has attracted financial support from over ninety organizations, including twenty-five local restaurants. By 2019, it attracted over six hundred people from Carrboro and had grown from an ad hoc group to an established institution. In 2014 the Carrboro Community Dinner was awarded a National League of Cities Award for promoting cultural diversity. Its success is an excellent example of how an ad hoc ritual can take hold over time and grow into a stable social institution. Every social institution has a heart made of ritual.

Finding a Rhythm

Chapter 6 discussed the power of ritual to mark time and give life a rhythm. We noted the importance of maintaining the many beats at which we live, from the micro-rhythms of our brainwaves to our organ pulses to the

Figure 12.5
Local talent

circadian rhythms of our sleep-wake cycles to the marking of years and life periods. Many of these cycles elude our awareness, operating at time scales too small and too big for us to comprehend. But we know when our rhythms are off: when our sleep cycle is disrupted, when we're forced to keep changing work shifts, when we face too many simultaneous demands, and when we are overwhelmed by too much stimulation. Disrupted rhythm inevitably spawns anxiety.

Modern life has created many challenges to maintaining healthy rhythms in our lives. Electric lights have allowed us to ignore the promptings of the sun and to ignore the rhythm of day and night, working at any time. People are often asked to work schedules for which their bodies are not suited and to change schedules at the employer's whim. Moreover, keeping busy has become a form of prestige so that when someone complains that they are too busy, they are both complaining and boasting. Activities have become the status currency of middle-class life, and the ability to "juggle" activities has led to an emphasis on multitasking. With many women in the work-force, families increasingly find themselves juggling work, childcare, and homelife.

The internet has brought us an endless flow of information. News is served up on a continuous twenty-four-hour cycle. It never stops. But the information explosion has been accompanied by an implosion of meaning, a need for significant patterns in our lives. How can we make sense of it all? Relentlessly assaulted by breaking news (usually defined as "bad news") and compulsively attached to the pixel dust on our cell phone screens, it is little wonder that we feel anxious, exhausted, and beset by a sense of uncontrol-lable chaos.

Historically, our sense of unease is not unique. Back in 1624 in his *Medi-tations*, the English poet John Donne, reacting to the new (Copernican) astronomy of his day, which had displaced the earth as the center of the universe, eloquently expressed the loss of balance he experienced trying to imagine himself moving around the sun while he was standing still. He phrases this paradox of motion as having lost his center. Four centuries ago, Donne expressed a powerful sense of losing his balance in the world that, despite the archaic spelling, is eerily familiar:

> I am up and I seeme to stand, and I goe round; and I am a new *argument* of the new *Philosophie*, That the *Earth* moves round, why may I not believe, that the *whole Earth* moves in a *round motion*, though that seeme to me to *stand*, when

as I seem to *stand* to my Company, and yet am carried, in a giddy, and *circular motion*, as I *stand*? Man hath no center but misery; there and onely *there*, he is *fixt*, and sure to finde himself. (Donne 1959, p. 140)

Donne's language may be archaic, and his concern with Copernican astronomy is distant history. But his feelings of disorientation and loss of balance should feel familiar enough to our twenty-first-century sensibilities.

While there is no quick fix for our overburdened schedules and compulsive multitasking, we can easily harness the power of ritual to provide some significant compensation for our sense of chaos and to lend some powerful rhythm to our lives. Chapter 6 noted how research supports ritualized behavior's effects on reducing anxiety. It does not take much for a ritual to do its healing work. By cultivating simple rituals in our schedules, we can regain some of the focus we have lost. There is no limit to the number or kinds of ad hoc rituals available to us. We all have our own ritual needs and tolerances.

Many of us will have already discovered the healing benefits of these ad hoc rituals. If you don't already use ritual in this way, give it a try. There is no one path to restoring balance and rhythm in our experience. While complex rituals like tai chi and yoga are available as individual or group rituals, simple homespun rituals are also surprisingly effective. For example, I like having a cup of tea in the evening, using a favorite teacup and my favorite Margaret's Hope Darjeeling tea. A morning coffee ritual can start the day just as my tea completes the day. Since I grind my coffee and brew it, the making of the coffee is almost as important as the drinking. Couples can enjoy a nightly session of reading aloud to each other before bed. A daily walk in a beautiful place is another simple ritual with a big payoff, including cardiovascular exercise for us elderly folks. Simple rituals can be simply powerful.

For the religiously inclined, prayer is another ritual that can provide a contemplative space in a busy day, and ritual meditation can serve a similar function for everyone. The possibilities are endless. The key to these ad hoc rituals is regular performance on a more or less fixed schedule and focusing on a single activity or object. A ritual can heal the sense of exhaustion produced by constant multitasking.

Ad hoc rituals need not be performed every day, just regularly. Our life should be experienced as a series of cycles of different duration: circles within circles. What matters is establishing a rhythm of meaningful action. Effective rituals can be done daily, weekly, monthly, annually, or even once in a lifetime. Many of our most popular family rituals are done annually. Birthday celebrations or wedding anniversaries, Christmas dinner, or the lighting of the Jewish *yahrzeit* (annual) candle of remembrance on the anniversary of a loved one's death are all ways people mark the year. The complex rhythm created by these ritual acts cultivates the feeling that our time is full of meaning and our time on earth is not empty. Many of these annual rituals are called "holidays," suggesting their religious origin. While we generally think of ritual as often repeated, we also have landmark rituals performed once in a person's life, rituals like a birth ceremony, a funeral, a fiftieth wedding ceremony, graduation, or a bar mitzvah that, taken together, establishes a meaningful pattern for a person's lifetime, connecting us to our larger society and in some cases to transcendent powers.

Figure 12.6 is a photo taken at my mother's one hundredth birthday party. Over a hundred relatives and friends attended, and each grandchild got up and gave my mother a specially prepared birthday greeting. We also hosted celebrations for her sixtieth, seventy-fifth, eightieth, ninetieth, and ninety-fifth birthdays. Rituals like these have the power to provide a satisfying rhythm for our lives. The celebrations were not just for her but a focus point for all of us providing landmarks in our family memory.

Ritual is often closely aligned with the ordering of space (Smith 1987). Ritually orchestrating our living space is a powerful way of creating a sense of rhythm. My wife is a gifted decorator, and throughout the year, our house always reflects the holiday season through the many decorations that Linda has acquired over the years. Under every bed and in every closet in our house are boxes full of holiday decorations awaiting their time to shine. Somehow, Linda knows where every decoration is stored, and on each Thanksgiving, Easter, Christmas, and Halloween, the house becomes attired with just the right holiday wardrobe. Figure 12.7 shows our home outfitted by Linda for Christmas. When I was growing up, my family never had Christmas, so, like many Jews who marry into Christmas, I especially enjoy these holiday decorations.

I used to think that all this decorating was over the top, not to mention quite expensive. But now, when I look back on our life with our two kids and our grandsons, I realize that in her constant redecoration of the house, Linda was providing a visual rhythm to our life together, a feeling of the changing year and that this cycling of decorations is powerfully inscribed

Figure 12.6
Landmark birthday celebration: My mother's 100th birthday party

Figure 12.7
The Shore house at Christmas

in our memories. Our house pulses with the seasons, a reflection of my wife's gorgeous vision of just how our time together flows over the year. Through seasonal rituals, our family time has been given a rhythm, reflected in every room of the house. Once again, we see the hidden power of ritual at work.

The Power of Ritual in Aging

Ritual has its special place at every stage of life. We have already noted the importance of the small interaction rituals for infants that are the key to producing a child's first experience of joint attention. As we age, the importance of rituals grows. While young children and teenagers may be impatient with ritual, preferring the buzz of novel experience to routine, that changes radically in old age. It is no secret that ritual has its special attractions for the elderly. Not only does routine tend to compensate for weakening memory ("Why did I come into this room?"), but ritualization of our day proves comforting, providing a sense of continuity and predictability. Rituals, including simple, homely routines, are the comfort food of the aging soul.

My friend and lunch brother, Bill Dillingham, Charles Howard Candler Professor of American Literature Emeritus at Emory University, sent me a moving commentary on the power of ritual in aging as a response to an early draft of this chapter. Bill has generously given me permission to add his wise words to my chapter:

> I am as you well know elderly; in fact, I am ninety-one years old. I am not eligible to analyze life in its entirety, but I know what it is like to be old, really old. That is why when I refer to ritual as the antidote to the archenemy of old age, depression, experience has qualified me as something of an authority. I am referring to sustaining ritual. I have found that ritual has sustained me, has made my life bearable as an old man. I have put together an array of acts that I undertake each day.
>
> My household usually consists of four persons, my wife, Elizabeth, one of my two daughters, Becky or Judy, my son, Paul, and I. I have a number of acts that I perform daily, not chores assigned to me but things that I do that I prescribed for myself a good while ago. For example, I arise each morning of the week at a certain time, 7:30. After that for a period of about an hour and a half to two hours, I wash dishes left from the night before, always doing it a certain way that has proved to be the most effective, prepare the coffee, a particular brand that has half-caffeine, feed the cat with the same food I have found to be most appetizing to her in precisely the same amount, go outside to retrieve the morning newspaper, always thrown in the same place in my driveway, then prepare my own breakfast always using exactly the same ingredients. Then I rest in the same chair until the rest of the household awakes.
>
> Believe it or not, I have left out some details always repeated because I realize this description of my sustaining ritual is probably boring. It is not boring to me, but redemptive. Throughout the day, I live this sustaining ritual consisting by and large of the same acts each day To it I owe a peace within me that is a form of victory over the depression that victimizes so many elderly people. Bradd, there are rich rewards to the elderly from ritual. Old age is the most challenging period that a person goes through (if he/she lives long enough). The road out of this hell is ready and available through ritual, self-formulated, and carefully constructed ritual. It sustains.

Bill felt he had to apologize for describing at length his daily ritual, fearing he would bore us. But, as he stressed, it does not bore him. And his reflection is so movingly written that I cannot imagine it boring any reader.

Bill's point is very important. Anthropologists and ritual studies scholars have generally focused on the big, showy rituals like the Balinese pelebon described in chapter 3 or the elaborate Samoan exchange ritual discussed in chapter 5. These elaborate rituals stick out from the stuff of everyday life and seem to demand attention and explanation. Bill is a devout Christian and a lifelong churchgoer. His religious commitments are a testament to the power of religious rituals. But it is striking that in this account, Bill skips the religious liturgy and goes straight to the "boring" rituals of his everyday life. That is significant.

Family Ritual

In several ways, the family is created by our rituals. One of the most important jobs of ritual is the shaping of family life, giving it form and meaning. I came to this conclusion after studying the role of ritual in American family life for over a decade, when I established and ran The MARIAL Center, a research institute at Emory University. The center was funded by the Sloan Foundation's Program on Working Families, which established seven research centers at major American universities to study middle-class working families.

A working family is any family where both parents (or a single parent) work full time. We wanted to know how middle-class families are faring with no one staying home to organize family life full time. Each Sloan Center on Working Families was tasked with studying a different aspect of family life: childcare, eldercare, marriage, everyday family life, time management, and so forth. Our job at MARIAL was to focus on how families find meaning in their lives through their rituals and stories. Over ten years, we funded over sixty scholars, faculty, postdoctoral fellows, graduate students, and undergraduate honors students, each pursuing a different research project. In addition to funding research, The MARIAL Center also sponsored a number of scholarly conferences (figure 12.8).

As an anthropologist, I was used to studying exotic rituals in far-off places, rituals like Samoan kava ceremonies, Balinese cremation ceremonies, Navajo sand painting rituals, initiation rites among Australian Aborigines, and Kwakiutl potlatch ceremonies. Anthropologists also studied American traditions, but usually the focus was on major civic and religious ceremonies like Memorial Day, Thanksgiving, Independence Day, or the Catholic Mass. The Sloan Foundation wanted something different. They were funding us to study the significant ritual events of family life and the

Figure 12.8
MARIAL conference on family and memory

more minor rituals hidden within the everyday lives of American families. Initially, I was skeptical. Would there be enough to study? How interesting would everyday rituals be to someone used to studying exotic symbol systems? Would the results be worth all the time and expense?

As it turned out, there was little need for worry. MARIAL generated dozens of fascinating projects on the making of American middle-class family life. Studying the ritual creation of family culture was very illuminating. One of our anthropologists studied black family reunion traditions in a small town. An undergraduate whose father owned a funeral home studied funeral traditions. A postdoctoral linguist studied the creation of "family-lects," distinctive speech and conversation styles of families. A pair of biological anthropologists studied the effects of family rituals on stress as measured by cortisone levels. An undergraduate honors student studied changes in the representation of dysfunctional families in films from the 1950s and 1990. I led a team of scholars to study Salem Camp Meeting over a period of five years (see chapter 7).

A graduate student in anthropology studied the lives of middle-class black working mothers in relation to black histories of work. A colleague from the Candler School of Theology studied the effect of Evangelical mega-churches on the family lives of their congregations. A pair of psychologists and their students studied the impact of regular family dinners and dinner-time conversations on family members. Twice we brought in the journalist and author Judith Martin (better known as Miss Manners) to talk about the relations between etiquette and ritual. Her talks were eye-opening. She was one of about 130 speakers on myth and ritual and the American family we invited to our seminars over the MARIAL decade at Emory.

My project focused on the various ritual cycles of family life in four middle-class families in small-town Georgia. We went through the daily, weekly, monthly, seasonal, and annual cycles of family rituals. I accompanied kids to school, shared holidays with the families, and listened every week to stories from their family lives as families sat down with me to share their lives.

In addition to the many specific findings of these diverse projects, we began to see some interesting general features of American middle-class family life that we had not previously understood. The American family, it turns out, has some unusual characteristics. Most family systems are per-petuated through inheritance rules regulating how identity and property are passed on to the next generation. Descent groups are usually conceived as ongoing institutions, reproduced generation after generation. But the American nuclear family usually lasts no more than two generations. Our families are individual enterprises established by a couple or a single parent who, on becoming adults, usually leave their childhood families to set up their own families. Except in rare cases, such as family businesses, siblings do not have joint property since inheritance is generally divided among offspring. Whereas in many societies where individuals remain members of their corporate descent groups, Americans aim for autonomy and self-sufficiency. However we may think about our family, it is established as a short-term institution, lasting until the children can set up their own house-holds. Every family system has a characteristic "developmental cycle." In middle-class America, the developmental goal of our nuclear family is to explode, to successfully self-destruct.

This is a shocking way to describe our family system, of course. We Americans are good at hiding this disturbing reality from ourselves by our insistent emphasis on family values and a tendency toward family nostal-gia. But to be successful, the American family has to prepare its children to leave home eventually, ideally to establish their own families. While we talk of our families as if they are secure havens for our kids, the truth is that the childhood "home" is a temporary placeholder for a future home that each of us will have to make.

College students learn this when they come back home for a visit late in their college years to discover that their bedroom has been turned into a study or a guest room. Families prepare their kids for this eventual exit. Early on, many middle-class families encourage their kids to do sleepovers at other houses. Many parents aspire to send their kids to sleepaway camp during summer vacations. These sleepaway traditions are a kind of dry run for what is to come when the kids are older. Touting family values, we may preach togetherness, but we practice training for independence and self-reliance.

Recognizing this unstated reality of American family life, we can understand the power of many of our American family rituals. Our family system produces both a striving for autonomy and countervailing anxiety about losing our homes. Our most treasured family holidays, like Thanksgiving, Christmas, and Passover, celebrate the return of family members who have dispersed to make their own homes and their jobs. Some of the cherished images of these holidays feature a big table around which are gathered at least three generations of family. Most famous is *Freedom from Want*, the nostalgic painting by Norman Rockwell of the American family at the Thanksgiving table, part of a quartet of poster paintings collectively titled *The Four Freedoms* commissioned by President Franklin Roosevelt to support the war effort in 1943.

These holidays are what anthropologists call "rites of reaggregation" since they realize the dream of a home where the whole family has magically reappeared at the table, if only for the holiday. The knowledge of a lost home remains buried for most Americans just beneath the nostalgic images of hearth and family purveyed in greeting cards, television sitcoms, dreamy paintings, and family-oriented advertising.

Some of the most famous American plays, novels, and films deal with the tragedy of the frustrated desire for homecoming. Arthur Miller's play *Death of a Salesman* features the return home of two sons, whose return to their childhood home signals not a warm return to the family hearth but the tragic failure to attain successful adulthood. Thomas Wolf's 1940 novel *You Can't Go Home* again explores the disillusionment of a fledgling writer named George Webber, who writes nostalgically of his hometown Libya Hills (based on Asheville, North Carolina) but discovers his dreams of returning are thwarted by the sad realities he finds there. Even the wildly popular *Home Alone* movies play with the idea of a repeated loss of home by a child except that the films reverse the loss, having his family abandoning him at home only to return by the movie's end.

Homecoming rituals for high schools and colleges are distinctly American nostalgic traditions, indirectly feeding off of the complex dynamics of American family life. Usually held in the fall, colleges and high schools welcome their alumni for a week of parades, parties, concerts, and other festivities. Many alumni come dressed in school colors. Since the college was initially where many American students went when they "left home," this annual ritual implicitly celebrates the school as a surrogate home to which you can return annually. Once going to college was going "away," and now it has become coming "home." Homecoming traditions began around 1910 at Baylor University, the University of Illinois, and the University of Missouri and were held at the start of the football season. These reunion rituals are more than just a good time. For colleges especially, the loyalty and affection for the school are also intended to transform alumni into donors and school boosters.

There's No Place Like Home

"There's No Place Like Home." Dorothy's famous spell in *The Wizard of Oz* had the power to bring her back to her lost home and family in Kansas. But people tend to overlook the ambiguity of those words, which simultaneously assert the draw of home and the fact that it is "no place." This sense of a lost home is buried deep in the American psyche. It is little wonder that the word "home" is so powerfully evocative for us.

The Victorian name for stay-at-home wives was "housewife," but in the 1950s, the housewife gradually became known as a "homemaker." More recently, as married women and single mothers have increasingly entered the workforce, the term homemaker has come to sound old-fashioned. The Sloan Foundation's massive investment in research on the status of the dual-wage-earner family starting back in 2000 was based on the question of what happens to the making of "home" with all adults in the workforce. The hidden meaning of "There's no place like home" emerges. The most common answer to what happens to home invokes the metaphor of a frantic juggling of time, obligations, and roles.

The rise of the dual-wage-earner family (or its single working parent variant) has intensified anxieties about homemaking. Transforming a household into a home is one of the essential obligations of new parents. Making a home does not only entail providing a secure place to live, along with adequate food, clothing, and other material necessities. Though many are not aware of what lies ahead, new parents have to create a miniature society within the four walls of their house, a family culture with its own rules of engagement. Out of the initial chaos of setting up a household and bringing children into the world, new parents have to produce a set of viable routines that gradually develop into an organized family life. The demands of family life keep changing, of course, and the cultivation of family routines and schedules is an ongoing challenge, at least until the nest is emptied.

Creating a family routine is among the most important things couples have to negotiate, and every family does it their own way. Traditionally in the United States, the mother—"the homemaker"—has been the chief architect of family time, responsible for organizing mealtimes, bedtimes, wake-up schedules, bathroom routines for children, and holiday celebrations. But there are plenty of exceptions to this pattern, especially with the increase in dual-wage-earner families and the advent of the stay-at-home dad. Rarely is the job of creating a family routine explicitly negotiated by a couple in the same way as cooking or food shopping. But gradually, as a pattern of family life solidifies, it becomes clear that one or another parent has assumed the dominant role in creating family routines.

I have used the term "routines" rather than "rituals" for the repeated patterns of family life because the most basic designs are more pragmatic than symbolic. Bedtime, homework, wake-up, and meal schedules have symbolic dimensions, but they serve primarily practical functions. However, creating family life inevitably includes the creation of family rituals that serve essential symbolic and spiritual functions for the family. Which holidays will be celebrated? What (if any) religious orientation will the family have, especially if the parents come from different religious or ethnic backgrounds? Which parent's family traditions will this new family take up?

These decisions will significantly affect the children's primary social identity and the family's identity. Many of these issues are decided by the realities of family relations and physical proximity. Suppose one parent has closer ties with their parents and siblings than another. In that case, those connections will likely figure more prominently in family visits, holiday celebrations, and even ethnic or religious identity. Complex holiday traditions may develop as a compromise between husband and wife, such as alternating Thanksgiving between the husband's and wife's families or allocating different holiday visits to different sides of the family.

Families develop unique ways of celebrating. When I was a child, my parents celebrated our birthdays by taking us all out to dinner and a Broadway show. Going out to a restaurant was a rare treat since our parents had five kids and not much money to spend on dining out. So the birthday dinner was memorable. And those Broadway musicals, which we watched from our seats in the highest balcony, had an enormous impact on us and come up again when I talk with my siblings. We saw the original Broadway casts perform *Westside Story*, *The Music Man*, *The Sound of Music*, and *My Fair Lady*. This birthday ritual was an invention of our parents, who loved to see shows, and they passed down to all of us their love of show tunes—a lasting birthday present.

While most family routines evolve gradually out of necessity, family rituals can easily be deliberate creations. I cultivated a tradition of having evening tea with my son when he was in high school, and when he visits now, he enjoys repeating our old father-son ritual. Now my daughter and I have begun a regular lunch-out tradition. Family rituals can involve the whole family or specific relationships like the father-daughter lunch or the father-son tea. If family schedules make it hard to have regular family dinners, then cultivating a traditional Sunday dinner tradition may provide missing family time. The emphasis has to be on the word "regular."

Fortunately, satisfying rituals tend to be self-enforcing. Once the rhythm takes hold and the activity has become ritualized, compliance will become automatic. This is one of the secret powers of ritual in that we all have a natural tendency to fall into ritual patterns. Families can take advantage of this power to create a set of family rituals that can choreograph family time in a healthy and satisfying way. But for family rituals to take root, someone needs to step up and become the family ritualist. It does not have to be one family member, but often one member tends to serve this function. These family rituals are significant at a time in history when we all find ourselves compulsively glued to a computer screen, a TV, or a cell phone. Here, harnessing the compulsive power of ritual may be one of the few effective ways to counteract the compulsive pull of the screen.

Consciously using the power of ritual to create family time (or relationship time), not only shapes relationships. It is a powerful shaper of family memory. As the years go by, these rituals, big and small, often become the memory framework by which we will remember our past and how we understand how we became who we are. When we narrate our family stories, we often use a special framing of the past tense reserved for reciting "the ritual past." "When I was young," we say, or "we used to go ice-skating at Memorial Park." Or "when we were kids, we always went to Jones Beach in the summer." These statements are not descriptions of specific events but repeated events that have taken hold of our memory and filtered into our sense of who we are. They are our ritual memory anchors. If the effect is powerful, the cause is simple. Like a vast underground spring, ritual is a surprisingly accessible resource. Built into the very fibers of our nervous systems, the powers of ritual lie within all of us, waiting to be harnessed.

Acknowledgments

Because this book draws on my lifetime of experiences with rituals, both as an anthropologist and as an ordinary person, it has benefited from the help and insights of many people and organizations in my life. To the extent that memory allows, I want to acknowledge my debts. First and foremost, I want to thank the Alfred P. Sloan Foundation for their generous funding of MARIAL at Emory University for a decade, making possible the research on American middle-class family ritual that has significantly shaped this book. Thanks also to Emory College for giving me released time from teaching to set up and run the center. I am especially indebted to Kathleen Christensen, our program officer at Sloan, who oversaw the administration of the grant and the development of the center as part of Sloan's larger initiative on middle-class working families.

At MARIAL, I want to recognize the work of our office manager Donna Day who kept the operation humming; our able communications director Beth Kurlyo; core faculty members Carol Worthman, Carla Freeman, Nancy Eiesland, Mark Auslander, Kathryn Yount, Marshall Duke, and Robyn Fivush; and our staff assistants, especially John Kerry, Nat Kendall-Taylor, Emily Katz, and Charles Jandreau as well as our many students, postdoctoral fellows, and graduate and undergraduate fellows who helped generate a stimulating decade of discussions of ritual and myth over the life of MARIAL.

My research on Salem Camp Meeting and the documentary film we made there benefited enormously from the work and talent of our lead videographer and editor Scott Edmundson, our consulting editor Peter Odabashian, and our research and filming team including Eric Panter, Rob Shore, Rebecca Morgan, and Charles Jandreau. Thanks also to the families at Salem who invited us into their tents and their lives at Salem, especially to Sam Ramsey, Becky Ramsey, and Alice Griffin. Also thanks to Paige Farley, Teresa Doster, and our host during our time at Salem, Laura Ramsey Kemp, who allowed our team to share her tent and sink our feet into its sawdust. Thanks also to the families in Covington, Georgia, who welcomed me into their lives as I attempted to understand the ritual life of Southern middle-class families: the Stillermans, the Laseters, the Dobbs, and the Schultzes. So compelling and revealing were the rhythms of their family life that they eventually convinced my wife and me to "go native" and move to Covington. We are still friends with each of these families today, twelve years after MARIAL ended its run.

Many of the most engaging conversations about our collective work during the MARIAL years came during of my interactions with the talented group of fellow Sloan Center directors: Arlie Hochschild and Barrie Thorne at the University of California at Berkeley, Barbara Schneider and Linda Waite at the University of Chicago, Phyllis Moen at Cornell University, Elinor Ochs at University of California at Los Angeles, Anne Bookman at MIT, and Tom Fricke at the University of Michigan, along with their many core faculty members and research fellows. Our annual gatherings to share our findings were always stimulating and mind-expanding occasions.

During my many years of research in Samoa, I greatly benefited from various kinds of help and support from my adoptive family, the Petaias, especially Memea, Iokapeta, Samuelu, Pita, Nu'ufou, Setu, To'afitu, and Kereti, My understanding of Samoa has been enriched by many of my Samoan friends, including my brilliant teacher Peseta Gatoloai Sio, Albert Wendt, Felix Wendt, Merita Wendt, Uelese Petaia, Tili Peseta Afamasaga, Masiofo Filia Tuiatua, Tuato Liko, Susana Tuato, Tuiatua Tupua Tamasese Efi, and Tofilau Eti Alesana.

Over the years, my understanding of ritual has benefited from the insights derived from conversations with, and reading the work of, many teachers, friends, colleagues, and former students: Jerome Bruner, Aaron Collett, Irving Goldman, Sherry Ortner, Putu Yasa, Victor Turner, Robert Paul, Mel Konner, Rob Shore, Emily Katz, Rima Shore, Ken Shore, Nancy Munn, Barbara Shore, Bill Chace, JoAn Chace, Alex Hinton, Riche Barnes, Eric Lindland, Ellen Schattschneider, Tenzin Namdul, Saia Kauko, Buncic Lanners, Shelly Errington, John Gillis, Stephanie Coontz, and Judith Martin. I have also learned so much about the power of ritual from my lunch buddies who have gathered regularly over the last quarter century: Frank Manley, Vincent Murphy, Shufei (Ha) Jin, Bill Dillingham, Tim McDonough, Jim Peck, Gary Hauk, Brooks Holifield, and Don Saliers. Closer to home, my wife Linda has taught me most of what I know about the power of ritually ordering family life and magically transforming our house in response to the ritual flow of the year.

I am grateful to my editor at MIT Press, Philip Laughlin, for his enthusiasm about this book project and for his help and encouragement in coaxing this book into print. Finally, I want to thank the anonymous reviewers that read the original manuscript for this book for several presses and who made many suggestions, many of which were followed and helped produce the book in its final form.

And, to anyone whom I may have inadvertently omitted from these acknowledgments, I offer my apologies and my embarrassed thanks.

Notes

Chapter 2

1. Goffman's most famous books dealing with social rituals are *The Presentation of Self in Everyday Life* (1956), *Asylums: Essays on the Social Situations of Mental Patients and Other Inmates* (1961), *Behavior in Public Places: Notes on the Social Organization of Gatherings* (1963), *Stigma: Notes on the Management of Spoiled Identity* (1963), a collection of six essays called *Interaction Ritual: Essays on Face-to-Face Behavior* (1967), *Strategic Interaction* (1969), and *Forms of Talk* (1981), where he applied his conception of interaction ritual to the analysis of face-to-face conversations.

Chapter 3

1. In addition to the information I collected on the pelebon during my visit to Bali in July of 2008, this chapter has benefitted from my consulting the following published sources: Samarth (2018), Geertz (1966, 2005), Covarrubias (1937), Bateson and Mead (1942), Wikan (1990), and Boon (1977). I also viewed several films of pelebon rituals including Timothy Asch, Patsy Asch, and Linda Conner, dir. *Releasing the Spirits: A Village Cremation in Bali* (Watertown, MA: Documentary Educational Resources, 1991) DVD; Lemelson (2012); and Yasuhiro Omori, *Balinese Requiem* (Watertown, MA: Documentary Educational Resources, 1992), DVD.

Chapter 5

1. Since the 1980s, the Kwakiutl have called themselves Kwakwaka'wakw. I am retaining the old name here to avoid confusion since the name Kwakiutl is used in all the older ethnographic literature.

2. The word *potlatch* comes from Chinook, the trading jargon used by various Indian nations of the Northwest. It means "to give."

3. While the main islands in the archipelago belong to the Independent State of Samoa, the small eastern islands of Tutuila, Ofu, Olosega, and Ta'u have been an American territory, American Samoa, since 1900.

4. Most Samoans were converted to Christianity shortly after the arrival of congre-
gational missionaries from Tahiti 1830, followed by the Wesleyans five years later.
Once the paramount chiefs had converted to the new religion, the rest of the population quickly followed suit. By 1870, Samoans claimed to have forgotten their own
indigenous religion.

5. My dissertation research on conflict and social control in Samoa was published in
a 1982 book (Shore 1982).

Chapter 6

1. Though Piaget's view of the primacy of an egocentric perspective for infants
has been very influential in developmental psychology, it was challenged by Russian psychologist Lev Vygotsky, among others. Reflecting his socialist worldview,
Vygotsky insisted that the newborn's experience of the world is intersubjective
from the get-go since the child's earliest experiences of the world are inherently
tied to those of its mother (Bruner 1984). Moreover, the child is, from the start
embedded in a web of social relations, developing in what Vygotsky called "the
zone of proximal development," where learning is necessarily mediated and guided
by caretakers.

2. On the ever-present possibility of play fighting spilling over its boundaries into
real violence, see "Playing With Rules: Sports at the Borderland of Time and Space"
in Shore (1996, chapter 4).

3. For classic discussions of the ambiguities of performance genres, see Schechner
(2020) and MacAloon (1984).

4. The classic work in anthropology on pollution and the ritual meaning of "dirt" as
the mixing of categories is Mary Douglas's influential book *Purity and Danger* (Douglas 1966).

5. Mary Klaus, "Roman Catholic Church Changes Mass to a More Formal Version,"
The Patriot News, https://www.pennlive.com/midstate/2011/03/catholic_mass_is
_changing.html.

6. Klaus, "Roman Catholic Church Changes Mass."

7. For a theoretical account of the basis of human religious practice that focuses
on experiencing transpersonal agency, see Lawson and McCauley (1990), especially
chapter 5.

8. See Rappaport (1999) for an important theoretical account of the role of ritual
in shaping the human experience of religious transcendence. For Rappaport, the
ritualization of language and behavior produces authoritative messages that are not
subject to disconfirmation, producing the human sense of the sacred.

Chapter 7

1. Our documentary film *Family Revival: Salem Camp Meeting*, which is the source of most of the interview quotes in this chapter, is available online at https://vimeo .com/18480085.

Chapter 8

1. For a vivid and detailed account of the Moore's Ford lynching and its aftermath, see Laura Wexler's excellent account in *Fire in the Canebrake* (Wexler 2003). Most of the details of the fight preceding the lynching in my account are taken from Wexler's book.

2. Wexler (2003, p. 51)

3. Wexler (2003, p. 62)

4. Eugene Talmadge died from cirrhosis of the liver before he ever took office. His life of heavy drinking had taken its toll. The state legislature voted to appoint his son Herman as Georgia's governor since he had gotten a significant number of write-in votes.

5. I became uncomfortably aware that I was doing my own "shooting."

Chapter 9

1. This chapter draws on Shore (1996, chapter 3).

2. But sometimes our personal rituals like morning coffee are not easily visible to others, having no markers other than our private sense of familiarity with a routine. The fact that the boundary markers of personal rituals are often invisible to others is one of the reasons that they are not generally recognized as rituals.

3. See especially D'Aquili, Loughlin, and McManus (1979).

4. On the relations between ritual and theater, see Turner (2001) and Schechner (1988, 2020).

5. On ritual as a form of play, see Huizinga (1971) and Bronkhorst (2012).

6. For a well-known essay on baseball rituals and superstations, see Gmelch (1992).

7. But there is no tailgating in baseball—a ritual tradition belonging largely to fans of football or outdoor concerts.

8. The only exceptions are the ancient British games of cricket and rounders, from which baseball developed.

9. Baseball can also be reconfigured to accommodate a more communitarian cultural vision. For example, Japanese baseball mimics its American cousin in many ways, but differences in cultural values have produced some subtle differences in how the Japanese game is played. For example, Japanese baseball allows for tie scores. Moreover, it understands batting as a collective enterprise rather than as a moment of heroic individualism. Batters will often be praised for their ability to move each other around the plate, treating the batter as a kind of fielder.

Chapter 10

1. See also Sturgill (2019).

2. "Choosing a New Church or House of Worship," Pew Research Center, August 23, 2016, https://www.pewresearch.org/religion/2016/08/23/choosing-a-new-church-or -house-of-worship/.

3. https://www.catholictv.org/catholictv-mass/.html.

4. https://congregationbethshalomnorthbrook.shulcloud.com/.

5. https://www.uptownchabad.com/.

6. http://www.centralsynagogue.org/.

7. https://www.ritualwell.org/ritual/radical-shabbat-guide.

8. "Nava Tehila Kabbalat Shabbat Live Stream," YouTube video, 1:32:13, posted by Nava Tehila, April 24, 2020, YouTube, https://www.youtube.com/watch?v=cZ _kNTmczo0.

9. For a fascinating comparison of the experience of worship in a Hindu virtual temple and a Christian virtual church, see Krueger (2004).

10. For an interesting set of essays on the influence of the internet on Buddhism, see Grieve and Veidlinger (2015) and Grieve (2016).

11. https://ryi.org.

12. Grieve 2016, p. 298.

13. http://faith.nd.edu/s/1210/faith/interior.aspx?sid=1210&gid=609&pgid=32742.

14. This technique of using words and images to reshape the imagination of worshippers has a distinguished history. In his fascinating book *Painting and Experience in Fifteenth-Century Italy*, the British art historian Michael Baxandall shows how paintings were used by fifteenth-century Italian artists to allow worshippers to project personal imagery onto the stereotyped or neutral Biblical faces and places depicted in the religious paintings to place themselves in the religious scenes and personalize conventional religious tales (Baxandall 1972; Shore 1995).

15. https://theamm.org/articles/317-these-states-are-where-you-can-and-can-t-get
-married-online.

16. Lighten, https://lightenarrangements.com/; SympathyNet, https://sympathynet
.com/; Willowise, https://willowise.com/.

Chapter 11

1. In chapter 13 of *The Elementary Structures of Kinship*, Claude calls this kind of
social organization a "disharmonic" marriage system in contrast to a harmonic
regime, where the norms of descent and those governing postmarital residence are
consistent (Lévi-Strauss 1969).

2. Charles Peirce calls such arbitrary symbols "legisigns," signs whose connection to
their referents is legislated by law, society, or pure convention (Peirce 1998).

3. The Catholic Church has traditionally recognized the power of ritual action to
promote a sense of spiritual communion. Interpretation and meaning have generally been relegated to theologians and other specialists. The Protestant Reformation
shifted this emphasis away from ritual to focus on worshippers' personal relationship with Christ and their understanding of the meaning of God's word. In so
doing, the Protestant churches deemphasized the work of ritual action in generating
community and spiritual commitment.

Chapter 12

1. Bob, who suffered from Parkinson's disease, died three months after my visit. But
Nerys is still very active in the Carrboro Community Dinner twenty-five years after
its founding. In 2019 she was elected chairman of its Planning Committee.

References

Anastasi, Matthew W., and Andrew B. Newberg. 2008. "A Preliminary Study of the Acute Effects of Religious Ritual on Anxiety." *The Journal of Alternative and Complementary Medicine* 14, no. 2: 163–165.

Auslander, Mark. 2013. "Touching the Past: Materializing Time in Traumatic 'Living History' Reenactments." *Signs and Society* 1, no. 1 (Spring): 161–183.

Bartlett, Frederic V. 1932. *Remembering: A Study in Experimental and Social Psychology.* Cambridge: Cambridge University Press.

Bateson, Gregory. 1955. "A Theory of Play and Fantasy." *Psychiatric Research Reports* 2: 39–51.

Barclay, Katie, and Nina Koefoed. 2021. "Family, Memory, and Identity: An Introduction." *Journal of Family History* 46, no. 1 (January): 3–12.

Bateson, Gregory, and Margaret Mead. 1942. *Balinese Character: A Photographic Analysis.* New York: New York Academy of Sciences.

Batista, Eva. 2009. "Mythical Re-Construction of the Past: War Commemoration and Formation of Northern Irish Britishness." *Anthropological Notebooks* 15, no. 3: 5–25.

Baxandall, Michael. 1972. *Painting and Experience in Fifteenth-Century Italy.* Oxford: Oxford University Press.

Beck, Mary G. 1993. *Potlatch: Native Ceremony and Myth on the Northwest Coast.* Portland, OR: Alaska Northwest Books.

Beatty, Geoffrey. 2003. *Visible Thought: The New Psychology of Body Language.* East Sussex and New York: Routledge.

Boon, James. 1977. *The Anthropological Romance of Bali 1597–1972.* Cambridge: Cambridge University Press.

Boswell, Thomas. 1984. *Why Time Begins on Opening Day.* New York: Doubleday.

Bourdieu, Pierre. 1977. *Outline of a Theory of Practice*. Translated by Richard Nice. Cambridge: Cambridge University Press.

Boyer, Pascal, and Pierre Liénard. 2006. "Why Ritualized Behavior? Precaution Systems and Action Parsing in Developmental, Pathological and Cultural Rituals." *Behavioral and Brain Sciences* 29: 1–56.

Bronkhorst, Johannes. 2012. "Can There Be Play in Ritual? Reflections on the Nature of Ritual." Chapter 11 in *Religions in Play: Games, Rituals and Virtual Worlds*, edited by Philippe Bornet and Maya Burger, pp. 1–15. Zurich: Pano Verlag.

Bruce, Dickson D. 1974. *And They All Sang Hallelujah: Plain-Folk Camp-Meeting Religion, 1800–1845*. Knoxville: University of Tennessee Press.

Bruner, Jerome. 1984. "Vygotsky's Zone of Proximal Development: The Hidden Agenda." *New Directions for Child Development* 23: 93–97.

Buford, Bill. 1990. *Among the Thugs: The Experience, and the Seduction, of Crowd Violence*. London: Secker & Warburg.

Carpenter, Malinda, Katherine Nagell, Michael Tomasello, George Butterworth, and Chris Moore. 1988. "Social Cognition, Joint Attention, and Communicative Competence from 9 to 15 Months of Age." *Monographs of the Society for Research in Child Development* 63, no 4: 1–174.

Casey, Cheryl. 2006. "Virtual Ritual, Real Faith: The Revirtualization of Ritual in Cyberspace." *Journal of Religions on the Internet* 2 no. 1: 73–90.

Codere, Helen. 1950. *Fighting with Property: A Study of Kwakiutl Potlatching and Warfare, 1792–1930*. New York: J. J. Augustin.

Covarrubias, Miguel. 1937. *Island of Bali*. New York: Alfred Knopf.

D'Aquili, Eugene, Charles D. Loughlin, and John McManus.1979. *The Spectrum of Ritual: A Biogenetic Structural Analysis*. New York: Columbia University Press.

Delafield-Butt, Jonathan T., and Colwyn Trevarthen. 2013. "Theories of the Development of Human Communication." In *Handbook of Communication Science*, pp. 199–222, edited by Paul Cobley and Peter J. Schultz. Berlin: Gruyter Mouton.

Deren, Maya. 1963. *The Divine Horsemen: The Living Gods of Haiti*. Kingston, NY: McPherson & Company.

de Tocqueville, Alexis. 2000. *Democracy in America*. Chicago: University of Chicago Press. First published 1835 by Saunders and Otley.

Donald, Merlin. 1991. *Origins of the Modern Mind: Three Stages in the Evolution of Culture and Cognition*. Cambridge, MA: Harvard University Press.

Donne, John. 1959. "Meditation." Chapter 10 in *Devotions upon Emergent Occasions*. Ann Arbor: University of Michigan Press. First published 1624 by Stationers' Company.

D'Orsi, Lorenzo, and Febio Dei. 2018. "What is a Rite? Émile Durkheim, A Hundred Years Later." *Open Information Systems* 2:115–126.

Douglas, Mary. 1966. *Purity and Danger*. London: Routledge & Kegan Paul.

Drucker, Philip, and Robert Heizer. 1967. *To Make My Name Good: A Reexamination of the Southern Kwakiutl Potlatch*. Berkeley: University of California Press.

Durkheim, Emile. 1995. *The Elementary Forms of the Religious Life*. Translated by Karen E, Fields. New York: The Free Press. First published in 1912.

Ejaz, Khadija. 1967. "Muslims in the Digital Age." In *Religion Online: How Digital Technology Is Changing the Way We Worship and Pray*, vol. 2, edited by August F. Grant, Daniel A. Stout, Chiung H. Chen, and Amanda F. C. Sturgill, 687–715. Santa Barbara, CA: Praeger.

Eliade, Mircea. 1954. *The Myth of the Eternal Return or Cosmos and History*. Princeton, NJ: Princeton University Press.

Eslinger, Ellen. 1999. *Citizens of Zion: The Social Origins of Camp Meeting Revivalism*. Knoxville: University of Tennessee Press.

Fast, Julius. 1970. *Body Language*. London: Souvenir Press.

Foley, John P. 2002. "The Church and the Internet." The Pontifical Council for Social Communications (February 22). https://www.vatican.va/roman_curia/pontifical_councils/pccs/documents/rc_pc_pccs_doc_20020228_church-internet_en.html.

Foster, Russel, and Leon Kreitzman. 2004. *The Rhythms of Life: The Biological Clocks That Control the Daily Lives of Living Things*. London: Profile Books.

Geertz, Clifford. 1966. *Person, Time, and Conduct in Bali: An Essay in Cultural Analysis*. New Haven: Yale University Press.

———. 2005. "Deep Play: Notes on the Balinese Cockfight." *Daedalus* 134, no. 4: 56–86.

Giulianotti, Richard, Norman Bonney, and Mike Hepworth, eds. 1994. *Football Violence and Social Identity*. London: Routledge.

Gmelch, George. 1992. "Superstition and Ritual in American Baseball." *Elysian Fields Quarterly* 11, no. 3: 25–36.

Goffman, Erving. 1956. *The Presentation of Self in Everyday Life*. New York: Doubleday.

———. 1961. *Asylums: Essays on the Social Situations of Mental Patients and Other Inmates*. New York: Doubleday.

———. 1963a. *Behavior in Public Places: Notes on the Social Organization of Gatherings*. New York: The Free Press.

———. 1963b. *Stigma: Notes on the Management of Spoiled Identity*. New York: Simon and Schuster.

———. 1967. *Interaction Ritual: Essays on Face-to-Face Behavior*. New York: Pantheon Books.

———. 1969. *Strategic Interaction*. Philadelphia: University of Pennsylvania Press.

———. 1981. *Forms of Talk*. Philadelphia: University of Pennsylvania Press.

———. 1986. *Frame Analysis: An Essay on the Organization of Experience*. Boston: Northeastern University Press.

Goldman, Irving, 1975. *The Mouth of Heaven: An Introduction to Kwakiutl Religious Thought*. New York: Wiley.

Grieve, Gregory P. 2016. *Cyber Zen: Imagining Authentic Buddhist Identity, Community, and Practices in the Virtual World of* Second Life. London: Routledge.

Grieve, Gregory P., and Daniel Veidlinger, eds. 2015. *Buddhism, the Internet, and Digital Media: The Pixel in the Lotus*. London: Routledge.

Homans, George C. 1941. "Anxiety and Ritual: The Theories of Malinowski and Radcliffe-Brown." *American Anthropologist* 43, no. 2 (April–June): 164–172.

Huizinga, Johan. 1971. *Homo Ludens: A Study of the Play-Element in Culture*. Boston: Beacon Press. First published 1938.

Humphries, Caroline, and James Laidlaw. 1994. *The Archetypal Actions of Ritual: A Theory of Ritual Illustrated by the Jain Rite of Worship*. Oxford: The Clarendon Press.

Johnson, Charles A. 1985. *The Frontier Camp Meeting: Religion's Harvest Time*. Houston, TX: Southern Methodist University Press.

Johnson, Mark. 1990. *The Body in the Mind: The Bodily Basis of Meaning, Imagination, and Reason*. Chicago: University of Chicago Press.

Kalinock, Sabine. 2006. "Going on Pilgrimage Online: The Representation of the Twelver-Shia in the Internet." *Heidelberg Journal of Religions on the Internet* 2, no. 1: 6–23.

Kertzer, David. 1989. *Ritual, Politics, and Power*. New Haven: Yale University Press.

Krueger, Oliver. 2004. "The Internet as Distributor and Mirror of Religious and Ritual Knowledge." *Asian Journal of Social Science* 32, no. 2: 183–197.

Kuhnke, Elizabeth. 2016. *Body Language: Learn How to Read Others and Communicate with Confidence*. New York: John Wiley & Sons.

Kurzweil, Ray. 2000. *The Age of Spiritual Machines: When Computers Exceed Human Intelligence*. New York: Penguin Books.

Lakoff, George, and Mark Johnson. 1980. *Metaphors We Live By*. Chicago: University of Chicago Press.

Lang, Martin, Jan Krátký, and Dimitris Xygalatas. 2020. "The Role of Ritual Behaviour in Anxiety Reduction: An Investigation of Marathi Religious Practices in Mauritius." *Philosophical Transactions of the Royal Society B, Biological Sciences* no. 375: 1–6.

Lawson, Thomas, and Robert McCauley. 1990. *Rethinking Religion: Connecting Cognition and Culture*. Cambridge: Cambridge University Press.

Leach, Edmund R. 1966. "Ritualization in Man in Relation to Conceptual and Social Development." *Philosophical Transactions of the Royal Society of London. Series B, Biological Sciences* 251, no. 772: 403–408.

Lemelson, Robert. 2012. *Ngaben: Emotion and Restraint in a Balinese Heart*. Los Angeles, CA: Elemental Productions. http://www.elementalproductions.org.

Lévi-Strauss, Claude. 1966. *The Savage Mind*. Translated by George Weidenfeld. Chicago: University of Chicago Press. First published 1962.

———. 1969. *The Elementary Structures of Kinship*. Translated by James Harle Bell, John von Sturmer, and Rodney Needham. Boston: Beacon Press.

Linnekin, Jocelyn. 1991. "Fine Mats and Money: Contending Exchange Paradigms in Colonial Samoa." *Anthropological Quarterly* 64, no. 1: 1–13.

Lorenz, Konrad. 1980. *King Solomon's Ring: New Light on Animal Ways*. New York: Time-Life Books. First published 1949.

———. 1966a. "Evolution of Ritualization in the Biological and Cultural Spheres." *Philosophical Transactions of the Royal Society of London. Series B, Biological Sciences* 251, no. 772: 273–284.

———. 1966b. "The Triumph Ceremony of the Greylag Goose." *Philosophical Transactions of the Royal Society of London. Series B, Biological Sciences* 251, no. 772: 477.

MacAloon, John J. 1984. *Rite, Drama, Festival, Spectacle: Rehearsals Toward a Theory of Cultural Performance*. Philadelphia: Institute for the Study of Human Issues.

Maghribi, Layla. 1921. "Experiencing Hajj in Virtual Reality." *The National News* (July 8). https://www.thenationalnews.com/world/uk-news/2021/07/08/experiencing-hajj -in-virtual-reality/.

Malinowski, Bronislaw. 1922. *Argonauts of the Western Pacific*. London: George Routledge.

———. 2015. *Magic, Science, and Religion*. New York: Martino Fine Books. First published 1954.

Mauss, Marcel. 2002. *The Gift: The Form and Reason for Exchange in Archaic Societies*. Translated by W. D. Halls. London: Routledge. First published 1925.

McNeill, David. 1996. *Hand and Mind: What Gestures Reveal about Thought*. Chicago: University of Chicago Press.

———. 2007 *Gesture and Thought*. Chicago: University of Chicago Press.

McNeill, William H. 1995. *Keeping Together in Time: Dance and Drill in Human History*. Cambridge, MA: Harvard University Press.

O'Leary, Stephen D. 1996. "Cyberspace as Sacred Space: Communicating Religion on Computer Networks." *Journal of the American Academy of Religion* 64, no. 4 (Winter): 781–808.

Ong, Walter. 1967. *The Presence of the Word: Some Prolegomena for Cultural and Religious History*. New Haven, CT: Yale University Press.

———. 1982. *Orality and Literacy: The Technologizing of the Word*. London: Routledge.

Perry, Susan, and Marco Smolla. 2020. "Capuchin Monkey Rituals: An Interdisciplinary Study of Form and Function." *Philosophical Transactions of the Royal Society B, Biological Sciences* 375 (June): 1–8.

Peirce, Charles S. 1998. *The Essential Peirce*. Vol. 2. Peirce Edition Project. Bloomington, IN: Indiana University Press.

Petito, Laura, Siobhan Horlowka, Lauren E. Sergio, and David Ostry. 2001. "Language Rhythms in Baby Hand Movements." *Nature* 413: 35–36.

Radcliffe-Brown, Alfred R. 1922. *The Andaman Islanders: A Study in Social Anthropology*. Cambridge: Cambridge University Press.

Radde-Antweiler, Kerstin. 2007. "Cyber-Rituals in Virtual Worlds, Wedding-Online in *Second Life*." *Masaryk UJL & Tech*: 185–197.

Rappaport, Roy. 1968. *Pigs for the Ancestors: Ritual in the Ecology of a New Guinea People*. New Haven, CT: Yale University Press.

———1999. *Ritual and Religion in the Making of Humanity*. Cambridge: Cambridge University Press.

Reiman, Tonya. 2008. *The Power of Body Language: How to Succeed in Every Business and Social Encounter*. New York: Pocket Books.

Rosman, Abraham, and Paula G. Rubel. 1971. *Feasting with Mine Enemy: Rank and Exchange in Northwest Coast Societies*. New York: Columbia University Press.

Rütten, Sylvia, and Gunther Fleissner. 2004. "On the Function of the Greeting Ceremony in Social Canids—Exemplified by African Wild Dogs Lycaon Pictus." *Canid News* 7.3. http://www.canids.org/canidnews/7/Greeting_ceremony_in_canids.pdf.

Samarth, Aditi G. 2018. "The Survival of Hindu Cremation Myths and Rituals in 21st Century Practice: Three Contemporary Case Studies." PhD diss. The University of Texas at Dallas.

Sherwood, Harriet. 2017. "Robot Priest Unveiled in Germany to Mark 500 Years since Reformation." *The Guardian*, May 30. https://www.theguardian.com/technology/2017/may/30/robot-priest-blessu-2-germany-reformation-exhibition.

Schechner, Richard. 1988. *Essays in Performance Theory*. London: Routledge.

———. 2020. *Performance Studies: An Introduction*. London: Routledge.

Schieffelin, Edward. 1976. *The Sorrow of the Lonely and the Burning of the Dancers*. New York: Palgrave.

Scriven, Jennifer. 2006. "Review of Humphries, Caroline, and James Laidlaw." *The Archetypal Actions of Ritual: A Theory of Ritual Illustrated by the Jain Rite of Worship, Lambda Alpha Journal* 36: 103–107.

Shore, Bradd. 1982. *Sala'ilua: A Samoan Mystery*. New York: Columbia University Press.

———. 1995. *What Culture Means, How Culture Means. The Heinz Werner Lectures*. Worcester, MA: Clark University Press.

———. 1996. *Culture in Mind: Culture, Cognition, and the Problem of Meaning*. Oxford: Oxford University Press.

———. 2008. "Spiritual Work, Memory Work: Revival and Recollection at Salem Camp Meeting." *Ethos* 36: 98–119.

———. 2022. *Shakespeare and Social Theory: The Play of Great Ideas*. London: Routledge.

Shore, Bradd, and Sara Kauko. 2018. "The Landscape of Family Memory." In *Handbook of Culture and Memory*, edited by Brady Waggoner, pp. 85–116. New York: Oxford University Press.

Smith, Jonathan Z. 1987. *To Take Place: Toward Theory in Ritual*. Chicago: University of Chicago Press.

Staal, Fritz. 1979. "The Meaninglessness of Ritual." *Numen* 26: 2–22.

Stein, Daniel H., Juliana Schroeder, Nick M. Hobson, Francesca Gino, and Michael I. Norton. 2021. "When Alterations Are Violations: Moral Outrage and Punishment in Response to (Even Minor) Alterations to Rituals." *Journal of Personality and Social*

Psychology: Interpersonal Relations and Group Processes. http://doi.org/10.31234/osf.io/yd7tg.

Sturgill, Amanda F. C. 2019. "Artificial Intelligence: Its Future Uses in Religious Compassion." In *Religion Online: How Digital Technology Is Changing the Way We Worship and Pray*, vol. 1, edited by August F. Grant, Daniel A. Stout, Chiung H. Chen, and Amanda F. C. Sturgill, 83–95. Santa Barbara, CA: Praeger.

Tomasello, Michael. 1999. *The Cultural Origins of Human Cognition*. Cambridge, MA: Harvard University Press.

———. 2009. *Why We Cooperate*. Cambridge, MA: MIT Press.

Travagnin, Stefania. 2020. "Cyberactivities and 'Civilized' Worship: Assessing Contexts and Modalities of Online Ritual Practices." In *Buddhism after Mao: Negotiations, Continuities, and Reinventions*, edited by Ji Zhe, Gareth Fisher, and André Laliberté, pp. 291–306. Honolulu: University of Hawai'i Press.

Turner, Jack. 2019. "Online Ritual and the Active Participation of the Faithful." In *Religion Online: How Digital Technology Is Changing the Way We Worship and Pray*, vol. 1, edited by August F. Grant, Daniel A. Stout, Chiung H. Chen, and Amanda F. C. Sturgill, 224–324. Santa Barbara, CA: Praeger.

Turner, Victor. 1969. *The Ritual Process: Structure and Anti-Structure*. London: Routledge.

———. 1970. *The Forest of Symbols*. Ithaca, NY: Cornell University Press.

———. 1973. "The Center Out There: Pilgrim's Goal." *History of Religions* 12, no. 3: 191–230.

———. 2001. *From Ritual to Theater: The Human Seriousness of Play*. New York: PAJ Books.

Turner, Victor, and Edith Turner. 1995. *Image and Pilgrimage in Christian Culture: An Anthropological Perspective*. New York: Columbia University Press.

van Gennep, Arnold. 1969. *Rites of Passage*. Translated by Monika Vizedom and Gabrielle Caffee. Chicago: University of Chicago Press. First published 1909.

Walens, Stanley. 1982. *Feasting with Cannibals: An Essay on Kwakiutl Cosmology*. Princeton, NJ: Princeton University Press.

Warner, W. Lloyd. 1959. *The Living and the Dead: A Study of the Symbolic Life of Americans*. New Haven: Yale University Press.

Weiss, Ellen. 1998. *City in the Woods: The Life and Design of an American Camp Meeting on Martha's Vineyard*. Boston: Northeastern University Press.

Wexler, Laura. 2003. *Fire in the Canebrake*. New York: Scribner.

Whitehouse, Harvey. 2022. *The Ritual Animal: Imitation and Cohesion in the Evolution of Social Complexity*. Oxford: Oxford University Press.

Wikan, Unni. 1990. *Managing Turbulent Hearts*. Chicago: University of Chicago Press.

Woo, Hai-Ran. 2013. "Buddhist Online Rituals in South Korea." Paper presented at the 32nd International Society for the Sociology of Religion Conference, Turku-Åbo, Finland (June 29). https://www.academia.edu/11899881/Buddhist_Online_Rituals _in_South_Korea.

Suggested Resources in Ritual Studies

Introduction to Ritual Studies

Grimes, Ronald. 1994. *Beginnings in Ritual Studies.* Columbia: University of South Carolina Press.

———. 2013. *The Craft of Ritual Studies.* Oxford: Oxford University Press

Grimes, Ronald, ed. 1995. *Readings in Ritual Studies.* Englewood Cliffs, NJ: Prentice Hall.

Segal, Robert, ed. 1998. *The Myth and Ritual Theory.* New York: Wiley & Sons.

Shore, Bradd. 2023. *The Hidden Powers of Ritual.* Cambridge, MA: MIT Press.

Stephenson, Barry. 2015. *Ritual: A Very Short Introduction.* Oxford: Oxford University Press.

Works on Ritual and Performance Theory

Aboujaoude, Elias. 2008. *Compulsive Acts: A Psychiatrist's Tales of Ritual and Obsession.* Berkeley: University of California Press.

Bell, Catherine. 2009. *Ritual: Perspectives and Dimensions.* Oxford: Oxford University Press.

———. 2009. *Ritual Theory, Ritual Practice.* Oxford: Oxford University Press.

Boyer, Pascal, and Pierre Liénard. 2006. "Why Ritualized Behavior? Precaution Systems and Action Parsing in Developmental, Pathological and Cultural Rituals." *Behavioral and Brain Sciences* 29: 1–56.

Caillois, Roger. 2001. *Man, Play, and Games.* Champaign: University of Illinois Press.

D'Aquili, Eugene, Charles Loughlin, and John McManus. 1979. *The Spectrum of Ritual: A Biogenetic Structural Analysis.* New York: Columbia University Press.

Douglas, Mary. 1966. *Purity and Danger*. London: Routledge & Kegan Paul.

Durkheim, Emile. 1995. *The Elementary Forms of the Religious Life*. Translated by Karen E, Fields. New York: The Free Press. First published in 1912.

Grimes, Ronald, ed. 2006. *Rite out of Place: Ritual, Media and the Arts*. New York: Oxford University Press.

Huizinga, Johan. 1949. *Homo Ludens: A Study of the Play-Element in Culture*. London: Routledge & Kegan Paul.

Humphries, Caroline, and James Laidlaw. 1994. *The Archetypal Actions of Ritual: A Theory of Ritual Illustrated by the Jain Rite of Worship*. Oxford: The Clarendon Press.

David Kertzer. 1989. *Ritual, Politics, and Power*. New Haven: Yale University Press.

Lawson, Thomas, and Robert McCauley. 1990. *Rethinking Religion: Connecting Cognition and Culture*. Cambridge: Cambridge University Press.

Leach, Edmund. 1966. "Ritualization in Man in Relation to Conceptual and Social Development." *Philosophical Transactions of the Royal Society of London. Series B, Biological Sciences* 251, no. 772: 403–408.

Lewis, Gilbert. 1988. *Day of Shining Red: An Essay on Understanding Ritual*. Cambridge: Cambridge University Press.

McNeill, William. 1995. *Keeping Together in Time: Dance and Drill in Human History*. Cambridge, MA: Harvard University Press.

Mauss, Marcel. 2002. *The Gift: The Form and Reason for Exchange in Archaic Societies*. London: Routledge.

Rappaport, Roy. 1968/1984. *Pigs for the Ancestors: Ritual in the Ecology of a New Guinea People*. New Haven: Yale University Press.

———. 1999. *Ritual and Religion in the Making of Humanity*. Cambridge: Cambridge University Press.

Sax, Willian, Johannes Quack, and Jan Weinhold, eds. 2010. *The Problem of Ritual Efficacy*. Oxford: Oxford University Press.

Schechner, Richard. 1988. *Essays in Performance Theory*. London: Routledge.

———. 2020. *Performance Studies: An Introduction*. London: Routledge.

Sennett, Richard. 2007. *Together: The Rituals, Pleasures, and Politics of Cooperation*. New Haven, CT: Yale University Press.

Smith, Jonathan Z. 1987. *To Take Place: Toward Theory in Ritual*. Chicago: University of Chicago Press.

Staal, Fritz. 1979. "The Meaninglessness of Ritual." *Numen* 26: 2–22.

Turner, Victor. 2001. *From Ritual to Theater: The Human Seriousness of Play*. New York: PAJ Books.

Turner, Victor, and Edith Turner. 1995. *Image and Pilgrimage in Christian Culture: An Anthropological Perspective*. New York: Columbia University Press.

van Gennep, Arnold. 1969. *Rites of Passage*. Translated by Monika Vizedom and Gabrielle Caffee. Chicago: University of Chicago Press. First published 1909.

Weiner, Annette. 1992. *Inalienable Possessions: The Paradox of Keeping while Giving*. Berkeley: University of California Press.

Classic Ethnographic Studies of Ritual

Codere, Helen. 1950. *Fighting with Property: A Study of Kwakiutl Potlatching and Warfare, 1792–1930*. New York: J. J. Augustin.

Deren, Maya. 1983. *The Divine Horsemen: The Living Gods of Haiti*. New York: McPherson & Company.

Geertz, Clifford. 1973. *The Interpretation of Cultures*. New York: Basic Books.

Gmelch, George. 1992. "Superstition and Ritual in American Baseball." *Elysian Fields Quarterly* 11, no. 3: 25–36.

Goldman, Irving. 1975. *The Mouth of Heaven: An Introduction to Kwakiutl Religious Thought*. New York: Wiley.

Luhrmann, Tanya M. 1989. *Persuasions of the Witch's Craft: Ritual Magic in Contemporary England*. Cambridge, MA: Harvard University Press.

Malinowski, Bronislaw. 1922. *Argonauts of the Western Pacific*. London: George Routledge.

Schieffelin, Edward. 1976. *The Sorrow of the Lonely and the Burning of the Dancers*. New York: Palgrave.

Shore, Bradd. 1996. *Culture in Mind: Culture, Cognition, and the Problem of Meaning*. Oxford: Oxford University Press.

Turner, Victor. 1969. *The Ritual Process: Structure and Antistructure*. London: Routledge.

———. 1970. *The Forest of Symbols*. Ithaca, NY: Cornell University Press.

Walens, Stanley. 1982. *Feasting with Cannibals: An Essay on Kwakiutl Cosmology*. Princeton, NJ: Princeton University Press.

Warner, W. Lloyd. 1959. *The Living and the Dead: A Study of the Symbolic Life of Americans*. New Haven, CT: Yale University Press.

————. 1964. *A Black Civilization: A Study of an Australian Tribe*. New York: Harper.

Weiner, Annette. 1983. *Women of Value, Men of Renown: New Perspectives in Trobriand Exchange*. Austin: University of Texas Press.

Weiss, Ellen. 1998. *City In The Woods: The Life and Design of an American Camp Meeting on Martha's Vineyard*. Boston: Northeastern University Press.

Witherspoon, Gary. 1977. *Language and Art in the Navajo Universe*. Ann Arbor: University of Michigan Press.

Studies of Animal Ritual

Lorenz, Konrad. 1980. *King Solomon's Ring: New Light on Animal Ways.* New York: Time-Life Books.

————. 1966a. "Evolution of Ritualization in the Biological and Cultural Spheres." *Philosophical Transactions of the Royal Society of London. Series B, Biological Sciences* 251, no. 772: 273–284.

————. 1966b. "The Triumph Ceremony of the Greylag Goose." *Philosophical Transactions of the Royal Society of London. Series B, Biological Sciences* 251, no. 772.

————. 1966c. *On Aggression*. London: Methuen & Co.

O'Connell, Caitlin. 2021. *Wild Rituals: 10 Lessons Animals Can Teach Us about Connection, Community, and Ourselves*. San Francisco: Chronicle Prism.

Perry, Susan, and Marco Smolla. 2020. "Capuchin Monkey Rituals: An Interdisciplinary Study of Form and Function." *Philosophical Transactions of the Royal Society B, Biological Sciences* 375, no. 1805.

Rogers, Lesley, and Gisela Kaplan. 2002. *Songs, Roars, and Rituals: Communication in Birds, Mammals, and Other Animals*. Cambridge, MA: Harvard University Press.

Rütten, Sylvia, and Günther Fleissner. 2004. "On the Function of the Greeting Ceremony in Social Canids—Exemplified by African Wild Dogs *Lycaon Pictus*." *Canid News* 7.3. http://www.canids.org/canidnews/7/Greeting_ceremony_in_canids.pdf.

Tinbergen, Nikolas. 1971. *The Herring Gull's World: A Study of the Social Behavior of Birds*. New York: Harper Collins.

Interaction Ritual

Collins, Randall. 2005. *Interaction Ritual Chains*. Princeton, NJ: Princeton University Press.

Goffman, Erving. 1956. *The Presentation of Self in Everyday Life*. New York: Doubleday.

———. 1961. *Asylum: Essays on the Social Situation of Mental Patients and Other Inmates*. New York: Doubleday.

———. 1963a. *Behavior in Public Places: Notes on the Social Organization of Gatherings*. Glencoe, IL: The Free Press.

———. 1963b. *Stigma: Notes on the Management of Spoiled Identity*. New York: Simon and Schuster.

———. 1967. *Interaction Ritual: Essays on Face-to-Face Behavior*. New York: Pantheon Books.

———. 1969. *Strategic Interaction*. Philadelphia: University of Pennsylvania Press.

———. 1981. *Forms of Talk*. Philadelphia: University of Pennsylvania Press.

———. 1986. *Frame Analysis: An Essay on the Organization of Experience*. Boston: Northeastern University Press.

Weininger, Elliott B., Annette Lareau, and Omar Lizardo, eds. 2019. *Ritual, Emotion, Violence: Studies on the Micro-Sociology of Randall Collins*. London: Routledge.

Ritual and Conflict

Chalkdust, Hollis. 2001. *Rituals of Power & Rebellion: The Carnival Tradition in Trinidad & Tobago, 1763–1962*. Chicago: Frontline Distribution International.

Gluckman, Max. 2004. *Rituals of Rebellion in Southeast Africa*. London: Routledge.

Spencer, Paul. 1988. *The Maasai of Matapato: A Study of Rituals of Rebellion*. London: Routledge.

Ritual in the Internet Age

Grant, August F., Daniel A. Stout, Chiung H. Chen, and Amanda F. C. Sturgill, eds. 2019. *Religion Online: How Digital Technology Is Changing the Way We Worship and Pray*. 2 vols. Santa Barbara, CA: Praeger.

Grieve, Gregory P. 2016. *Cyber Zen: Imagining Authentic Buddhist Identity, Community, and Practices in the Virtual World of* Second Life. London: Routledge.

Grieve, Gregory P., and Daniel Veidlinger, eds. 2015. *Buddhism, the Internet, and Digital Media: The Pixel in the Lotus*. London: Routledge.

Grimes, Ronald, ed. 2006. *Rite Out of Place: Ritual, Media and the Arts*. Oxford: Oxford University Press.

Hutchings, Tim. 2017. *Creating Church Online*. London: Routledge.

McKnight, Scot. 2020. *Analog Church: Why We Need Real People, Places, and Things in the Digital Age.* Downers Grove, IL: InterVarsity Press.

Radde-Antweiler, Kerstin. 2007. "Cyber-Rituals in Virtual Worlds: Wedding-Online in *Second Life.*" *Masaryk UJL & Tech*: 185–197.

Self-Help Books on Ritual

Cheung, Theresa. 2019. *21 Rituals to Ignite Your Intuition.* London: Watkins Publishing.

Currey, Mason. 2019. *Daily Rituals: Women at Work.* New York: Knopf.

Fajardo, Glenn. 2021. *Rituals for Virtual Meetings.* New York: Wiley.

Kuhnke, Elizabeth. 2016. *Body Language: Learn How to Read Others and Communicate with Confidence.* New York: John Wiley & Sons.

O'Connell, Caitlin. 2021. *Wild Rituals: 10 Lessons Animals Can Teach Us about Connection, Community, and Ourselves.* San Francisco: Chronicle Prism.

Ozenc, Kursat. 2019. *Rituals for Work.* New York: Wiley.

Piastrelli, Becca. 2021. *Root and Ritual: Timeless Ways to Connect to Land, Lineage, Community, and the Self.* Boulder, CO: Sounds True.

ter Kuile, Casper. 2020. *The Power of Ritual: Turning Everyday Activities into Soulful Practice.* New York: Harper.

Selected Documentary Films on Ritual

A Balinese Trance Séance, directed by Linda Connor, Patsy Asch, and Timothy Asch in Bali, https://search.alexanderstreet.com/preview/work/bibliographic_entity%7Cvideo_work%7C764348.

Catholic Mass, directed by John Beugen in Naperville, IL, https://www.youtube.com/watch?v=aVV-sGi-x0o.

Coming of Age in Africa: Initiation in the Bwa Village of Dossi, directed by Christopher D. Roy in Burkina Faso, https://www.youtube.com/watch?v=2HDjh5kZnoc.

Dead Birds, directed by Robert Gardner in Papua New Guinea, https://video-alexanderstreet-com.proxy.library.emory.edu/watch/dead-birds?context=channel:academic-video-online.

Extraordinary Rituals, directed by Simon Reeve, https://www.imdb.com/title/tt8877116/.

Family Revival: Salem Camp Meeting, directed by Bradd Shore in Covington, Georgia, https://vimeo.com/18480085.

Kawelka: Onka's Big Moka, directed by Charlie Naim in New Guinea, https://www.youtube.com/watch?v=W_gBYVfqtWM.

Kinaalda: A Navajo Puberty Ceremony, directed by Navajo people in New Mexico, https://www.facebook.com/watch/?v=579312205815611.

Magical Death: An Account of Kanaima Assault Sorcery, directed by Sago Williams and Neal Whitehead in Amazonia, https://www.youtube.com/watch?v=e3awSW0cno8.

Ngaben: Emotion and Restraint in a Balinese Heart, directed by Robert Lemelson in Bali, https://www.youtube.com/watch?v=Sesmyp3ZVAo.

Ritual Burdens, directed by Robert Lemelson in Bali, https://www.youtube.com/watch?v=N6qS3g7uM1w.

Rituals: How and Why? directed by Ajahn Brahm in Western Australia, https://www.youtube.com/watch?v=wHS8_D0nnOg.

The Feast, directed by Timothy Asch near Orinoco River, Amazonia, https://archive.org/details/thefeast_20170105.

The Holy Ghost People, directed by Peter Adair in Scrabble Creek, West Virginia, https://www.youtube.com/watch?v=QZIa4kutkIM.

Trance and Dance in Bali, directed by Gregory Bateson and Margaret Mead in Bali, https://www.youtube.com/watch?v=Z8YC0dnj4Jw.

Widi's dhapi'—initiation ceremony, directed by Ididg in Galiwinku, Australia, https://www.youtube.com/watch?v=MLWvLIeJB6o.

Carnival in Q'eros: Where the Mountains Meet the Jungle, directed by Juan Nuñez del Prado and John Cohen in the Peruvian Andes, https://video-alexanderstreet-com.proxy.library.emory.edu/watch/carnival-in-q-eros-where-the-mountains-meet-the-jungle?context=channel:academic-video-online.

Choqela, directed by John Cohen in Peru, https://video-alexanderstreet-com.proxy.library.emory.edu/channel/academic-video-online?q=Choqela&sort=relevance.

Dance for the King, directed by Wendy Arbeit in Tonga, https://video-alexanderstreet-com.proxy.library.emory.edu/watch/dance-for-the-king?context=channel:academic-video-online.

Enga Mass, directed by Philip Gibbs in New Guinea, https://video-alexanderstreet-com.proxy.library.emory.edu/watch/enga-mass?context=channel:academic-video-online.

Misek—The Spark, directed by Carlos Gomez in Eastern Nepal, https://video-alexanderstreet-com.proxy.library.emory.edu/watch/misek-the-spark?context=channel:academic-video-online.

The Hanmaneak Su in a Routuman Wedding, directed by Vilsoni Hereniko on Rotuma Island, https://video-alexanderstreet-com.proxy.library.emory.edu/watch/the-hanmaneak-su-in-a-routuman-wedding?context=channel:academic-video-online.

The Peyote Road: Ancient Religion in Contemporary Crisis, directed by Phil Cousineau in the American Southwest, https://video-alexanderstreet-com.proxy.library.emory.edu/watch/the-peyote-road-ancient-religion-in-contemporary-crisis?context=channel:academic-video-online.

The Sanma Yam Festival, directed by Larry Thomas on Malo Island, New Caledonia, https://video-alexanderstreet-com.proxy.library.emory.edu/channel/academic-video-online?q=The%20Sanma&sort=relevance.

Easter in Kandep, directed by Philip Gibbs in Kandep, New Guinea, https://video-alexanderstreet-com.proxy.library.emory.edu/watch/easter-in-kandep?context=channel:academic-video-online.

Index

Action clusters, 14

Ad hoc ritual groups, 281–282

Agency, power of rituals to reverse, 153–158

Age of Spiritual Machines: When Computers Exceed Human Intelligence, The (Kurzweil), 222

Aggression, 72–73
  ritual control of violence and, 90–92

Aging, power of ritual in, 291–293

Agonistic display, 75–76

Agung, Ida Anuk Agung Gde, 39–40

Alesana, Tofilau Eti, 109–110, 116–117

Alfred Sloan Foundation, 4

Analogies, 66

Animal rituals
  anxiety reduction through, 87–90
  ceremonies, 76–77
  communicating with and without language, 67–71
  compared to human rituals, 64–66, 78–83, 92–94
  displays in, 74–76
  evolution of, 66
  formalization of, 83
  functions of, 83–92
  instincts and, 65
  mating and, 72, 84
  modular organization of, 78–82
  ritual control of violence, 90–92
  ritualization and, 63–65, 71–73

scholarly debate over, 63

species-specific, 63–64

structure of, 74–77

synchronization and coordination of behavior through, 84–87

Anxiety reduction, 87–90, 125–129

Arbitrary association, 262–263

Archetypal Actions of Ritual: A Theory of Ritual Illustrated by the Jain Rite of Worship, The (Humphrey and Laidlaw), 266

Argonauts of the Western Pacific (Malinowski), 98

Aristotle, 120

Arnall, Ellis, 182, 188

Arrhythmia, 121

Artificial intelligence (AI), 222, 251

Asymmetrical coordination, 132–133

Auslander, Mark, 183, 200–201

Automating action power of rituals, 133–134

Autonomic nervous system, 17–18

Bali
  boisterous funeral procession in, 49–52
  ceremonial dancing in, *41*
  cockfight game and ritual in, 137–139
  gamelan orchestra in, *42*
  genocide in, 42–43
  Hinduism in, 38, 44, 53, 55